Rethinking Productivity in Software Engineering

Edited by
Caitlin Sadowski
Thomas Zimmermann

Rethinking Productivity in Software Engineering

Caitlin Sadowski
Mountain View, CA, USA

Thomas Zimmermann
Bellevue, WA, USA

ISBN-13 (pbk): 978-1-4842-4220-9
https://doi.org/10.1007/978-1-4842-4221-6

ISBN-13 (electronic): 978-1-4842-4221-6

Library of Congress Control Number: 2019934471

Managing Director, Apress Media LLC: Welmoed Spahr
Acquisitions Editor: Susan McDermott
Development Editor: James Markham
Coordinating Editor: Jill Balzano

Cover image designed by Freepik (www.freepik.com)

Distributed to the book trade worldwide by Springer Science+Business Media New York, 233 Spring Street, 6th Floor, New York, NY 10013. Phone 1-800-SPRINGER, fax (201) 348-4505, e-mail orders-ny@springer-sbm.com, or visit www.springeronline.com. Apress Media, LLC is a California LLC and the sole member (owner) is Springer Science + Business Media Finance Inc (SSBM Finance Inc). SSBM Finance Inc is a **Delaware** corporation.

For information on translations, please e-mail rights@apress.com, or visit www.apress.com/rights-permissions.

Apress titles may be purchased in bulk for academic, corporate, or promotional use. eBook versions and licenses are also available for most titles. For more information, reference our Print and eBook Bulk Sales web page at www.apress.com/bulk-sales.

Any source code or other supplementary material referenced by the author in this book is available to readers on GitHub via the book's product page, located at www.apress.com/9781484242209. For more detailed information, please visit www.apress.com/source-code.

Printed on acid-free paper

To Mr. Wiggles.
—Caitlin Sadowski

To my parents.
—Thomas Zimmermann

Table of Contents

About the Editors

Dr. Caitlin Sadowski is a software engineer at Google in Mountain View, California, where she aims to understand and improve developer workflows. Currently, she is helping Chrome developers make data-driven decisions as the manager of the Chrome Metrics team. In the past, she made static analysis useful at Google by creating the Tricorder program analysis platform, and then co-founded a team that provides ongoing insight into how developers spend their time and what makes them effective (the Engineering Productivity Research team). She is a committee member of top software engineering and programming language conferences (ICSE, ESEC/FSE, OOPSLA, and PLDI). She has a PhD from the University of California at Santa Cruz where she worked on a variety of research topics related to programming languages, software engineering, and human computer interaction. She enjoys baking with her three-year-old, Naru (otherwise known as Mr. Wiggles).

Dr. Thomas Zimmermann is a senior researcher at Microsoft Research, where he analyzes data for a living. Currently, he works on the productivity of software developers and data scientists at Microsoft. In the past, he analyzed data from digital games, branch structures, and bug reports. He is the co-editor in chief of the Empirical Software Engineering journal and serves on the editorial boards of IEEE Transactions on Software Engineering, IEEE Software, Journal of Systems and Software, and Journal of Software: Evolution and Process. He is a committee member of top software engineering conferences (ICSE, ESEC/FSE, and ASE) and the chairman of ACM SIGSOFT. He previously edited books on recommender systems (Springer) and data science in software engineering (Morgan Kaufmann). He has a PhD from Saarland University where he worked on mining software repositories. He likes movies, enjoys football at -6 degrees Fahrenheit, and collects unicorns.

Acknowledgments

There are many people who made this book possible. We gratefully acknowledge the extensive and professional work of our authors and the Apress team, especially Todd Green, Jill Balzano, and Susan McDermott. Special thanks to the staff and the organizers of Schloss Dagstuhl (`https://www.dagstuhl.de`, where computer scientists meet), who hosted the original meeting that was the genesis of this book. Special thanks also to Jaeheon Yi and Ambrose Feinstein, without whom it would have been impossible to find the time to work on this.

Introduction

Caitlin Sadowski
Thomas Zimmermann

As Marc Andreessen put it, software is eating the world [1], and there is an ever-growing demand on software being built. Despite the immense growth in the number of professional software developers, there is still a shortage. To satisfy this demand, we need more productive software engineers.

Over the past four decades, there has been significant research on understanding and improving the productivity of software developers and teams. A substantial amount of work has examined the meaning of software productivity. Much of this introduced definitions of productivity (many of them!), considered organizational issues associated with productivity, and focused on specific tools and approaches for improving productivity. In fact, most of the seminal work on software productivity is from the 1980s and 1990s (Peopleware, Mythical Man-Month, Personal Software Process).

Why This Book?

Historically, this book began as a weeklong workshop in Dagstuhl, Germany [2]. The motivation for this seminar was that since the 1980s and 1990s many things have changed and that it was time to revisit what makes *modern* software engineers productive.

What has changed since the 1980s and 1990s? Today's software teams and engineers are often global and collaborate across borders and time zones, practice agile software development, frequently use social coding tools such as Stack Overflow and GitHub, and often work on laptops or their own personal devices. Today's software engineers must deal with unprecedented complexity, can build large systems fast in the cloud, can store millions (or even billions) of lines of code in a single repository, and can release software frequently, often multiple times a day. They use on average 11.7 communication channels such as web search, blogs, Q&A sites, and social networking sites [85]; in 1984, the primary communication channels for software engineers were phone calls and in-person meetings [27]. The human-computer interaction (HCI) and computer-supported cooperative work (CSCW) communities have made significant advances in supporting knowledge workers to become more productive that one might also transfer to software engineers. Furthermore, the wide availability of data about software development enables a more sophisticated analysis of software productivity.

The goal of this seminar was to rethink, discuss, and address open issues of productivity in software development and figure out how to measure and foster productive behavior of software developers. Specifically, the discussion at the seminar focused on the following questions:

- What does productivity mean for individuals, teams, and organizations?

- What are the dimensions and factors of productivity?

- What are the purposes and implications of measuring productivity?

- What are the grand challenges in research on productivity?

This book explores what productivity means for modern software development. The chapters were written by participants at the Dagstuhl seminar (see Figure 1), plus numerous other experts. Our goal is to summarize and distribute their combined experience, wisdom, and understanding about software productivity.

Figure 1. *The attendees of the Dagstuhl seminar called "Rethinking Productivity in Software Engineering" in March 2017. The two editors of this book are in the second row on the right hand side.*

About This Book

This book is organized into five topic areas. We begin with a set of essays outlining challenges with measuring productivity ("Measuring Productivity: No Silver Bullet"). This is followed by essays focused on breaking down productivity into its components ("Introduction to Productivity") and essays that identify productivity factors and how they may give a different perspective on productivity ("The Context of Productivity"). Even though productivity is difficult to measure in general, we include specific case studies focused on measuring some aspect of productivity ("Measuring Productivity in Practice"). We finish with a series of essays on interventions that do work to improve productivity ("Best Practices for Productivity").

Measuring Productivity: No Silver Bullet

Are some programmers indeed ten times more productive than others, as some people claim? Lutz Prechelt digs into the data to address this question in Chapter 1. Ciera Jaspan and Caitlin Sadowski then explain what is inherently wrong with focusing on a single productivity metric (and what you can do instead) in Chapter 2. Amy J. Ko describes a thought experiment identifying the unintended consequences of measuring productivity in Chapter 3.

An Introduction to Productivity

We begin this part with an overview of ways that productivity has been defined in the past with Chapter 4 by Stefan Wagner and Florian Deissenboeck. In Chapter 5, Caitlin Sadowski, Margaret-Anne Storey, and Robert Feldt describe a framework for breaking down productivity into three dimensions: quality, velocity, and satisfaction—and how to apply that framework when considering productivity metrics. Amy J. Ko then describes how it is important to consider productivity in context through a particular lens in Chapter 6. Emerson Murphy-Hill and Stefan Wagner conclude this introduction to productivity concepts with an overview of productivity research in a related context (knowledge work) in Chapter 7.

The Context of Productivity

There are many different factors that may affect the productivity of software engineers. Stefan Wagner and Emerson Murphy-Hill overview the space of these factors in Chapter 8. We do a deep dive into two of these factors in the following two chapters: Duncan Brumby, Christian Janssen, and Gloria Mark provide an overview of research on interruptions in Chapter 9, and then Daniel Graziotin and Fabian Fagerholm discuss research about the relationship between happiness and productivity in Chapter 10. We end this part with Pernille Bjørn's cautionary tale about the importance of considering social factors for productivity in Chapter 11.

Measuring Productivity in Practice

André N. Meyer, Gail C. Murphy, Thomas Fritz, and Thomas Zimmermann dig into the varying ways developers perceive productivity and the implications for self-reported productivity measurement in Chapter 12. Brad A. Myers, Amy J. Ko, Thomas D. LaToza, and YoungSeok Yoon then discuss how qualitative research methods can aid in understanding productivity challenges or improvements in Chapter 13. Marieke van Vugt then overviews the benefits and limitations of using eye trackers and electroencephalography (EEG) scans to measure productivity in Chapter 14. Christoph Treude and Fernando Figueira Filho discuss the importance of awareness of what is going on in the larger team (team awareness) for productivity and investigate how team awareness can be measured in Chapter 15. In Chapter 16, Margaret-Anne Storey and Christoph Treude overview benefits and challenges of presenting productivity metrics in dashboards.

Some organizations perform productivity benchmarking using International Organization for Standardization (ISO) standard methods; the final two chapters give a perspective into this world. Charles Symons overviews one such measurement (COSMIC) in Chapter 17. Frank Vogelezang and Harold van Heeringen describe a case study of how organizations use a benchmarking method like COSMIC in Chapter 18.

Best Practices for Productivity

There are too many "best practices" for improving the productivity of software engineers to include in this book, so we give an overview of different interventions that provide a variety of perspectives into what such an intervention could look like. Todd Sedano, Paul Ralph, and Cécile Péraire describe how changing the mindset from "improving productivity" to "reducing waste" can make productivity improvements tractable in Chapter 19. Bill Curtis describes the importance of having clear, mature processes in Chapter 20. In Chapter 21, Franz Zieris and Lutz Prechelt give an answer to the question of whether pair programming pays off.

There are also tool-supported interventions to improve productivity. The benefits and challenges of self-tracking for productivity are described by André N. Meyer, Thomas Fritz, and Thomas Zimmermann in Chapter 22. Manuela Züger, André N. Meyer, Thomas Fritz, and David Shepherd present a system to surface information about when to interrupt software engineers in Chapter 23. In Chapter 24, Gail C. Murphy, Mik Kersten, Robert Elves, and Nicole Bryan review an evolution of technologies focused on improving the access and flow of information between the humans and tools involved in creating software systems. Lastly, Marieke van Vugt focuses inward and overviews the role of mindfulness in productivity in Chapter 25.

The Future of Software Productivity

While these essays were written by experts, they are hardly complete. Software development is always changing, and there is a lot we don't know yet about software productivity. At the Dagstuhl seminar, the attendees identified several open questions and grand challenges. The three main grand challenges are building a body of knowledge about what we know about software productivity, improving the measurement of productivity, and affecting and improving software productivity through interventions.

Building a Body of Knowledge About Software Productivity

The following are the next steps towards building a body of knowledge about software productivity:

- Develop a theoretical framework for productivity.

- Define *laws or rules of productivity* similar to the laws of software evolution. For example, a happier developer is a more productive developer; a participatory culture in a team is more productive.

- Examine the difference of software development to all other kinds of knowledge workers and learn what is unique about software development and what is not.

- Develop a mapping from questions on productivity to a methodology of studying it.

Improving the Measurement of Productivity

The following are the next steps for improving the measurement of productivity:

- Collect examples of where measuring productivity was done well with good outcomes. Distill the insights and guidelines from this collection.

- Develop an approach that can track "everything" at every moment, including detailed data across a company; biometric data from individuals; and data on aspects such as satisfaction, mood, fatigue, and motivation. Use the data to profile development work and productivity. *Obviously, it will be hard (if not impossible) to get the privacy right for an approach like this.*

Improve the Productivity of Software Engineers

The following are the next steps for improving the productivity of software engineers:

- Understand how to support and facilitate productivity.

- Conduct a multitude of comparative studies on productivity at different companies and on different interventions.

Exciting times are ahead. We hope you enjoy this book!

References

[1]   Marc Andreessen. Why Software Is Eating The World. Wall Street Journal 2011. https://www.wsj.com/articles/SB1000142405311 19034809045765122509915629460

[2]   Thomas Fritz, Gloria Mark, Gail C. Murphy, Thomas Zimmermann. Rethinking Productivity in Software Engineering (Dagstuhl Seminar 17102). Dagstuhl Reports, Volume 7, Number 3, March 2017, pages 19–26. http://dx.doi.org/10.4230/ DagRep.7.3.19

[3] M.-A. Storey, A. Zagalsky, F. F. Filho, L. Singer, and D. M. German. How social and communication channels shape and challenge a participatory culture in software development. IEEE Transactions on Software Engineering, 43(2):185–204, 2017.

[4] T. DeMarco and T. Lister. Programmer performance and the effects of the workplace. In Proceedings of the 8th international conference on Software engineering, pages 268–272. IEEE Computer Society Press, 1985.

PART I

Measuring Productivity: No Silver Bullet

PART I

Measuring Productivity: No Silver Bullet

CHAPTER 1

The Mythical 10x Programmer

Lutz Prechelt, Freie Universität Berlin, Germany

Are some programmers indeed ten times more productive than others, as some people claim? To a shocking degree, the answer depends on what exactly the question is intended to mean. In this chapter, we will work our way toward this insight by way of a fictious dialogue that is based on actual programming research data.

   Alice: "I've heard the claim that 'Some programmers are ten times as productive as others.' Sounds a bit exaggerated to me. Do you happen to have data on this?"

   Bob: "Indeed I do." (Bob is an evidence buff.)

Some Work Time Variability Data

Bob (pointing at Figure 1-1): "Look at this plot. Each circle shows the work time of one person for a particular small program, and each of the programs solves the same problem. The box indicates the 'inner half,' from the 25th percentile to the 75th percentile, leaving out the lower and upper fourth of the data points. The fat dot is the median (or a 50/50 split point), the *M* shows the mean and its standard error, and the whiskers extend from minimum to maximum."

© The Author(s) 2019
C. Sadowski and T. Zimmermann (eds.), *Rethinking Productivity in Software Engineering*,
https://doi.org/10.1007/978-1-4842-4221-6_1

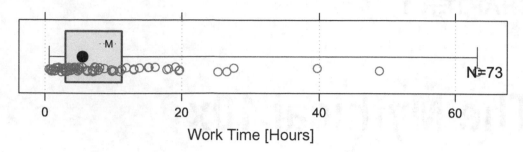

Figure 1-1. *Distribution of work times for 73 developers for the same small program*

Alice: "Wait. Not so fast. Are all these implementations working correctly?"

Bob: "23 of them have minor defects left in them; 50 work perfectly. All are more than 98 percent reliable and can be considered acceptable."

Alice: "I see. So min to max...that is how much?"

Bob: "Minimum is 0.6 hours; maximum is 63. That's a **105x** ratio."

Insisting on Homogeneity

Alice: "Wow, impressive. And are these data points indeed comparable?"

Bob: "What do you mean, comparable?"

Alice: "I don't know. Um, for instance...were these solutions all written in the same programming language? Maybe some languages are better suited to the problem than others. What type of problem is that anyway?"

Bob: "It's an algorithmic problem, a search-and-encode task. The data set mixes seven different languages, and some of those are indeed less suitable for the task than others."

Alice: "So, could we kick those out, please?"

Bob (showing Figure 1-2): "We can do even better because one of the seven groups provides 30 percent of the whole. This is what it looks like for only the Java solutions."

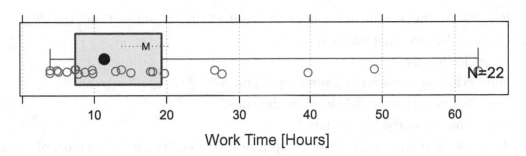

Figure 1-2. *Distribution of work times for 22 developers for the same small Java program*

Alice: "Uh-huh. Five of the six slowest are still there, but many of the fastest are not. So, that is still how much? 20x?"

Bob: "3.8 to 63, so it's **17x.**"

Deciding What We Even Mean

Alice (shaking her head): "Okay, but I think I see the problem now. I said 'faster than *other* programmers,' but if those others are the worst possible ones, the difference can be *any* size because some people may need an arbitrarily long time."

Bob: "I agree. The experimenters for this data had expected this to be a half-day task for most people and a full day for the slower ones, but apparently the slowest ones instead came back every day for a week. Dogged folks!"

Alice: "So, I think what the statement really ought to mean is 'faster than *normal* programmers.'"

Bob: "And 'normal' is just the average? No, I don't agree with that definition. The comparison group then would include everybody and also those who are fast or even very fast. Would anybody expect to be 9x faster nevertheless?"

Alice: "Good point. So, then the statement should mean 'faster than ordinary-not-so-great programmers'?"

Bob: "Probably. And that means what?"

Alice: "Hmm, I suggest those are the slower half of all."

Bob: "Sounds fair to me. And how are they represented, by the slower-half mean or the slower-half median?"

Alice: "Median. Or else a single super-obstinate slow person taking 1,000 hours could still make it easy to be 10x as fast."

Bob: "Okay. The median of the slower half is the 75th percentile. That's simply the right edge of the box. That leaves 'some.'"

Alice: "Excuse me?"

Bob: "What do we mean by '*some* programmers?'"

Alice: "Ah, yes. There should be more than one."

Bob: "How about the top 2 percent?"

Alice: "No, that is almost irrelevant in practice. We need to have a few more of these people before it starts to matter that they exist. I'd say we take the top 10 percent. Programmers overall need to be pretty intelligent people, and to be among the top 10 percent of those is quite elite. Where does that get us?"

Bob: "The median of the top 10 percent is the 5th percentile. For the Java people, that comes out at 3.8 as well. And the 75th percentile is 19.3. That's a **5x** ratio."

Alice: "Ha! I knew it! 10x is just too much. On the other hand..."

Alice stares into the distance.

Uninsisting on Homogeneity

Bob: "What?"

Alice: "Who picked the programming language used?"

Bob: "Each programmer decided this for him or herself."

Alice: "Then the suitability of the language and all its effects should be part of the performance we consider. Insisting on a fixed language will artificially dampen the differences. Let's go back to the complete data. What's the ratio then?"

Bob: "The 5th percentile is 1; the 75th percentile is 11. An **11x** ratio."

Alice (shaking her head): "Gosh. Over ten again—a wild ride."

Questioning the Base Population

Alice: "So, maybe I was wrong after all. Although...who *were* these people?"

Bob: "Everybody essentially. It is a diverse mix from students to seasoned professionals, people with much language experience to little, scruffy ones and neat, and what-have-you. The only thing similar about them is their motivation to take part in the experiment."

Alice (looking hopeful): "So, can we make the set a little more homogeneous?"

Bob (grinning sardonically): "Based on what? Their productivity?"

Alice: "No, I mean…there must be *something*!"

Her face lightens up. "I bet there are freshmen and sophomores among the students?"

Bob: "No. All seniors or graduate students. Besides, many places in industry have some people with no formal computer science training at all!"

Alice: "So, you mean this is an adequate population to study our question?"

Bob: "Probably. At least it is unclear what a better one ought to look like."

Alice: "So 11x is the answer?"

Bob: "At least approximately, yes. What else?"

Alice thinks hard for a while.

It's Not Only About Development Effort

Alice: "Oops."

Bob: "Oops what?"

Alice: "We've overlooked a big part of the question. We've assumed development time is all there is to productivity because the resulting programs are all equivalent. But you said it was an algorithmic problem. What if the program is run often or with large data in a cloud computing scenario? Then the programs could have wildly different execution costs. High cost means the program is less valuable; that must be factored into the productivity."

Bob: "Good thinking."

Alice: "But I guess your data does not contain such information?"

Bob: "In fact it does. For each program there is a benchmark result stating run time and memory consumption."

Are Slower Programmers Just More Careful?

Alice: "Fantastic! I bet some of the slower programmers have spent time on producing faster and leaner programs, and once we factor that in, the productivity becomes more even. Can we please look at a scatterplot with work time on the x-axis and memory consumption multiplied by run time on the y-axis? Both those latter factors produce proportional execution cost increases in the cloud, so they ought to be multiplied."

Bob (showing Figure 1-3): "Here we are. Note the logarithmic axes. Some of those costs are extreme."

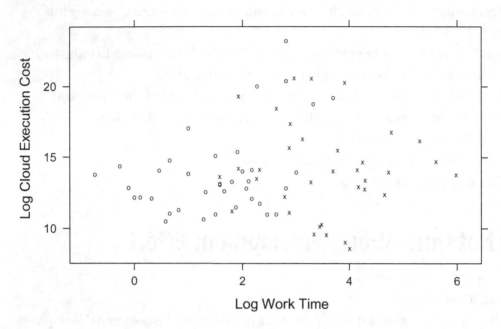

Figure 1-3. *Work time versus cloud execution cost (memory consumption times run time), log scale*

Alice: "Oh, there's hardly any correlation at all. I wouldn't have expected this."

Bob: "Do you still think the ratio will go down?"

Alice: "No, I guess not."

Secondary Factors Can Be Important

Alice: "By the way, what's the difference between the plot symbols?"

Bob: "The circles represent programs written in a dynamically typed scripting language; the Xs are statically typed programs."

Alice: "The scripts tend to be written much faster, so picking a scripting language was a clever move."

Bob: "Yes. That's because scripts get only half as long. This is what drove up the ratio compared to the Java-only group."

Alice: "Interesting. Yet scripts compete okay in terms of execution cost."

Bob: "Except against the very best nonscripts, yes."

The Productivity Definition Revisited

Alice: "But back to our question. Let's incorporate this execution cost idea: productivity is value per effort. Effort is our work time. Value goes down as cost goes up; so, value is the inverse of cost. Can you show that?"

Bob (showing Figure 1-4): "Sure. Here's the resulting plot."

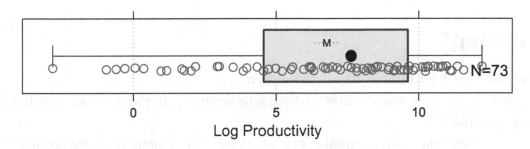

Figure 1-4. *"Productivity" for 73 developers for the same small program*

Bob: "It's hopeless without the logarithm and has a really strange unit of measurement, so it is difficult to make sense of intuitively. Larger is better now, so for our ratio we look at the 95th percentile, which is 2200, and the 25th percentile, the left box edge, which is 23.6, which makes the ratio **93x**. I guess you should get used to the fact that 10x differences exist."

How Would Real People Work?

Alice: "Perhaps. On the other hand, I now recognize that even with our refined understanding of what the question should mean we are asking the wrong question."

Bob: "Why is that?"

Alice: "I see two reasons. First, in a real scenario, one would not assign a task with cost implications as big as this one has to a developer from the lower half. Few people would be so shortsighted. Let's ignore the lower half."

Bob: "And instead of the 25th percentile of everybody take the 25th percentile of the upper productivity half?"

Alice: "Hmm, nobody can know that exactly in advance, but for simplicity's sake let's say yes."

Bob: "That would be the 62.5th percentile then. That's 385 and leads to a ratio of **6x**."

Alice: "Aaaaah, that sounds a lot more reasonable to me."

Bob: "I'm always happy to help."

Alice: "But that's not all. Second, if you build a solution with very high execution cost, you will go and optimize it. And if the original developer is not capable enough to do that properly, somebody else will come to the rescue. Or should at least. Productivity is about teams, really, not individuals!"

So What?

The next day, Bob runs into Alice in the kitchen.

Bob: "That was a really interesting discussion yesterday. But what is your take-home message from it?"

Alice: "My answer to the question of whether some programmers are indeed 10x more productive than others?"

Bob: "Yes."

Alice: "My answer is that is a misleading question. Other productivity facts are way more useful."

Bob: "And that would be which?"

Alice: "First, as the data showed, the low end of productivity can be *reeeeeally* low. So, do your best not to have such people on your team. Second, productivity is a lot about quality. There was not much information about this in your particular data set, but in the real world, I am strongly convinced that it makes little sense to talk about effort without talking about quality as well. Third, my personal conclusion is to assign critical tasks to the best engineers and noncritical tasks however they fit. Finally, although the data didn't have a lot to say about this, I firmly believe in improving a product over time. Productivity differences are a fact of life, but if you invest incrementally where it matters, they will not hurt very much."

The End.

Key Ideas

Here are the key ideas from this chapter in a nutshell:

- The low end of productivity can be really low.

- Quality matters, too, not only raw development speed.

- Assign critical tasks to your best engineers.

- Do your best not to have very weak engineers on your team at all.

References

The original study for the data used in this chapter is [1]. You can find a shorter report at [2] but will miss the add-on analyses. The data itself can be downloaded from [3].

[1]   Lutz Prechelt. "An empirical comparison of C, C++, Java, Perl, Python, Rexx, and Tcl for a search/string-processing program." Technical Report 2000-5, 34 pages, Universität Karlsruhe, Fakultät für Informatik, March 2000. `http://page.mi.fu-berlin.de/prechelt/Biblio/jccpprtTR.pdf`

[2]   Lutz Prechelt. "An empirical comparison of seven programming languages." IEEE Computer 33(10):23–29, October 2000.

[3]   Lutz Prechelt. `http://page.mi.fu-berlin.de/prechelt/packages/jccpprtTR.csv`

CHAPTER 2

No Single Metric Captures Productivity

Ciera Jaspan, Google, USA

Caitlin Sadowski, Google, USA

> *"Measuring software productivity by lines of code is like measuring progress on an airplane by how much it weighs."*
>
> —Bill Gates

> *"The purpose of software engineering is to control complexity, not to create it."*
>
> —Pamela Zave

The urge to measure the productivity of developers is not new. Since it is often the case at organizations that more code needs to be written, many attempts have been made to measure productivity based on lines of code (LOC). For example, in early 1982, the engineering management of developers working on software for the Apple Lisa computer decided to start tracking LOC added by each developer. One week, the main user interface designer, Bill Atkinson, optimized QuickDraw's region calculation machinery and *removed* about 2,000 LOC. The management stopped asking for his LOC [3].

© The Author(s) 2019

C. Sadowski and T. Zimmermann (eds.), *Rethinking Productivity in Software Engineering*,
https://doi.org/10.1007/978-1-4842-4221-6_2

Although measuring engineer productivity by LOC is clearly fraught, anecdotes like this abound on the Internet [7]. Organizations have continued to search for better and easier ways to measure developer productivity [6]. We argue that there is no metric that adequately captures the full space of developer productivity and that attempting to find one is counterproductive. Instead, we encourage the design of a set of metrics tailored for answering a specific goal.

What's Wrong with Measuring Individual Performers?

Tracking individual performance can create a morale issue, which perversely could bring down overall productivity. Research has shown that developers *do not like* having metrics focused on identifying the productivity of individual engineers [5]; this has also been our experience at Google. Developers are concerned about privacy issues and about how any measurement could be misinterpreted, particularly by managers who do not have technical knowledge about inherent caveats any metric has. If productivity metrics directly feed into an individual's performance grading, then they will impact how developers are compensated and whether they continue to keep their jobs—a serious consequence for getting it wrong. These high stakes further incentivize gaming the metrics, for example, by committing unnecessary code just to increase LOC ratings.

Measuring productivity to identify low performers may not even be necessary. It is our experience that managers (and peers) frequently already know who the low performers are. In that case, metrics serve only to validate a preexisting conception for why an individual is a low performer, and so using them to identify people in the first place is not necessary and serves only to demoralize the higher-performing employees.

Why Do People Want to Measure Developer Productivity?

As critiqued earlier, one possible motivation for measuring developer productivity is identifying high/low-performing individuals and teams. However, there are many reasons why a company may want to measure the productivity of their engineers. Other motivations include surfacing global trends across a company, rating the effectiveness of different tools or practices, running comparisons for an intervention meant to improve productivity, and highlighting inefficiencies where productivity can be improved.

While each of these scenarios has a goal of measuring productivity, the metrics, aggregations, and reporting are different. For example, identifying high- and low-performing individuals means aggregating a metric on an individual level, while running a comparison would mean aggregating across a group of developers. More important, the type of productivity metric used for these scenarios is different. There are many different stakeholders who may be interested in measuring productivity with different goals. If the goal is to identify low performers or to surface global trends, the stakeholders interested in the metric will be looking for metrics that measure task completion. If the goal is to run a comparison for a specific intervention or to highlight inefficiencies within a specific process, the productivity metrics used will be measuring subtasks that address the goals of the intervention or the process being investigated. What is actionable for an individual is different than what is actionable for a team.

What's Inherently Wrong with a Single Productivity Metric?

Any single productivity metric is intrinsically problematic. Productivity is too broad of a concept to be flattened into a single metric, and confounding factors will exacerbate the challenges with attempting such a flattening.

Productivity Is Broad

Productivity is a broad concept with many aspects. The problem is that productivity metrics are poor proxies of the underlying behavior or activity that we want to measure. As poor proxies, they are ripe for misuse.

When we create a metric, we are examining a thin slice of a developer's overall time and output. Developers engage in a variety of other development tasks beyond just writing code, including providing guidance and reviewing code for other developers, designing systems and features, and managing releases and configuration of software systems. Developers also engage in a variety of social tasks such as mentoring or coordination that can have a significant impact on overall team or organization output.

Even for the narrow case of measuring productivity of developers in terms of code contributions, quantifying the size of such contributions misses critical aspects of code such as quality, or maintainability. These aspects are not easy to measure; measuring code readability, quality, understandability, complexity, or maintainability remain open research problems [2, 4].

Flattening/Combining Components of a Single Aspect Is Challenging

Furthermore, flattening all of these into a single measure along with quantity has limited applicability and risks, reducing the actionability of a metric. Is a developer with few code contributions of very high quality more or less productive than a developer with many contributions but some quality issues? Does it make a difference if the engineer with some quality issues comes back and fixes the issues later? It is not clear which is more productive because it depends on the trade-offs of the project in question.

An additional problem with flattening or combining metrics is that flattened metrics may not make intuitive sense and so may be distrusted or misinterpreted. For example, if a variety of factors (e.g., cyclomatic complexity, time to complete, test coverage, size) are compressed into one number representing the productivity impact of a patch, it will not be immediately clear why one patch scores 24 and another one scores 37. Furthermore, a single score is not directly *actionable* since a variety of interrelated factors contribute to that score.

Confounding Factors

Even if we are able to tease out a single metric that holistically covers some aspect of productivity, confounding factors can make the metric meaningless. Take the case of comparing programming languages. It is difficult to measure the productivity of languages in particular because of the number of confounding factors. There is the language itself, the tools, the libraries, the culture, the types of projects, and the types of developers who are attracted to that language.

As another example, a Google team wanted to show that high test coverage improves code quality. To do this, they compared the test coverage of different teams with the number of bugs filed. They found no correlation. Was there really no improvement in code quality, though? In this case, there may have been a confounding *cultural component*. Teams that have high test coverage may also file more bug reports. The projects with low test coverage may have been prototypes or just teams that don't track bugs accurately.

There can also be confounds from *intrinsic complexity differences* between teams. For example, two teams may have a difference in their average patch completion time. One likely explanation is that these teams are working on different projects. There may be project-specific differences in the size of patches they submit or their overall complexity.

There can even be *externalities* that are not captured within a metric. For example, one team might appear to be submitting fewer lines of code than another team. There are many possible causes for such a difference that do not mean the team has lower productivity; perhaps the team is taking more steps to improve quality and therefore has fewer bugs down the road, or perhaps the team has taken on several new employees and is ramping them up. Again, confounding factors are at play. We can't separate those out because they come from nonmeasurable sources.

What Do We Do Instead at Google?

Although there is no general-purpose measurement that can be used in any situation focused on developer productivity, it is still possible to make data-driven improvements to a software engineering *workflow*. Given a specific research question, it is possible to break measurements down into a specific context and know what the caveats are.

At Google, we work with teams to figure out how they can leverage metrics to help make data-driven decisions. The process starts with clarifying the research questions and motivation. We then come up with custom metrics targeted toward those specific questions. This kind of thinking is similar to the Goal–QuestionMetric paradigm [1]. We validate these metrics against qualitative research (encompassing techniques such as surveys and interviews) to ensure that the metrics measure the original goal.

For example, a team at Google working on a distributed version control layer wanted to show that using multiple smaller patches speeds up the review process (perhaps because they are easier to review). After investigating and rejecting not meaningful metrics related to the number of changes or LOC committed per week, the team investigated how long it took developers to commit code *scaled by the size of code changes*. They were able to show improvement in the time to commit per LOC changed.

We can likewise find improvements for other tools, investigate the current cost on developers, and then put those into a Return on Investment (ROI) calculation. For example, we have determined how much time is lost because of waiting for builds (or because of unnecessary context switching as a result of builds). After contrasting this with the cost of speeding up builds (through human or machine resources), we have provided an estimated ROI for different build improvements.

We often see teams that either don't have a research question that matches their motivation for coming up with a metric or have a mismatch between the metrics and the research questions of interest. For example, we talked to one team that wanted to measure codebase modularity. After some discussion, we determined that they wanted to see whether developers were faster at developing software after an intervention and needed to consider ways to measure velocity. Teams also need to carefully consider the time window and aggregations (for example, team versus individual versus larger organization) of interest, as well as any selection criteria for individuals being measured.

Qualitative analysis helps understand what a metric is actually measuring, and data analysis and cross-validation can make sure the results are sensible. For example, by examining distributions of log events for individual developers, we discovered logs that show developers making an action on a web page tens of thousands of times – actions that were actually the result of a Chrome extension. Similarly, we found out during an interview that developers have good reasons for doing something we had thought was an anti-pattern.

Our approach works because we explicitly do not attempt to create a single metric to measure engineering productivity. We instead narrow down the problem into a concrete research statement and seek metrics that address precisely the question at hand. This allows us to validate each individual metric against a specific goal, rather than against the vague concept of productivity. In practice, we find that several of our metrics get reused from one productivity question to the next. While this approach does not scale as fast as applying a single productivity metric, it scales well enough while providing precise, reliable data that we can trust when making investment decisions.

Key Ideas

The following are the key ideas from this chapter:

- There is no single productivity metric for software engineers.
- Instead, focus on a set of custom metrics targeted to a specific question.

References

[1] Basili, V., Caldiera, G., and H. Dieter Rombach. (1994). The goal question metric approach. Encyclopedia of Software Engineering 2, 528–532.

[2] Buse, R. P., & Weimer, W. R. (2010). Learning a metric for code readability. IEEE Transactions on Software Engineering, 36(4), 546–558.

[3] Hertzfeld, A. -2000 Lines Of Code. `https://www.folklore.org/StoryView.py?project=Macintosh&story=Negative_2000_Lines_Of_Code.txt`

[4] Shin, Y., Meneely, A., Williams, L., & Osborne, J. A. (2011). Evaluating complexity, code churn, and developer activity metrics as indicators of software vulnerabilities. IEEE Transactions on Software Engineering, 37(6), 772–787.

[5] Treude, C., Figueira Filho, F., & Kulesza, U. (2015). Summarizing and measuring development activity. In Proceedings of Foundations of Software Engineering (FSE), 625–636. ACM.

[6] Thompson, B. Impact: a better way to measure codebase change. `https://blog.gitprime.com/impact-a-better-way-to-measure-codebase-change/`

[7] Y Combinator. Thread on -2000 LOC Story. `https://news.ycombinator.com/item?id=7516671`

CHAPTER 3

Why We Should Not Measure Productivity

Amy J. Ko, University of Washington, USA

Software moves faster every year. Markets shift rapidly, releases are ever more frequent, and languages, APIs, and platforms evolve at a relentless pace. And so the interest in productivity, both by developers who want to keep up with these changes and by managers and organizations that need to compete, appears entirely rational. Moreover, improving software faster holds even greater promise to the rest of humanity: getting more work done with less effort may mean an increased quality of life for everyone.

In pursuit of productivity, however, there can be unintended consequences from trying to measure it. Here are some examples:

- Measuring productivity can warp incentives, especially if not measured well.

- Sloppy inferences from measurements could result in *worse* management decisions rather than better ones.

Are these bad enough that we shouldn't even try to measure it? To find out, let's do a thought experiment. I want you to imagine an organization that you've worked for or are working for now. Let's consider what might happen if it invested seriously in trying to measure productivity. As we go, test the argument against your own experience.

© The Author(s) 2019
C. Sadowski and T. Zimmermann (eds.), *Rethinking Productivity in Software Engineering*,
https://doi.org/10.1007/978-1-4842-4221-6_3

Unintended Consequences

The first unintended consequence comes from trying to use any single concrete measure of productivity. Take, for example, a measure of productivity that focuses on *time to release*. An individual developer committing faster means a team reviewing faster, which ultimately means shipping faster, right? But unless your organization also measures the outcomes of shipping—positive outcomes such as adoption, customer growth, and sales increases, or negative outcomes such as software failures or harm to brand—one risks optimizing for an intermediate outcome at the expense of an organization's ultimate goal.

For example, in the race to release, a team might ship more defects than it would have otherwise or take on more technical debt than is desirable for longer-term goals. Most other single metrics have the same problems. Counting the number of bugs closed, the number of lines of code written, the number of user stories completed, the number of requirements met, and even the number of customers acquired—if your organization tried to measure these, optimizing any one of them would almost always come at the expense of others.

But this is a bit obvious. I bet it's even more obvious if you've been in an organization that did this because you probably lived those unintended consequences every day, feeling tension between the official measures of productivity and the other concerns that related to that measure. So, let's take our thought experiment in a more radical direction.

Imagine it was possible for your organization to measure *all* dimensions of productivity. After all, software has a vast array of quality dimensions Redundant, as do software development methodologies. Perhaps measuring all of these dimensions can overcome any overfitting to one metric. Let's put aside for the moment that we don't know how to measure most of these dimensions well, imagining a future in which we can accurately observe and measure every dimension of work. Would a holistic, multidimensional metric of productivity be any better?

It would certainly make the activities of a team more *observable*. Developers and managers would know every aspect of every developer's work, able to observe every dimension of progress or lack thereof. It would provide a perfect model of developer activity.

But this omniscient vision of software development work still comes with significant unintended consequences. First, if this monitoring were done at a team or organization level by managers, how would being monitored change developers' behavior? The effect of being observed so thoroughly might actually result in developers self-monitoring their every action, unintentionally *reducing* productivity. Even if this were a net increase in productivity, it might also lead to developers leaving the organization, moving to organizations that were a little less like Big Brother.

Explaining Productivity

For the sake of our thought experiment, let's imagine that you and every developer in your organization fully embraced rich monitoring of productivity of all kinds. What would a manager actually do with this data to improve productivity?

- They could use the data to rank the productivity of individual developers and teams to make promotion or investment decisions.

- If the data were real-time enough, they might use it to intervene in teams that are seeing drops in productivity.

- With enough detail, the data might even reveal which practices and tools are associated with increased productivity, allowing an organization to change practices to increase productivity.

This rich stream of real-time data could empower an organization to fine-tune its activities to more rapidly achieve its goals.

Unfortunately, there's a hidden requirement to achieve this vision. For a manager to actually go from data to intervention, they need to make a creative leap: a manager has to take all of the measures, correlations, and models to ultimately infer a theory for what *explains* the productivity they're observing. Making these inductive leaps can be quite challenging, and coming up with a wrong theory means any intervention based on that theory would likely not be effective and may even be harmful.

Even if we assume that every manager is capable of creatively and rigorously inferring explanations of a team's productivity and effectively testing those theories, the manager would need richer data about causality. Otherwise, they'd be blindly testing interventions, with no sense of whether improvements are because of their intervention or just the particular time and context of the test. Where would this causal data come from?

One source of richer data is *experiments*. But designing experiments requires control groups that are as close to identical as the treatment group or sufficiently randomized to control for individual differences. Imagine trying to create two teams that are identical in nearly every way, except for the process or tools they use, and randomizing everything else.

As a scientist of software engineering, I've tried, and not only is it extremely time-consuming and therefore expensive, but it's almost always impossible to do, even in the laboratory, let alone in a workplace.

Another source of rich data about causality is qualitative data. For example, developers could report their *subjective* sense of their team's productivity. Every developer could write a narrative each week about what was slowing them down, highlighting all of the personal, team, and organizational factors that they believe are influencing all of those elaborate quantitative metrics being measured in our omniscient vision. This would help support or refute any theories inferred from productivity data and might even surface some recommendations from developers about what to do about the problems they're facing.

This would be ideal, right? If we combine holistic *qualitative* data from developers with holistic *quantitative* data about productivity, then we'll have an amazingly rich and precise view into what is either causing or preventing an organization's desired level of productivity. What could be more valuable for improving developer productivity?

Dealing with Change

As usual, there's another fatal flaw. Such a rich model of productivity would be incredibly powerful if developers, teams, and organizations were a relatively stable phenomena to model. But new developers arrive all the time, changing team dynamics. Teams disband and reform. Organizations decide to enter a new market and leave an old one. All of these changes mean that the phenomena one might model are under constant change, meaning that whatever policy recommendations our rich model might suggest would likely need to change again in response to these external forces. It's even possible that by having such a seamless ability to improve productivity, one would accelerate the pace at which new productivity policies would have to be introduced, only creating more entropy in an ever-accelerating system of work.

One final flaw in this thought experiment is that, ultimately, all productivity changes will come from changes in the behavior of developers and others on a team. Depending on their productivity goals, they'll have to write better code, write less code, write code faster, communicate better, make smarter decisions, and so on. Even with a perfect model of productivity, a perfect understanding of its causes in an organization, and a perfect policy for improving productivity, developers will have to learn new skills, changing how they program, communicate, coordinate, and collaborate to implement more productive processes. And if you've had any experience changing developer or team behavior, you know how hard it is to change even small things about individual and team behavior. Moreover, once a team changes its behavior, one has to understand the causes of behavior all over again.

This thought experiment suggests that regardless of how accurately or elaborately one can measure productivity, the ultimate bottleneck in realizing productivity improvements is behavior change. And if our productivity utopia relies on developer insight into their own productivity to identify opportunities for individuals to change, why not just focus on developers in the first place, working with them individually and in teams to identify opportunities for increased productivity, whatever the team and organizational goals? This would be a lot cheaper than trying to measure productivity accurately, holistically, and at scale. It would also better recognize the humanity and expertise of the people ultimately responsible for achieving productivity. A focus on developers' experiences with productivity also leaves room for all the *indirect* components of productivity that are far too difficult to observe, including factors such as developers' motivation, engagement, happiness, trust, and attitudes toward the work they are doing. These factors, likely more than anything else, are the higher-order bits in how much work a developer gets one per unit time.

Managers as Measurers

Of course, all these individual and emotional factors about probing developer experience are just fancy ways of talking about *good management*. Great managers, by respecting the humanity of the people they are managing and understanding how their developers are working, are constantly building and refining rich models of their developers' productivity all the time and using them to make identify opportunities for improvements. The best ones already achieve our productivity measurement ideal but through interpersonal communication, interpretation, and mentorship. The whole idea of *measuring* productivity is really just an effort to be more objective about the subjective factors that are actually driving software development work.

So, what does this mean for improving productivity? I argue that instead of *measuring* productivity, we should instead invest in finding, hiring, and growing managers who can *observe* productivity as part of their daily work with developers. If organizations grow good managers and can trust that their great managers will constantly seek ways to improve productivity, developers will be more productive, even if we can't objectively measure it.

Of course, part of growing good management *can* involve measurement. One can think of measurement like a form of self-reflection scaffolding, helping a manager to reflect on process in more structured ways. That structure might help inexperienced managers develop more advanced skills of management observation that do not necessarily involve counting things. More advanced managers can be more intuitive, gathering insights as they work with their team and making changes to team dynamics as the world around the team changes. This vision of management ultimately frames measurement as just one small tool in a much larger toolbox for organizing and coordinating software development work.

Now all we need is a measure of good management.

Key Ideas

The following are the key ideas from the chapter:

- Improving productivity requires explaining the factors that affect it, but that requires qualitative insights into team behavior.

- Teams are always changing, making it even harder to get insights about team behavior through data.

- Managers are best positioned to get these qualitative insights by interacting with their team.

PART II

Introduction to Productivity

CHAPTER 4

Defining Productivity in Software Engineering

Stefan Wagner, University of Stuttgart, Germany

Florian Deissenboeck, CQSE GmbH, Germany

Successful software systems are subject to perpetual change as they need to be continuously improved and adapted to continuously changing requirements. *Software evolution* is the term used in software engineering to refer to this process of developing software initially and then repeatedly updating it. It is an essential goal to minimize the cost and to maximize the benefits of software evolution. In addition to financial savings, for many organizations, the time needed to implement software changes largely determines their ability to adapt their business processes to changing market situations and to implement innovative products and services. With the present yet increasing dependency on large-scale software systems, the ability to develop and change existing software in a timely and economical manner is essential for numerous enterprises and organizations in most domains.

We commonly call this *productivity,* which across disciplines and domains refers to the ratio between output and input. The input side—the cost spent—is relatively easy to measure in software development. The challenge lies in finding a reasonable way to define output as it involves software quantity and quality. The software engineering community has so far been unable to develop a thorough understanding of productivity in software evolution and the significance of the factors influencing it, let alone universally valid methods and tools to analyze, measure, compare, and improve productivity. Perhaps the most difficult issues are the many factors that influence

C. Sadowski and T. Zimmermann (eds.), *Rethinking Productivity in Software Engineering,*
https://doi.org/10.1007/978-1-4842-4221-6_4

productivity—and that they are different in every project, which makes it so hard to compare them. What complicates the situation is the lack of an established, clearly defined terminology that serves as a basis for further discussions.

Hence, we see the disambiguation of the terms that are central to productivity as a first important step toward a more mature management of productivity in software engineering. For that, we make use of the existing work from other research areas with a focus on *knowledge work*. We discuss the terms frequently associated with productivity, namely, *efficiency*, *effectiveness*, *performance*, and *profitability*, and explain their mutual dependencies. As a first constructive step, we propose a clear and integrated terminology.

To better put the terminology in the perspective of software engineering, we start with a description of the history of software productivity.

A Short History of Software Productivity

A wide variety of definitions of software development productivity have been discussed for more than four decades. In the beginning, however, this discussion was usually based on anecdotal evidence presented by renowned researchers and practitioners of the field. For example, Brooks stressed in 1975 the importance of people-related factors for software productivity [3], which was more recently followed up on by DeMarco and Lister [4], as well as Glass [5]. First isolated experiments were carried out to investigate productivity variations and its causes as early as 1968 [7, 11].

The late 1970s and early 1980s brought the first attempts to tackle software development productivity in a more comprehensive manner. As measuring productivity requires a well-defined notion of the size of the generated product, considerable effort was spent on the definition of size metrics that do not suffer from limitations of the classic lines of code (LOC) metric. In 1979, Albrecht introduced *function points* to express the amount of functionality of an information system rather than the size of its code. Based on the specification of a system instead of on its implementation, function points were designed to support early development effort estimation and to overcome limitations inherent to the measurement of LOC, e.g., comparability between different languages. Function points provide a basis for productivity measures such as function points per week or work-hours per function point.

In parallel, Boehm developed his cost estimation model COCOMO—now COCOMO II [1]—which is part of the standard software engineering knowledge today. While not directly based on function points but on LOC, COCOMO addresses development productivity by explicitly including productivity factors such as *required reliability* or the *capability of the analysts*. Boehm also recognized the importance of reuse, a phenomenon unknown in manufacturing, for software productivity and introduced a separate factor that should cover this influence.

The 1980s deepened the understanding of software productivity by significantly enlarging the then poor empirical knowledge base. Most notably, Jones contributed to this through his systematic provision and integration of a large amount of data relevant for productivity analyses. In his books, he discusses various factors for productivity and presents industrial averages for these factors that potentially form a basis for productivity assessments. Nevertheless, one of his insights [6] is that for each project a different set of factors may be most influential.

In the beginnings of the 2000s, several researchers proposed economic-driven or value-based software engineering as an important paradigm in future software engineering research. For example, Boehm and Huang [2] point out that it is not only important to track the costs in a software project but also the real earned value, i.e., the value for the customer. They explain that it is important to develop the software business case and keep it up-to-date. By doing so, they open up a new perspective on software productivity that reaches beyond development costs and explicitly includes the benefits provided for the customer.

During the 2000s and the recent years, agile software development has made a strong impact on many organizations that develop software. One of the core principles of agile development is to create *customer value*. Hence, many aspects of agile development aim to focus on this value generation. One example is the evolution from continuous integration to continuous delivery [13], i.e., to deliver value to customers not at the end of the project or a sprint but continuously. Another aspect related to productivity brought in by agile development was the counting of *story points* and the calculation of *velocity* as the number of story points per sprint. However, many proponents of agile development recommend not to use this measure of velocity as a productivity measure because it can lead to unwanted effects. For example, Jeffreys [15] states, "Velocity is so easy to misuse that one cannot recommend it." The effects can include that story points are inflated instead of used as a means to identify too large stories and keeping developers from working on stories with a small number of story points. Hence, agile software development has no clear definition of *productivity* or a solution for measuring productivity.

31

Terminology in the General Literature

Our starting point is Tangen's [12] Triple-P-Model, which is a well-established model in knowledge work research to differentiate *productivity*, *profitability*, and *performance* as well as the programming productivity Wikipedia article (`https://en.wikipedia.org/wiki/Programming_productivity`). Especially in software engineering, *efficiency* is used instead of *productivity*; we also discuss it and differentiate it from *effectiveness*. Finally, following Drucker [8], we include a short discussion on the influence of quality on productivity. We discuss each of these terms separately in the following sections and will integrate them afterward.

Productivity

While there is no commonly agreed on definition of *productivity*, there appears to be consensus that productivity describes the ratio between output and input.

Productivity = Output / Input

Across the various disciplines, however, different notions and different measurement units for input and output can be found. The manufacturing industry uses a straightforward relation between the number of units produced per time unit and the number of units consumed in production. Nonmanufacturing industries use person-hours or similar units to enable comparison between outputs and inputs.

As long as classical production processes are considered, a metric of productivity is straightforward: how many units of a product of specified quality are produced at which costs? For intellectual work, productivity is much trickier. How do we measure the productivity of authors, scientists, or engineers? Because of the rising importance of "knowledge work" (as opposed to manual work; see also "What We Can Learn from Productivity Research About Knowledge Workers" [8]), many researchers have attempted to develop productivity measurement means that can be applied in a nonmanufacturing context. It is commonly agreed on that the nature of knowledge work fundamentally differs from manual work and, hence, factors besides the simple output/input ratio need to be taken into account, e.g., quality, timeliness, autonomy, project success, customer satisfaction, and innovation. However, the research communities in neither discipline have been able to establish broadly applicable and accepted means for productivity measurement yet [9].

Profitability

Profitability and productivity are closely linked and are, in fact, often confused. However, *profitability* is most often defined as the ratio between revenue and cost.

Profitability = Revenue / Cost

The number of factors that influence profitability is even greater than the number of factors that influence productivity. Particularly, profitability can change without any change to productivity, e.g., due to external conditions such as cost or price inflation.

Performance

The term *performance* is even broader than productivity and profitability and covers a plethora of factors that influence a company's success. Hence, well-known performance control instruments such as the Balanced Scorecard [14] do include productivity as a factor that is central but not unique. Other relevant factors are, for example, the customers' or stakeholders' perception of the company.

Efficiency and Effectiveness

Efficiency and *effectiveness* are terms that provide further confusion as they are often mixed up themselves; additionally, efficiency is often confused with productivity. The difference between efficiency and effectiveness is usually explained informally as "efficiency is doing things right" and "effectiveness is doing the right things." While there are numerous other definitions [12], an agreement prevails that *efficiency* refers to the utilization of resources and mainly influences the required input of the productivity ratio. *Effectiveness* mainly aims at the usefulness and appropriateness of the output as it has direct consequences for the customer.

Influence of Quality

Drucker [8] stresses the importance of quality for the evaluation of knowledge worker productivity. Productivity of knowledge work therefore has to aim first at obtaining quality—and not minimum quality but optimum if not maximum quality. Only then can one ask, "What is the volume, the quantity of work?" However, most of the literature in nonsoftware disciplines does not explicitly discuss the role of quality in the output of the productivity ratio [8]. More recent work from nonmanufacturing disciplines have a stronger focus on knowledge, office, or white-collar work and hence increasingly discuss the role of quality with respect to productivity [4, 9, 10]. Still, it appears that these efforts to include quality in the determination of productivity have not yet led to an operationalizable concept.

An Integrated Definition of Software Productivity

As discussed, for measuring software productivity we need a measurement of input and output of a software project. The input is the effort dedicated to its development and evolution. The output is the value of the software for its users or customers. The value cannot always be defined by the market value of the software as it is often developed and used internally by organizations and as such does not have a market value. Furthermore, the market value may be influenced by factors that we put to the level of profitability or performance, such as currency valuations or competition on the market.

Hence, we suggest a purpose-based definition of software value. Given a purpose (a business goal or an application vision), we ask, how well does the software address its purpose in terms of functional and nonfunctional requirements? The answer to this question is determined by the functionality as well as the nonfunctional quality of the software.

On the basis of the purpose-based view, we build a consolidated summary of the productivity-related terms. As shown in Figure 4-1, from the purpose, we derive an ideal functionality and quality as well as the ideal effort to serve the purpose correctly. The ideal functionality means the optimal set of features (nothing missing, nothing too much) to fulfil the purpose. Similarly, the ideal quality is the level of the various quality attributes that fit to the purpose in an optimal way. For example, the application scales easily to the needed number of parallel users but not beyond. The ideal effort denotes the number of person-hours if people trained well for the problems to be solved (i.e., the ideal functionality and quality) would have worked in a supportive environment on the software. Comparing the ideal with the actually produced functionality and quality shows the effectiveness of the software development activities; the relation of the ideal to the actual effort gives the efficiency. Both have an influence on productivity.

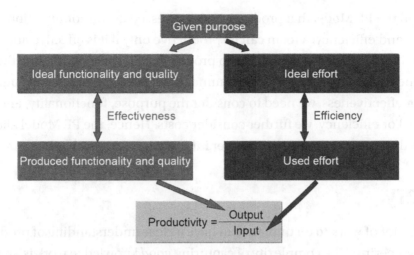

Figure 4-1. *Purpose-based effectiveness and efficiency*

We embed this in the Triple-P-Model from Tangen [12] so that it results in the *PE Model* that illustrates how purpose, functionality, quality, and effort relate to effectiveness, efficiency, productivity, profitability, and performance (Figure 4-2). The original Triple-P-Model already provided the idea that profitability contains productivity but adds further factors such as inflation and pricing. In turn, performance contains profitability and adds factors such as customer perception.

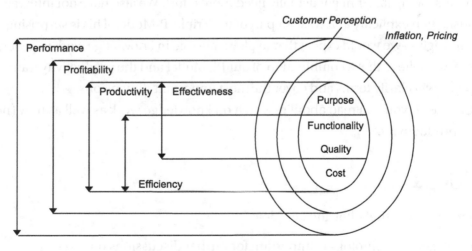

Figure 4-2. *PE Model for software evolution productivity*

We add in the PE Model that productivity is expressed as the combination of effectiveness and efficiency: a team can be productive only if it is effective and efficient! We would neither consider a software team productive if it was not building the features needed by the customers nor if it spent an unnecessary amount of effort on building the software. For effectiveness, we need to consider the purpose, functionality, and quality of the software. For efficiency, we further consider costs. Hence, the PE Model allows us to set all terms discussed earlier in this chapter into relation with each other.

Summary

There is still a lot of work to do until we can have a clear understanding of productivity in software engineering. The complexity of capturing *good* knowledge work is an obstacle in general to unambiguously measuring the productivity of such work. We hope that at least our classification of the relevant terms and the resulting PE Model can help to avoid confusion and to focus further efforts.

Our discussion of the related terms complements the productivity framework in Chapter 5. The framework focuses on the three dimensions of *velocity*, *quality*, and *satisfaction*. While quality is covered in both chapters, we have not incorporated velocity. Velocity can be different from effort as it concentrates on how fast features are delivered to customers. Being faster might actually need more effort. We also have not integrated work satisfaction explicitly as it was not part of the Triple-P-Model. This is surprising as—in hindsight—we would expect that to play a big role in knowledge work in general. Therefore, we believe that a combination of our PE Model and the productivity framework in Chapter 5 will clarify terms and cover the most important dimensions.

In Chapter 7, you can read about research on knowledge work as well as how (not) to measure productivity.

Key Ideas

This chapter covers the following key ideas:

- A clear terminology is important for further discussions on productivity factors and productivity measurement.

- We should reflect on the history of productivity research in software engineering.

- We need to learn from research on knowledge work productivity and use compatible terms.

- The purpose of the software is the necessary basis for all definitions of productivity and related terms.

Acknowledgements

We are grateful to Manfred Broy for fruitful discussions on definitions of productivity in software engineering.

References

[1]   Boehm, B. et al. Software Cost Estimation with COCOMO II, 2000

[2]   Boehm, B. and Huang, L. Value-Based Software Engineering: A Case Study. IEEE Software, 2003

[3]   Brooks, F. P. The mythical man-month. Addison-Wesley, 1975

[4]   DeMarco, T. and Lister, T. Peopleware: Productive Projects and Teams. B&T, 1987

[5]   Glass, R. L. Facts and Fallacies of Software Engineering. Addison-Wesley, 2002

[6]   Jones, C. Software Assessments, Benchmarks, and Best Practices. Addison-Wesley, 2000

[7]   Sackman, H.; Erikson, W. J. and Grant, E. E. Exploratory experimental studies comparing online and offline programming performance, Commun. ACM, ACM, 1968, 11, 3–11

[8]   Drucker, P. F. Knowledge-Worker Productivity: The Biggest Challenge. California Management Review, 1999, 41, 79-94

[9]   Ramírez, Y. W. and Nembhard, D. A. Measuring knowledge worker productivity: A taxonomy. Journal of Intellectual Capital, 2004, 5, 602–628

[10]   Ray, P. and Sahu, S. The Measurement and Evaluation of White-collar Productivity.

International Journal of Operations & Production Management, 1989, 9, 28–47

[11]   Sackman, H.; Erikson, W. J. and Grant, E. E. Exploratory experimental studies comparing online and offline programming performance, Commun. ACM, ACM, 1968, 11, 3–11

[12]   Tangen, S.; Demystifying productivity and performance. International Journal of Productivity and Performance, 2005, 54, 34–36

[13]   Jez Humble, David Farley. Continuous Delivery. Reliable Software Releases Through Build, Test, and Deployment Automation. Addison-Wesley, 2010.

[14]   Robert S. Kaplan, David P. Norton: The Balanced Scorecard – Measures that Drive Performance. In: Harvard Business Review. (January–February), 1992, S. 71–79.

[15]   Ron Jeffries. Should Scrum die in a fire? `https://ronjeffries.com/articles/2015-02-20-giles/`

CHAPTER 5

A Software Development Productivity Framework

Caitlin Sadowski, Google, USA
Margaret-Anne Storey, University of Victoria, Canada
Robert Feldt, Chalmers University of Technology, Sweden

Productivity is a challenging concept to define, describe, and measure for any kind of knowledge work that involves nonroutine creative tasks. Software development is a prime example of knowledge work, as it too often involves poorly defined tasks relying on extensive collaborative and creative endeavors. As in other areas of knowledge work, defining productivity in software development has been a challenge facing both researchers and practitioners who may want to understand and improve it by introducing new tools or processes.

In this chapter, we present a framework for conceptualizing productivity in software development according to three main dimensions that we propose are essential for understanding productivity. To help clarify productivity goals, we also propose a set of *lenses* that provide different perspectives for considering productivity along these three dimensions. We contend that any picture of productivity would be incomplete if the three dimensions and various lenses are not considered.

C. Sadowski and T. Zimmermann (eds.), *Rethinking Productivity in Software Engineering*,
https://doi.org/10.1007/978-1-4842-4221-6_5

Productivity Dimensions in Software Development

The three dimensions in the proposed productivity framework for software engineering are as follows:

- *Velocity*: How fast work gets done

- *Quality*: How well work gets done

- *Satisfaction*: How satisfying the work is

When trying to define productivity goals or measure productivity, it is important to consider all three of these dimensions because they work together synergistically. Even though productivity is often considered in terms of increased output (higher velocity), an increase in velocity may not correspond to an actual productivity improvement if there is a corresponding drop in the quality of that output. Velocity and quality taken together make up overall work efficiency and effectiveness, while velocity and quality may impact satisfaction in different ways. An increase in velocity may lead to reduced costs (and improve the satisfaction of managers), but at the same time it can lead to increased stress for developers (and reduce their satisfaction and in turn incur future costs). A detailed example of the perils of low satisfaction, even with high velocity and quality, can be found in Chapter 11.

Velocity

The velocity dimension captures how productivity is often conceptualized in terms of the time spent doing a task or the time taken (or cost) to achieve a given quantity of work. How one may conceptualize or measure velocity is highly task dependent, and the type of task needs to be considered, as well as the granularity, complexity, and routineness of a particular task. For example, developer velocity metrics could include the number of story points per sprint or the time taken to go from code to a release.

Quality

The quality dimension encapsulates doing a good job when producing artifacts (such as software) or the quality of provided services. Quality may be an internal consideration in a project (e.g., code quality) or external to a project (e.g., product quality from the perspective of the end users). Metrics for quality in a software project could include counts of negative characteristics such as post-release defects or self-reported ratings of delays incurred by technical debt.

Satisfaction

Engineering satisfaction is a multifaceted concept, which makes it challenging to understand, predict, or measure. This dimension captures human factors of productivity and has several possible subcomponents, including physiological factors such as fatigue, team comfort measures such as psychological safety, and individual feelings of flow/focus, autonomy, or happiness. Learning or skill development that may positively impact long-term quality, developer retention, or velocity may manifest as an increase in satisfaction. For developers, satisfaction may be impacted by the real or perceived effectiveness of their personal work or their team's work.

Lenses

The three dimensions of productivity can be viewed through different lenses. These lenses may help to narrow a research goal and provide perspective on the subsequent methods we may use to understand or measure productivity. The following are the main types of lenses we feel are important to consider:

- *Stakeholders*: Different stakeholders (e.g., developer, manager, vice president, etc.) may have varied goals and interpretations of any sort of productivity measurement. Before trying to understand and measure productivity, it is essential to identify which stakeholders are of concern and what is important to those stakeholders. It may not be immediately obvious which stakeholders should be considered; a researcher or practitioner may need to carefully elicit which stakeholder perspectives are important.

- *Context*: Particular project, social, and cultural factors will change perceptions of productivity. For example, if developers feel that helping others is valued by their team, then they will feel that time spent answering questions is productive. The underlying development context (e.g., open source projects versus projects focused on profits) affects productivity goals. Though context lenses are often implicit, sometimes it may be necessary to explicitly consider the impact of any norms, values, or attitudes.

- *Level*: Each lens in the level category represents a particular scale (in terms of group size) at which productivity is considered. Individual developers, teams, organizations and the surrounding community will lead to different perceptions of productivity, and productivity goals may also be in tension across these different groups. An intervention that may benefit one level may not hold at all levels. As a concrete example, interruptions that negatively impact the person who is interrupted may lead to a net gain from a team perspective. For an in-depth look at four different level lenses, see Chapter 6.

- *Time period*: Productivity perceptions vary greatly according to the period of time that is considered (shorter terms such as days, weeks, or sprints or longer terms such as months, years, or milestones). For example, a process change may slow down velocity in the short term but lead to enhanced team learning over time and thus speed up velocity over a longer time period. Similarly, short-term velocity enhancements may lead to fatigue and lower developer satisfaction over a longer period of time.

The Productivity Framework in Action: Articulating Goals, Questions, and Metrics

Given a particular high-level productivity goal, a common desire is to derive specific metrics that track such a goal. Unfortunately, going from goals to metrics is not trivial as metrics are typically proxies for specific aspects of a goal. One technique to bridge this divide is to have an intermediate state under consideration. For example, the goal-question-metric (GQM) approach for understanding and measuring the software process [1, 2] works by first generating "questions" that define goals and then specifying measures that could answer those questions. GQM suggests a systematic approach to do the following:

- **Conceptualize goals** aimed at understanding or improving software engineering tools and processes

- Specify **research questions** to operationalize those goals

- Define **metrics** for understanding or measuring tools and processes

Similar to GQM, the HEART framework is used for measuring usability in design projects [3]. HEART first decomposes a high-level usability goal (such as "my app is awesome") into subgoals, abstract "signals" that could measure those subgoals (e.g., time spent with app), and specific metrics for those signals (e.g., number of shares or number of articles read in app). In addition to this goals-signals-metrics breakdown, the HEART framework splits usability into five dimensions: happiness, engagement, adoption, retention, and task success.

Inspired by the way that the HEART framework involves both splitting by dimensions and breaking down from goals to metrics, we propose splitting into goals, questions, and metrics in combination with the productivity dimensions and lenses. This technique can guide the development of specific questions and metrics toward the concrete productivity goals identified. Such goals include measuring the impact of an intervention, identifying anti-patterns or problem spots causing productivity losses, comparing groups, or understanding productivity for a particular context. To illustrate how the framework may be used, we sketch two hypothetical examples in the following sections.

Example 1: Improving Productivity Through an Intervention

A manager of a software development team (the stakeholder) in a large software company (the context) would like to *improve productivity through the introduction of a new continuous integration system* (the stakeholder's productivity goal). She hopes that productivity will be improved for both individual developers and the team overall (the levels) and intends to measure the change over the time frame of a few months (the time period).

A set of specific questions about productivity improvements arises from considering the productivity goal through the identified lenses along each dimension. Since these questions are specific, it is possible to identify a set of metrics that may help to answer them, as shown in Table 5-1. Note that productivity metrics are always proxies for what you really want to measure, and there is a many-to-one relationship between metrics and a specific question, as well as between a set of specific questions and one or more productivity goals.

Productivity Goal 1: Improve Productivity at the Individual and Team Levels Through the Introduction of a New Continuous Integration System

Table 5-1. *Breaking Down Productivity Goal 1 Along the Three Dimensions*

Productivity Dimensions	Questions	Example Metrics
Quality	Is the committed code of a higher quality?	Test coverage. Number of bugs post release.
Velocity	Are developers able to deploy their features more quickly?	Time from creating a patch to patch release. Time to reach team milestones.
Satisfaction	Are developers more satisfied with the engineering process using the new tool?	Developer ratings for the new system. Developer ratings of team communication enabled by tool.

Example 2: Understanding How Meetings Impact Productivity

For this example, we consider a situation where the stakeholder wants to understand rather than try to improve productivity (although improving it may be a longer-term goal). The scenario we present here is the case where developers (the stakeholders) working in a team that also collaborates with other teams at their large company (the context) would like to *understand how meetings impact productivity* (the goal). Here the developers are more interested in an exploratory approach to understanding the impact of meetings on productivity. The dimensions and the lenses help form research questions, as shown in Table 5-2. In this example, even though no metrics have been defined, research questions can help sharpen an exploratory analysis by making it more concrete. Since the needs and goals of individual developers might conflict with those of the team and/or organization an exploratory analysis can help clarify such conflicts and form a basis for later change. Note that in the table we show only a sample of possible relevant questions along each dimension.

Productivity Goal 2: Develop an Understanding of How Meetings May Impact Productivity

Table 5-2. *Breaking Down Productivity Goal 2 Along the Three Dimensions*

Productivity Dimensions	Questions
Quality	Which meetings prompt follow-up work?
	Which meetings feel like a waste of time?
	Were all meeting participants needed in the meeting?
Velocity	What characterizes meetings that are the right length?
	What is the right length for meetings?
Satisfaction	What characterizes meetings where people feel good after attending?

Caveats

The framework we propose is abstract by its nature and thus may not suit all studies of productivity, nor may it match every nuanced definition of productivity. Other researchers and practitioners may want to consider additional dimensions or lenses depending on their needs. For example, learning/education could be considered as an explicit fourth dimension if this is important to the productivity goals under consideration.

When the dimensions framework is used with GQM, it may not be immediately evident to the researcher or practitioner what should be framed as a goal and what should be framed as one or more questions, as a goal could be stated as a research question or vice versa. As mentioned earlier, the HEART framework offers an alternative of using signals instead of questions. We have found it useful in practice to iteratively break down productivity measures along these three dimensions, and GQM is one approach for this.

As we noted earlier, any metrics defined are proxies for the concepts being measured. It is important to choose metrics that adequately capture key aspects of measured concepts and to be aware that every metric has limitations. We also stress that measuring engineer satisfaction is challenging, as satisfaction is influenced by and refers to many different concepts. The lenses together with the research goal may help in identifying how satisfaction should be conceptualized or measured. When it comes to satisfaction in particular, we stress there is no one-size-fits-all solution.

Finally, identifying/focusing on the right goals is outside the scope of this framework. A researcher or practitioner may assume the work being done is the right work when in fact it may not be (that is, the wrong tasks may be worked on in a productive manner!).

Key Ideas

Here are the key ideas from this chapter:

- Productivity should be considered along three dimensions: quality, velocity, and satisfaction.

- These three dimensions complement each other but often are in tension with each other.

- The dimensions have several possible attributes; measuring them is highly task and situation dependent.

- Productivity goals may be refined by considering the three dimensions through a set of perspective lenses.

- The main lenses we suggest include the stakeholders, the development context, the levels, and the time scale.

References

[1] Victor R. Basili, Gianluigi Caldiera, and H. D. Rombach. The Goal Question Metric Approach. In Encyclopedia of Software Engineering (John J. Marciniak, Ed.), John Wiley & Sons, Inc., 1994, Vol. 1, pp.528–532.

[2] V. R. Basili, G. Caldiera, and H. Dieter Rombach. The Goal Question Metric Approach. NASA GSFC Software Engineering Laboratory, 1994. (ftp://ftp.cs.umd.edu/pub/sel/papers/gqm.pdf)

[3] HEART framework for measuring UX. https://www.interaction-design.org/literature/article/google-s-heart-framework-for-measuring-ux

CHAPTER 6

Individual, Team, Organization, and Market: Four Lenses of Productivity

Amy J. Ko, University of Washington, USA

When we think about productivity in software development, it's reasonable to start with a basic concept of work per unit of effort. The more work a developer accomplishes with their efforts, the better.

But when researchers have investigated how developers think about productivity, some surprising nuances surface about what software engineering "work" actually is and at what level this work should be considered [14]. In particular, there are four lenses through which one can reason about productivity, and each of these has different implications for what actions one might take to increase productivity in a company.

The Individual

The first and most obvious lens is the *individual* perspective. For a developer, a tester, or any other contributor to a software team, it's reasonable to think about the tasks they are assigned, how efficiently those tasks can be completed, and what affects how efficiently those tasks are completed. Obviously, a developer's experience—what they've learned in school, online, or in other jobs—can affect how efficiently they accomplish tasks. For example, one study showed that in terms of task completion time, the skill of *comprehending* what a program does explains much of the variance in task completion

© The Author(s) 2019

C. Sadowski and T. Zimmermann (eds.), *Rethinking Productivity in Software Engineering*,

https://doi.org/10.1007/978-1-4842-4221-6_6

time [3]. But these skills aren't static. For example, while one might expect inexperienced developers to always be less efficient than experts, teaching novices expert strategies can make them match expert performance quite quickly [17]. As any developer knows, however, there's no such thing as mastery; even senior developers are always engaged in learning new concepts, architectures, platforms, and APIs [5]. This constant learning is even more necessary for new hires, whose instincts are often to hide their lack of expertise from the people they need help from [1].

But experience isn't the only factor that affects individual productivity. For example, we know that tools strongly influence how efficiently a development task can be completed. IDEs, APIs, and programming languages, for example, pose many barriers, including finding relevant APIs, learning to use them correctly, and learning to test and debug them correctly [7]. For example, one study found that simply using rudimentary tools for navigating code (scroll bars, text search, etc.) can account for up to a third of the time spent debugging code [8]. Another study found that tracking the specific structural elements in code that a developer navigates and making those structures and their dependencies visible can nearly reduce this overhead [6].

Having the right documentation with the right information (e.g., Stack Overflow or other sources of information about API usage) can also accelerate program construction [11], but when that documentation is wrong, it can actually have the opposite effect on time to complete tasks [18].

These discoveries have some simple implications for individual developer productivity. For example, teaching developers strategies that have proven to be more effective seems like an unqualified win. Training developers on tools that increase productivity is a potentially cheap way to help developers get more work done in the same amount of time.

The Team

And yet, when we use a *team* lens on productivity, some of these improvements to developer productivity suddenly seem less important. For example, if one developer is twice as efficient as others on a team but is constantly blocked waiting for work from others, is the team really more productive? Research shows that team productivity is actually bounded not by how efficiently individual developers work but by communication and coordination overhead [5]. This is partly because teams work only as fast as decisions can be made, and many of the most important decisions are not made individually but collaboratively. However, this is also because even for individual decisions, developers often need information from teammates, which studies have shown is always one or two orders of magnitude slower to obtain than referencing documentation, logs, or other automatically retrievable content [10]. These interactions between individual productivity and team work are also affected by changes in team membership: one study found that *slowly* adding people to a team (i.e., waiting for them to successfully onboard) *reduced* defects, but *quickly* adding them *increased* in defects [13].

Other team needs can lower productivity for individuals but increase it for the team. For example, interruptions can be a nuisance for individual developers, but if they have knowledge that others need to be unblocked, it may improve team productivity overall. Similarly, senior developers may need to teach skills or knowledge to junior developers to help junior developers be independently productive. That will reduce the senior developer's productivity for a time but will probably increase the team's long-term productivity.

If we view a team's work as correctly meeting requirements, then the influence of communication and collaboration on a team is clearly just as important as the productivity of individual developers on meeting those requirements. Finding a way to manage teams that streamlines communication, coordination, and decision-making is therefore key and perhaps more impactful than making individual developers faster. All of these responsibilities fall upon an engineering manager, whose notion of productivity isn't about how *efficiently* individual engineers work but rather about how efficiently a team can meet high-value requirements.

The Organization

Even a team lens, however, is a narrow view. An *organizational* lens reveals other important factors. For example, companies often set norms around how projects are managed, and these norms can greatly influence how efficiently work can move at the individual and team levels [4]. Organizations also set policies on whether developers are collocated, work down the hall, work at home, or work in entirely different countries. These policies, and their implications for coordination, can directly affect the speed of decisions proportionally to distance [16]. Organizations can also set formal policies and informal expectations about work-life balance, which can inadvertently lead to fatigue and defects [9]. Organizations have different norms of code ownership, which affects coordination within and between teams and can lead to defects when no one owns part of an implementation [2]. Organizations also invest infrastructure for maintaining awareness of work in other parts of the organization [12], such as Google, which has a single company-wide repository, versus other companies that have vast numbers of disconnected repositories. Companies also have different norms about how interruptions are handled, which can have organization-wide detrimental effects on productivity [15]. All of these cultural and policy factors can also complicate the recruiting and retention of productive developers, as we observed with Yahoo's decision to require that all engineers work on the main Yahoo campus.

Given all of these complex factors of organizational culture, one might imagine that a fruitful way to think about productivity from an organizational perspective is to reason about the unintended consequences of norms and policies on individual and team productivity. An organization's executives might be charged with monitoring for these problems and developing new policies, norms, and processes with fewer impacts on productivity.

The Market

Finally, the organizational lens has its own limitations. Viewing productivity from a *market* lens acknowledges that the whole purpose of an organization that creates software is to provide *value* to customers and other stakeholders. When Google says its mission is to "organize the world's information," it's stating the goal by which the entire organization's performance is judged. Google is therefore more effective when its users are more productive at finding information and answering questions relative to other organizations with similar goals. To measure productivity in terms of value, a company has to define *value propositions* for its product, which is some hypothesis about what value a product is offering to people relative to competing solutions. Some research has framed the refinement and measurement of value propositions as an organization's primary goal [9]. These ever-evolving understandings of an organization's goal then filter down to new organizational policies, new team-level project management strategies, and new developer work strategies targeted at improving this top-level notion of productivity.

Full-Spectrum Productivity

While it's easy to assume that each individual in an organization might have to concern themselves with only one of these lenses, studies of software engineering expertise show that great developers are capable of reasoning about code through *all* of these lenses [5]. After all, when a developer writes or repairs a line of code, not only are they getting an engineering task done, they're also meeting a team's goals, achieving an organization's strategic objectives, and ultimately enabling an organization to test its product's value proposition in a market. And the code they write can be seen as a different thing through each of these lenses, including not just code but also systems, software, platforms, and services, and products.

What does all of this mean for *measuring* productivity? It means you're not going to find one measure for everything. Individuals, teams, organizations, and markets need their own metrics because the factors that affect performance at each of these levels are too complex to reduce to a single measure. I actually believe that individual developers, teams, organizations, and markets are so idiosyncratic that each may need its own unique measures of performance that capture a valid notion of their work output (productivity, speed, product quality, actual versus plan, etc.). That might mean a core competency of everyone in an organization needs to be finding valid ways of conceiving of performance so one can measure and improve it.

Key Ideas

The following are the key ideas from this chapter:

- Individuals, teams, organizations, and markets need different productivity metrics.

- Productivities for these different lenses are often in tension.

References

[1]   Begel, A., & Simon, B. (2008). Novice software developers, all over again. ICER.

[2]   Bird, C., Nagappan, N., et al. (2011). Don't touch my code! Examining the effects of ownership on software quality. ESEC/FSE.

[3]   Dagenais, B., Ossher, H., et al. (2010). Moving into a new software project landscape. ICSE.

[4]   DeMarco, T. & Lister, R. (1985). Programmer performance and the effects of the workplace. ICSE.

[5]   Li, P.L., Ko, A.J., & Zhu, J. (2015). What makes a great software engineer? ICSE.

[6]   Kersten, M., & Murphy, G. C. (2006). Using task context to improve programmer productivity. FSE.

[7]   Ko, A. J., Myers, B. A., & Aung, H.H. (2004). Six learning barriers in end-user programming systems. VL/HCC.

[8]   Ko, A.J., Aung, H.H., & Myers, B.A. (2005). Eliciting design requirements for maintenance-oriented IDEs: a detailed study of corrective and perfective maintenance tasks. ICSE.

[9]   Ko, A.J. (2017). A Three-Year Participant Observation of Software Startup Software Evolution. ICSE SEIP.

[10] LaToza, T.D., Venolia, G., & DeLine, R. (2006). Maintaining mental models: a study of developer work habits. ICSE SEIP.

[11] Mamykina, L., Manoim, B., et al. (2011). Design lessons from the fastest Q&A site in the west. CHI.

[12] Milewski, A. E. (2007). Global and task effects in information-seeking among software engineers. ESE, 12(3).

[13] Meneely, A., Rotella, P., & Williams, L. (2011). Does adding manpower also affect quality? An empirical, longitudinal analysis. ESEC/FSE.

[14] Meyer, A.N., Fritz, T., et al. (2014). Software developers' perceptions of productivity. FSE.

[15] Perlow, L. A. (1999). The time famine: Toward a sociology of work time. Administrative science quarterly, 44(1).

[16] Smite, D., Wohlin, C., et al. (2010). Empirical evidence in global software engineering: a systematic review. ESE, 15(1).

[17]   Benjamin Xie, Greg Nelson, and Amy J. Ko (2018). An Explicit Strategy to Scaffold Novice Program Tracing. ACM Technical Symposium on Computer Science Education (SIGCSE).

[18]   Fischer, F., Böttinger, K., Xiao, H., Stransky, C., Acar, Y., Backes, M., & Fahl, S. (2017). Stack overflow considered harmful? The impact of copy&paste on android application security. IEEE Symposium on Security and Privacy (SP).

CHAPTER 7

Software Productivity Through the Lens of Knowledge Work

Emerson Murphy-Hill, Google, USA
Stefan Wagner, University of Stuttgart, Germany

While this book focuses on software developer productivity, other fields have studied productivity more broadly. Such work lends a perspective that can contribute to a solid foundation to what we know about software developer productivity. In this chapter, we provide an overview of related work about perhaps the most relevant allied field outside of software engineering, namely, the productivity of *knowledge workers*.

A Brief History of Knowledge Work

The term *knowledge work* was coined by the management guru Peter Drucker in 1959 [1]. Unlike manual labor where the main output is largely physical goods, knowledge workers deal primarily with information, where each task is usually different from the last, and the main output of the work is knowledge.

Later, Drucker challenged the field of management research to improve the productivity of knowledge workers in the same way they improved the productivity of manual laborers [2]. Drucker's contrast of knowledge worker productivity against manual worker productivity is insightful. While productivity of the manual worker can

C. Sadowski and T. Zimmermann (eds.), *Rethinking Productivity in Software Engineering*,
https://doi.org/10.1007/978-1-4842-4221-6_7

be improved by understanding and automating the routine steps involved in creating a physical good, the steps involved in the tasks performed by knowledge workers are so nonroutine that similar kinds of automation cannot be easily employed.

For the past half-century, studies in management and other social sciences have examined how to improve the productivity of the knowledge worker. Because software developers are one kind of knowledge worker, it stands to reason that much of what such studies have learned will be applicable to software developer productivity as well.

Studies about knowledge workers can teach us at least two things about productivity of software developers: techniques for measuring productivity and a set of drivers that have been shown to affect knowledge worker productivity. We next discuss each in turn.

Techniques for Measuring Productivity

As we discuss elsewhere in this book, measuring software developers' productivity is challenging, and likely no single metric will do (see Chapters 2 and 3). This problem also afflicts researchers in knowledge work, yet they have made progress on the problem by developing a breadth of techniques for measuring productivity. We next describe the techniques used to measure knowledge worker productivity by turning to a taxonomy of techniques from Ramírez and Nembhard [4]. We describe some of those techniques and discuss the trade-offs in using each technique. Further, we group these techniques into four categories, which we call outcome-oriented, process-oriented, people-oriented, and multi-oriented techniques. Software engineering practitioners and researchers can use these categories to choose appropriate productivity measures for their contexts.

Outcome-Oriented Techniques

In the original literature on improving the productivity of manual workers, it was common to measure productivity by looking primarily at the output of work per unit time. For software developers, this could be realized by measuring the number of lines of code written per day, for instance. This measurement technique has also been extended in knowledge worker research by accounting for inputs to the process—such as resources or salaries used by the workers. Such outcome-oriented techniques have the advantage of being relatively straightforward to measure. However, as Ramírez and Nembhard point out, the knowledge worker research community has largely converged on the opinion that such outcome-oriented techniques are generally inadequate because they fail to take into account output *quality*, which they generally regard as a critical aspect of productivity. See Chapter 5 for an in depth discussion of the importance of quality when measuring productivity. An additional challenge to outcome-oriented metrics for software engineering is that difficult software problems may have similar-appearing output to easy problems.

Another refinement of these outcome-oriented techniques is using organizational economic output as the outcome, such as a company's earnings. The main advantage of this approach is that economic output is arguably the most direct measure of productivity, at least at a large scale—if a developer's work does not produce profit directly or indirectly, are they really being productive? The disadvantages of this approach is that, as Ramírez and Nembhard point out, tracing profits down to individual knowledge workers is difficult and also that present economic output is not necessarily indicative of future potential economic output. In complex software organizations, measuring the economic effect of key but indirect developers—such as open source developers or infrastructure teams—is relatively challenging.

Process-Oriented Techniques

Rather than looking at the outcomes of work, some studies examine how knowledge workers' tasks are performed. For instance, using the *multiminute measurement* technique, knowledge workers fill out forms at regular intervals, reporting what they have done from a predefined list of tasks. Building on this, productivity measurement techniques can measure the time spent in value-added activities, which looks at what percentage of time knowledge workers spend doing desirable activities compared to the total number of hours worked. In software engineering, we could define desirable activities as activities that add value to the software product. This could include constructive activities, such as writing code, but also analytical, improving activities, such as performing code reviews. The advantage of such techniques is that they are amenable to some amount of automation, such as through experience sampling tools (for example, `www.experiencesampler.com/`) or instrumentation like RescueTime (`https://www.rescuetime.com/`). The primary disadvantages are that simply measuring activities doesn't measure how well knowledge workers conduct those activities and that it doesn't take into account quality. To the latter point, some activity-tracking techniques have also been extended to measure quality-enhancing activities, such as by counting thinking and organizing as activities that enhance quality and thus enhance productivity. This shows, however, that it is difficult to clearly distinguish between value-adding and non-value-adding activities. Potentially, the categorization of *waste* could be useful (see Chapter 19).

People-Oriented Techniques

In contrast to the prior techniques, which seek to define productive outcomes and activities up-front, people-oriented techniques empower knowledge workers to define metrics for productivity for themselves. One way to do this is through the *achievement method*, which measures productivity by determining the ratio of completed goals to planned goals. An extension of the achievement method is the *normative productivity measurement* methodology, which works to establish consensus among knowledge workers about the different dimensions of productivity. The advantage of these techniques is that measuring productivity as completion of self-determined goals has good construct validity, as research suggests that task or goal completion is the top reason that software developers report having a productive workday [5].

Using interviews and surveys to measure productivity is "a straightforward and commonly used method" to measure knowledge worker productivity and to determine knowledge worker compensation [4]. Such techniques have the advantage of being relatively easy to administer with existing instruments from the literature and can capture a wide variety of productivity factors. On the other hand, such techniques may have low reliability. To increase the reliability of these techniques, many studies have used *peer evaluations*, where knowledge workers rate their peers' productivity. However, the disadvantage of this technique is the so-called halo effect, where a peer might rate a knowledge worker's past performance as indicative of their current performance, even if past and present productivity are unrelated.

Multi-oriented Techniques

As we describe in Chapters 5 and 6, productivity can be measured through multiple facets within an organization; likewise, the knowledge worker literature has sought to understand productivity through multiple facets. For example, the *multiple output productivity indicator* can be used to measure productivity when a knowledge worker has more than one output. For instance, a software developer not only produces code but also produces infrastructure tools and trains peers in organizational development practices. A multiple-level productivity measurement technique is the *macro, micro, and mid-knowledge worker productivity models*, which seeks to measure productivity at the factory, individual contributor, and department levels, respectively. This technique measures productivity over time using attributes such as quality, cost, and lost time. The main advantage of these techniques is that they provide a more holistic view of organizational productivity than many other metrics, but at the same time, collecting them can be complex.

These three kinds of techniques—process-, people-, and multi-oriented—provide a variety of options for practitioners and researchers to use. One way these techniques can be used is to enable those who want to measure productivity to use off-the-shelf, validated techniques, rather than creating new techniques with unknown validity. Another way these techniques can be used is as a framework to broaden productivity-measurement efforts; if an organization is already using process-oriented productivity techniques, they could broaden their portfolio by adding people-oriented techniques. Similarly, researchers can choose multiple techniques to increase the validity of their studies through triangulation.

Drivers That Influence Productivity

The second major contribution of research on knowledge workers that can be applied to software engineers is an understanding of what drivers can change knowledge workers' productivity. Understanding productivity drivers is valuable because it tells organizations what changes they can make to improve knowledge worker productivity. While some productivity drivers are specific to software development, such as code complexity (see also Chapter 8), other drivers probably apply equally well to knowledge workers generally and software developers specifically, such as the need for quiet spaces required for concentration.

We draw on prior research, which we have found personally insightful, that catalogs productivity drivers among knowledge workers. In an attempt to measure knowledge worker productivity, Palvalin created SmartWoW, a survey that captures all the drivers that affect productivity, according to the knowledge work literature [3]; readers who want to know the strength of the scientific evidence for each factor are encouraged to explore the research cited by Palvalin. Palvalin showed that his survey has reasonable validity and reliability by assessing it at nine companies with almost 1,000 knowledge workers. SmartWoW divides productivity drivers into five types, which we describe here:

Physical environment. The physical environment refers to the place where the work occurs, whether that's in the office or at home. Studies of knowledge workers have found that a physical environment that increases productivity is one where there is adequate space for solitary work for concentration, official and unofficial meetings, and informal collaboration. A physical environment that enhances productivity also has good ergonomics with low noise and few interruptions. Software developers' frequent complaints about open offices underscore the importance of work environment drivers.

Virtual environment. The virtual environment refers to the technology that knowledge workers use. A virtual environment that enhances productivity is one where the technology is easy to use and available wherever the knowledge worker is working. Knowledge work studies have also identified several specific types of technology as productivity-enhancing, including use of instant messaging, video conferencing, access to co-workers' calendars, and other collaborative groupware. This research suggests that usable programming languages and powerful tools, as well as collaboration platforms like GitHub, are important for improving software developer productivity.

Social environment. The social environment refers to the attitudes, routines, policies, and habits performed by workers in an organization. Productive social environments are those where knowledge workers are given freedom to choose their work methods, work times, and work locations; information flows freely among workers; meetings are efficient; clear technology usage and communication policies exist; goals are cohesive and clearly defined; work is assessed in terms of outcomes, not just in terms of activities; and experimentation with new work methods is encouraged. A social environment for software development that enhances productivity is one where, for example, developers are given freedom to try new tools and methodologies. The importance of the social environment is underscored by Google's finding that psychological safety—that members of a team should be able to take risks without fear— is the most important predictor of effective teams.

Individual work practices. While the prior environmental drivers *enable* productive work through organizational practices, individual work practices measure to what extent knowledge workers will actually implement these practices. Productive individual work practices include knowledge workers using technology to reduce unnecessary travel, using mobile devices when waiting (e.g., during travel), prioritizing important tasks, using quiet spaces and shutting down disruptive software during tasks that require concentration, preparing for meetings, taking care of their well-being, using the organizations' official communication channels, planning out their workday, and experimenting with new tools and work methods. This suggests that developers are productive when, for example, they can code, test, and push while commuting to work on shared transit.

Well-being at work. Finally, Palvalin includes a knowledge worker's well-being at work both as a driver of productivity at work and as an outcome of productivity. A productive knowledge worker is one who enjoys and is enthusiastic about their work, finds meaning and purpose in their work, is not continuously stressed, is appreciated, has a work-life balance, finds the work atmosphere pleasant, and resolves conflicts with co-workers quickly. This suggests that the famous 80-hour workweek developer is not a productive developer.

Software Developers vs. Knowledge Workers: Similar or Different?

In this chapter, we've drawn parallels between software developer and knowledge worker productivity, so it's natural to ask whether one should consider their productivity the same or different. Our opinion is that each extreme is a cop-out; considering software developer productivity the same as knowledge worker productivity would abdicate our responsibility to study the productivity of software developers, while considering them as entirely different would allow us to reinvent the wheel by ignoring prior studies about knowledge worker productivity.

The reality is that knowledge workers and software developers are similar in some ways and different in others, both in kind and in degree. In kind, arguably everything that could possibly affect software developer productivity can be pigeonholed into one the five types of productivity drivers described in the prior section, but doing so elides some drivers that software developers may be uniquely positioned to measure and change, such as software complexity. In degree, software developers' productivity is similar in some ways and different in others. For instance, while surveying Google's employees, the first author found that job enthusiasm affects productivity to a nearly identical degree for both Google's knowledge workers and its software developers; on the other hand, he also found that time management autonomy affected knowledge workers' productivity substantially *more* than it affected software developers' productivity.

In sum, those who want to understand the productivity of software developers should also understand the productivity of knowledge workers, not because the latter can replace the former but instead so they can make informed choices about when existing measures and factors ought to be used and when new measures and factors ought to be invented.

Summary

While software development has its specific characteristics, there is a lot to learn from studies of general knowledge work. First, it is not sufficient to look at quantity of output but to include the quality of the work as well (see Chapters 4 and 5). Second, it provides approaches to measure productivity besides outcome. Still, knowledge work research has not found a suitable way to capture all important aspects of productivity. Third, it provides a set of drivers for productivity that are directly applicable to software development, such as enough space for solitary work and a pleasant work atmosphere.

Key Ideas

The following are the key ideas from the chapter:

- Software developers are a specific kind of knowledge worker. Knowledge worker productivity has been studied in a variety of contexts, and those studies can be used to understand software developers.

- There are four main techniques for measuring knowledge worker productivity: outcome-, process-, people-, and multi-oriented productivity measurement techniques.

- There are five categories of drivers that knowledge worker research suggests influence productivity: the physical environment, the virtual environment, the social environment, individual work practices, and well-being at work.

References

[1]   Drucker, P. F. (1959). Landmarks of tomorrow. Harper & Brothers.

[2]   Drucker, P. F. (1999). Knowledge-worker productivity: The biggest challenge. California management review, 41(2), 79-94.

[3]   Palvalin, M. (2017). How to measure impacts of work environment changes on knowledge work productivity–validation and improvement of the SmartWoW tool. Measuring Business Excellence, 21(2).

[4]   Ramírez, Y. W., & Nembhard, D. A. (2004). Measuring knowledge worker productivity: A taxonomy. Journal of intellectual capital, 5(4), 602–628.

[5]   Meyer A. N., Fritz T., Murphy G. C., Zimmermann T. (2014). Software developers' perceptions of productivity. SIGSOFT FSE 2014: 19–29.

PART III

The Context of Productivity

CHAPTER 8

Factors That Influence Productivity: A Checklist

Stefan Wagner, University of Stuttgart, Germany

Emerson Murphy-Hill, Google, USA

Introduction

In all areas of professional work, there are a lot of factors that influence productivity. Especially in knowledge work, where we do not have easily and clearly measurable work products, it is difficult to capture these factors. Software development is a type of knowledge work that comes with even more specific difficulties, as software developers deal nowadays with incredibly large and complex systems.

Yet, developers have to run software projects, manage other software developers, and optimize software development to make projects more competitive. Hence, we need a good overview of factors influencing productivity in software development so that developers and managers know what to focus and work on. Developers and managers probably have learned some factors that affect individual productivity, as well as team productivity, from experience. Even more useful, however, would be a list of factors that empirically have been shown to impact productivity in a more general way.

We provide such a list in this chapter as a kind of checklist that a developer or software manager can use to improve productivity. We will discuss technical factors related to the product, the process, and the development environment, as well as soft factors related to the corporate culture, the team culture, individual skills and experiences, the work environment, and the individual project.

© The Author(s) 2019

C. Sadowski and T. Zimmermann (eds.), *Rethinking Productivity in Software Engineering*,
https://doi.org/10.1007/978-1-4842-4221-6_8

A Brief History of Productivity Factors Research

There has been research on productivity in software development since the 1970s. The first studies have been very influential, and several of the factors we have compiled in this chapter were identified back then. However, some of the factors from the 1970s, such as chief programmer team usage or previous experience with operational computers, have become less important over time.

The 1980s saw a more systematic collection of data with, for example, a series of books by Jones [7]. But researchers also realized the importance of psychological and sociological factors. Most important, as De Marco and Lister discuss in Peopleware [3], are aspects such as employee turnover and the developers' workplace. They also emphasize product quality as an important factor for productivity. Around the same time, the most famous effort prediction model was published, COCOMO [6].

Maybe as a result of Peopleware, the 1990s saw more research on soft factors. There were studies on project duration and the usage of object-oriented approaches. In the 2000s, no completely new aspects were introduced, but the understanding of several factors, such as requirements volatility or customer participation, was investigated.

We will summarize the main factors from these decades of research and add a brief review of newer factors that have been investigated in the 2010's so far.

The List of Technical Factors

The following three tables show the product, process, and environment factors that have been found in the literature to have an impact on software development productivity. The factors in the tables are sorted alphabetically.

Product Factors

The list of product factors has seen little change over the past ten years. There are several factors related to size and complexity. Software size usually means the size of the code needed for the software system. Product complexity tries to capture how difficult it is to implement the system with more or less code. In any case, the extent and complexity of the software including its data is a major factor that reduces productivity. Related are also technical dependencies. Newer studies have focused on the dependencies between different software modules or components and how this is reflected in social dependencies in the development team. A high number of dependencies reduces productivity.

Factor	Description	Source
Developed for reusability	To what extent should the components be reusable?	[1]
Development flexibility	How strong are the constraints on the system?	[1]
Execution time constraints	How much of the available execution time is consumed?	[1]
Main storage constraint	How much of the available storage is consumed?	[1]
Precedentedness	How similar are the projects?	[1]
Product complexity	The complexity of the function and structure of the software.	[1]
Product quality	The quality of the product influences motivation and hence productivity.	[1]
Required software reliability	The level of reliability needed.	[1]
Reuse	The extent of reuse.	[1]
Software size	The amount of code in the system.	[1]
User interface	The degree of complexity of the user interface.	[1]
Technical dependencies	Data-related or functional dependencies such as call graphs or coupled changes.	[5, 11]

A further set of factors that are related are constraints on execution time, main storage constraints, and constraints overall, what we term development flexibility. This could be integrated into a single factor. However, the first two describe more specific real-time and embedded systems, while the latter can also cover other constraints. An example of these constraints might be the use of specific operating systems or database systems or a high number of concurrent users. Additional constraints potentially slow down development.

Furthermore, the requirements on the user interface play an important role. It is a difference if a graphical user interface has to be developed or if the product is a background service. Sophisticated user interfaces typically reduce productivity.

The next product factors are related to quality. The current product quality makes it easier or more complicated to work on the software. Higher requirements on reliability and reusability can increase the effort needed. New publications widen this also to other quality attributes.

Finally, what the organization has done before plays a role: precedentedness describes how similar the project in question is to existing software, and reuse describes how much of the new software can be achieved by reusing existing software (e.g., internal or open source).

Process Factors

The next category of factors are still technical but relate more to the process than the product itself. These factors are related to the project: project length and project type. Longer projects are more difficult to organize but benefit more from rules and custom tools. A more recent study [8] distinguished between development and integration projects. Development projects create most of the software during the project, while integration projects mostly connect and configure existing software. They found that integration projects are more productive.

Factor	Description	Source
Agile	Is an agile development process used?	[10, 12, 13]
Architecture risk resolution	How are the risks mitigated by architecture?	[1]
Completeness of design	The amount of the design that is completed when coding starts.	[1]
Early prototyping	Early in the process prototypes are built.	[1]
Effective and efficient V&V	The degree to which defects are found and the required effort therein.	[1]
Hardware concurrent development	Is the hardware developed concurrently?	[1]
Outsourcing and global distribution	Degree of outsourcing of the work of the project.	[9]
Platform volatility	Time span between major changes.	[1]
Process maturity	The well-definedness of the process.	[1]
Project duration	Length of the project.	[1]
Project type	Integration or development project.	[8]

From the next factors, we see that different development activities have an impact on productivity. Architecture risk resolution is important in architecture design and evolution. The completeness of design before the start of coding impacts how much changes need to be done later. Finally, effective and efficient V&V (verification & validation) describes suitable tests, reviews, and automated analysis. Early prototyping can increase productivity because requirements can be clarified and risks can be resolved. Today, this is often replaced by iterative and incremental development. Such a development probably is able to better deal with volatile requirements, but the completeness of the design during initial coding is low.

Most systems today are not completely stand-alone but rely on specific platforms or hardware. If the platform changes frequently (platform volatility), it creates a lot of adaptation effort. The concurrent development of hardware also means that it is difficult to rely on the hardware and might require adaptation efforts in the software.

The last factors are about the process model and the distribution of the work. A general factor is the process maturity, meaning how well-defined the development process is. In the recent years, research has focused on agile processes and found that they impact productivity. A further aspect of recent studies is outsourcing and global distribution of the project.

Development Environment

In the last category, we group factors that are not part of the product but not directly part of the process either.

Factor	Description	Source
Documentation match to life-cycle needs	How well the documentation fits the needs	[1]
Domain	Application domain such as embedded software, management information system, or web application	[4]
Programming language	The programming language used	[1, 21]
Use of software tools	The degree of tool use	[1]
Use of modern development practices	For example, continuous integration, automated testing, or configuration management	[1]

A very general factor is the domain of the application to be developed. Embedded software systems, for example, often have specific aspects such as cross-compiling that make development more difficult. Also quite general is the programming language used and the use of modern development practices. The latter includes methods such as continuous integration or automated tests that often come with agile development processes but are not restricted to them. Furthermore, the use of software tools such as modern IDEs or test frameworks impacts productivity. Finally, we also count the match of documentation to environmental factors. In particular, it is important if the documentation fits the needs of the current state of development.

The List of Soft Factors

As most people in a software engineering team have a technical background, we tend to focus on technical aspects. Yet, especially for productivity, many more soft factors play an important role. We will discuss the soft factors we have found in the following five categories: Corporate Culture contains the factors that are on a more company-wide level, whereas Team Culture denotes similar factors on the team level. In Individual Skills and Experiences, we summarize factors that are related to individuals. Work Environment stands for properties of the environment such as the workplace itself. Finally, project-specific factors are in the Project category. We sort the factors in each category again alphabetically.

Corporate Culture

We start with the factors related to the culture of the complete organization. All these factors could also be interesting on the team level, but the culture of a company overall reflects down to the teams as well. Researchers have studied the three factors credibility, fairness, and respect especially on the organizational level.

Factor	Description	Source
Credibility	Open communication and competent organization	[1]
Fairness	Fairness in compensation and diversity	[1]
Respect	Opportunities and responsibilities	[1]

Credibility is probably the most general factor that describes that communication is open overall in the company and the organization is competent in what it is doing. In our context, this could mean, for example, that there is an understanding on the organizational level of how to plan and run software projects. In fairness, we include equal payment opportunities for all employees and diversity in terms of gender or background in the organization. Respect, finally, means that the organization sees their employees not only as "human resources" but as people; management gives the employees opportunities and trusts them with responsibilities.

Team Culture

There has been considerably more research on the team level than on the corporate level. There can be strong differences between teams in the same company. The higher number of studies brought us eight factors in team culture influencing productivity.

Factor	Description	Source
Camaraderie	Social and friendly atmosphere.	[1]
Clear goals	How clearly defined are the group goals?	[1]
Communication	The degree and efficiency of which information flows in the team.	[1]
Psychological safety	The atmosphere is safe for risk-taking.	[14, 15]
Sense of eliteness	The feeling in the team that they are superior.	[1]
Support for innovation	To what degree assistance for new ideas is available.	[1]
Team cohesion	The cooperativeness of the stakeholders.	[1]
Team identity	A common identity of the team members.	[1]
Turnover	The amount of change in the personnel.	[1]

Camaraderie means a social and friendly atmosphere where team members socialize but also help each other. The second factor in this category consists of clear goals that are necessary so that all team members work toward the same objective. Most general is the factor communication that includes the degree as well as the efficiency of information flow inside the team. In general, what is surprising in the studies is that communication effort is positive for productivity. In discussions, we often hear that communication should be reduced to decrease unnecessary work. However, the actual problems seems to be the increase of communication effort when putting more and more people on a project. Yet, a high fraction of effort on communication seems like a good investment.

Psychological safety is similar to camaraderie but more specifically refers to an atmosphere where individual developers can take risks and share personal information, but know that teammates will handle these risks with respect and kindness. This is a factor that more recently came into productivity discussions in the context of software projects because of a large study at Google [14]. Also similar but aiming in a different direction is the sense of eliteness of the team. If the team believes that they are the best engineers always building the highest-quality software, they are more likely to go the extra mile to actually achieve this.

Also related to psychological safety is support for innovation. This contains to some degree safety for taking risks, but it also means that the team members are open to bring in innovations and also change the way they work. Yet another view on this is team cohesion. Team cohesion describes how well all team members are willing to work together. This does not necessarily include a social and friendly atmosphere but a professional approach to working together.

A common team identity also seems to support productivity, probably by influencing other factors such as camaraderie or the sense of eliteness. Finally, the turnover in the team might be influenced by the factors mentioned so far. Team changes could also be ordered by management because of other influences. In any case, less turnover is better for productivity, and it is one of the few factors that we can easily measure.

Individual Skills and Experiences

Besides teams, individual skills and experiences are the most well-studied. We found it notable that although experience is often brought up and is in interviews considered important, in empirical studies it is rather insignificant. By far more interesting is the capability of the developers. Hence, this suggests that being in a profession for a long time does not necessarily make one productive.

Factor	Description	Source
Analyst capability	The skills of the system analyst	[1]
Application domain experience	The familiarity with the application domain	[1]
Developer personality	Individual personality and the mix of different personalities on the team	[1, 19]
Developer happiness	Positive experiences leading to positive emotions	[16–18]
Language and tool experience	The familiarity with the programming language and tools	
Manager application domain experience	The familiarity of the manager with the application	[1]
Manager capability	The control of the manager over the project.	[1]
Platform experience	The familiarity with the hardware and software platforms	[1]
Programmer capability	The skills of the programmer	[1]

Therefore, we have factors for the analyst capability, the manager capability, and the programmer capability. Each refers to the skills of the individuals in their respective roles. For each role, these skill sets will differ, but there is thus far no fixed set of skills necessary for the roles that came out of the studies.

Experience does play a role but more in the sense of the experience with application domains and platforms. We have the three factors of application domain experience, manager application domain experience, and platform experience. The first two refer to how long and with what intensity the developers and managers have worked on software in a specific application domain. The latter refers to the experience of the individuals with a hardware and/or software platform such as the iOS operating system for mobile Apple devices.

Developer personality has been investigated in many empirical studies. Few measure personality according to the state of the art in personality psychology. A more recent study [19] found only one personality trait—conscientiousness—impacted productivity (positively).

Similarly to the study of personalities, another important psychological area has recently been investigated: the emotions of developers. Several studies [16–18] looked at the relationship of happiness of developers and their productivity. They found indeed that happy developers are more productive. You can find more details in Chapter 10.

Work Environment

This category of factors could be seen on the organizational or team level. Yet, as there are five factors, we decided to put them in their own category. They describe the direct work environment of the software engineers.

Factor	Description	Source
E-factor	This environmental factor describes the ratio of uninterrupted hours and body-present hours.	[1]
Office layout	Private or open-plan office layout.	[22]
Physical separation	The team members are distributed over the building or multiple sites.	[1]
Proper workplace	The suitability of the workplace to do creative work.	[1]
Time fragmentation	The amount of necessary "context switches" of a person.	[1]
Telecommunication facilities	Support for work at home, virtual teams, video conferencing with clients.	[1]

The e-factor introduced by DeMarco and Lister in Peopleware [3] emphasizes that uninterrupted time for work is important for productivity. Chapter 9 discusses this in more detail, and Chapter 23 shows an idea to improve the e-factor.

Although we have not found studies focusing specifically on software engineering teams, there are several studies on office layout that should apply in our context. In software companies, we frequently see open-plan offices with the reasoning that interaction between team members is important. A recent large study [22] found no evidence that this is actually the case. Instead, interruptions are much higher; hence, the e-factor becomes worse in open-plan offices.

Distributed development of software, meaning software teams physically distributed over several locations in potentially several different time zones, is common today. There is a considerable body of work on the potential problems with this working mode. It can have a negative effect on productivity.

Also, the workplace itself has an effect on productivity. There are studies investigating aspects such as if there are windows and natural light or the size of the room and space on a desk. Time fragmentation is related to the e-factor but covers more the aspect of how many different projects and kinds of tasks you have to work on. This results in costly context switches that could be avoided if you could focus on a single project.

Finally, proper telecommunication facilities are important so that you can work from home, work efficiently part-time, or interact efficiently with other team members who are in another physical location.

Project

Finally, there are factors related to the individual project that are not technical in the sense that they come from the technology or programming language. Instead, the people associated with the project influence them.

Factor	Description	Source
Average team size	Number of people on the team	[1]
Requirements stability	The number of requirements changes	[1, 4, 20]
Schedule	The appropriateness of the schedule for the development task	[1]

There are many studies looking into the relationship of team size and productivity. It is well established that larger teams lead to exponentially increasing communication efforts that, in turn, lead to lower productivity. Newer, agile software development processes therefore often recommend team sizes of about seven.

Also, the requirements stability over a project has been the subject of several studies. Highly unstable requirements lead to time, effort, and budget overruns; overall demotivation; decreased efficiency; and the need for post-implementation [20]. Again, agile development processes focus on this problem by reducing development cycles to a few weeks.

Finally, the planned project schedule needs to fit the actual work to be done. Several studies show that schedules that are too tight in effect reduce the productivity.

Summary

Our taxonomy of factors influencing software development productivity is extremely diverse. The technical factors range from detailed product factors, such as execution time constraints, to general environment factors such as the use of software tools. The soft factors have been investigated on the corporate, team, project, and individual levels. For specific contexts, it will be necessary for practitioners to look into each of these factors in more detail. We hope that this chapter can be used as a starting point and checklist for productivity improvement in practice.

Key Ideas

These are the key ideas from this chapter:

- The major factors influencing software development productivity can be summarized in a checklist for developers and managers.

- Some of the relevant research on productivity factors is decades old.

Acknowledgments

We are grateful to Melanie Ruhe for previous discussions on productivity and productivity factors.

Appendix: Review Design

This chapter is not meant to be a full-fledged academic literature review. Instead, we used our prior literature review [1] as a start and updated it with a search on Google Scholar. For the analysis, we also reused the search string from [1] to stay consistent: software AND (productivity OR "development efficiency" OR "development effectiveness" OR "development performance")

In contrast to the old review, however, we looked at only the first 30 results from 2017 to 2018 in Google Scholar. Of those results, we extracted any new relevant productivity factors from empirical studies. We did not use studies that only validated factors already on the list to keep this article concise. We also noted that while most of the factors come from academic papers investigating these factors in more detail, the old literature review [1] also included the books by Boehm [6] and Jones [7] as a baseline. They do not investigate single factors but use a set of factors to discuss productivity.

Finally, the extracted academic studies have limitations, such as some of them use lines of code per person-hour as a productivity measure. This is easy to measure but has significant problems because more code is not necessarily good. In many instances, less code is actually better as long as it fulfils the customer's requirements and needs. We decided to not exclude these studies, however, as the identified factors still might be interesting.

References

[1] Wagner, Stefan and Ruhe, Melanie. "A Systematic Review of Productivity Factors in Software Development." In Proc. 2nd International Workshop on Software Productivity Analysis and Cost Estimation (SPACE 2008). Technical Report ISCAS-SKLCS-08-08, State Key Laboratory of Computer Science, Institute of Software, Chinese Academy of Sciences, 2008.

[2] Hernandez-Lopez, Adrian, Ricardo Colomo-Palacios, and Angel Garcia-Crespo. "Software engineering job productivity—a systematic review." International Journal of Software Engineering and Knowledge Engineering 23.03 (2013):387–406.

[3] T. DeMarco, T. Lister. "Peopleware. Productive Projects and Teams." Dorset House Publishing, 1987.

[4] Trendowicz, Adam, Münch, Jürgen. "Factors Influencing Software Development Productivity – State of the Art and Industrial Experiences." Advances in Computers, vol 77, pp. 185–241, 2009.

[5] Cataldo, Marcelo, James D. Herbsleb, and Kathleen M. Carley. "Socio-technical congruence: a framework for assessing the impact of technical and work dependencies on software development productivity." Proceedings of the Second ACM-IEEE international symposium on Empirical software engineering and measurement. ACM, 2008.

[6] B. W. Boehm, C. Abts, A. W. Brown, S. Chulani, B. K. Clark, E. Horowitz, R. Madachy, D. Reifer, and B. Steece. Software Cost Estimation with COCOMO II. Prentice-Hall, 2000.

[7] C. Jones. Software Assessments, Benchmarks, and Best Practices. Addison-Wesley, 2000.

[8] Lagerström, R., von Würtemberg, L.M., Holm, H., Luczak, O. Identifying factors affecting software development cost and productivity. Software Qual J (2012) 20: 395. `https://doi.org/10.1007/s11219-011-9137-8`.

[9]   Tsunoda, M., Monden, A., Yadohisa, H. et al. Inf Technol Manag
       (2009) 10: 193. https://doi.org/10.1007/s10799-009-0050-9.

[10]   Kautz, Karlheinz, Thomas Heide Johanson, and Andreas Uldahl.
       "The perceived impact of the agile development and project
       management method scrum on information systems and software
       development productivity." Australasian Journal of Information
       Systems 18.3 (2014).

[11]   Cataldo, Marcelo, and James D. Herbsleb. "Coordination
       breakdowns and their impact on development productivity and
       software failures." IEEE Transactions on Software Engineering 39.3
       (2013): 343–360.

[12]   Cardozo, Elisa SF, et al. "SCRUM and Productivity in Software
       Projects: A Systematic Literature Review." EASE. 2010.

[13]   Tan, Thomas, et al. "Productivity trends in incremental and
       iterative software development." Proceedings of the 2009 3rd
       International Symposium on Empirical Software Engineering and
       Measurement. IEEE Computer Society, 2009.

[14]   Duhigg, Charles. "What Google learned from its quest to build the
       perfect team." The New York Times Magazine 26 (2016): 2016.

[15]   Lemberg, Per, Feldt, Robert. "Psychological Safety and Norm
       Clarity in Software Engineering Teams." Proceedings of the 11th
       International Workshop on Cooperative and Human Aspects of
       Software Engineering. ACM, 2018.

[16]   Graziotin, D., Wang, X., and Abrahamsson, P. 2015. Do feelings
       matter? On the correlation of affects and the self-assessed
       productivity in software engineering. Journal of Software:
       Evolution and Process. 27, 7, 467–487. DOI=10.1002/smr.1673.
       Available: https://arxiv.org/abs/1408.1293.

[17]   Graziotin, D., Wang, X., and Abrahamsson, P. 2015. How do you
       feel, developer? An explanatory theory of the impact of affects
       on programming performance. PeerJ Computer Science. 1, e18.
       DOI=10.7717/peerj-cs.18. Available: https://doi.org/10.7717/
       peerj-cs.18.

[18]   Graziotin, D., Fagerholm, F., Wang, X., & Abrahamsson, P. (2018).
       What happens when software developers are (un)happy. Journal
       of Systems and Software, 140, 32-47. doi:10.1016/j.jss.2018.02.041.
       Available: https://doi.org/10.1016/j.jss.2018.02.041.

[19]   Zahra Karimi, Ahmad Baraani-Dastjerdi, Nasser Ghasem-
       Aghaee, Stefan Wagner, Links between the personalities, styles
       and performance in computer programming, Journal of Systems
       and Software, Volume 111, 2016, Pages 228–241, https://doi.
       org/10.1016/j.jss.2015.09.011.

[20]   D. Méndez Fernández, S. Wagner, M. Kalinowski, M. Felderer,
       P. Mafra, A. Vetrò, T. Conte, M.-T. Christiansson, D. Greer,
       C. Lassenius, T. Männistö, M. Nayabi, M. Oivo, B. Penzenstadler,
       D. Pfahl, R. Prikladnicki, G. Ruhe, A. Schekelmann, S. Sen,
       R. Spinola, A. Tuzcu, J. L. de la Vara, R. Wieringa, Naming the
       pain in requirements engineering: Contemporary problems,
       causes, and effects in practice, Empirical Software Engineering
       22(5):2298–2338, 2017.

[21]   Ray, B., Posnett, D., Filkov, V., & Devanbu, P. (2014, November). A
       large scale study of programming languages and code quality in
       github. In Proceedings of the 22nd ACM SIGSOFT International
       Symposium on Foundations of Software Engineering (pp. 155–
       165). ACM.

[22]   Jungst Kim, Richard de Dear, "Workspace satisfaction: The
       privacy-communication trade-off in open-plan offices," Journal of
       Environmental Psychology 36:18–26, 2013.

CHAPTER 9

How Do Interruptions Affect Productivity?

Duncan P. Brumby, University College London, UK

Christian P. Janssen, Utrecht University, The Netherlands

Gloria Mark, University of California Irvine, USA

Introduction

When was the last time you were interrupted at work? If you use a computer for work and if it has been more than a couple of minutes, count your blessings and be prepared for an upcoming interruption. Modern information work is punctuated by a constant stream of interruptions [16]. These interruptions can be from external events (e.g., a colleague asking you a question, a message notification from a mobile device), or they can be self-initiated interruptions (e.g., going back and forth between two different computer applications to complete a task). A recent observational study of IT professionals found that some people interrupt themselves after just 20 seconds of settling into focused work [38].

Given the omnipresence of interruptions in the modern workplace, researchers have asked what impact these have on productivity. This question has been studied in many application domains, from the hospital emergency room to the open-planned office, using a variety of different research methods.

© The Author(s) 2019

C. Sadowski and T. Zimmermann (eds.), *Rethinking Productivity in Software Engineering*,
https://doi.org/10.1007/978-1-4842-4221-6_9

In this chapter, we provide a brief overview of three prominent and complementary research methods that have been used to study interruptions. The methods we review are as follows:

- Controlled experiments that demonstrate that interruptions take time to recover from and lead to errors

- Cognitive models that offer a theoretical framework for explaining why and how interruptions are disruptive

- Observational studies that give a rich description of the kinds of interruptions that people experience in the workplace

For each of these three research approaches, we will explain the aim of the method, why it is relevant to the study of interruptions, and some of the key findings. Our aim is not to offer a comprehensive review of all studies in this area but rather an introduction focusing on our own past research, which spans each of these three methods. We direct the interested reader to more comprehensive reviews of the interruptions literature [28, 44, 45].

Controlled Experiments

There is a long tradition of experiments being conducted to learn about the effect of interruptions on task performance. The earliest studies were conducted in the 1920s and focused on how well people remembered tasks that they had previously worked on. In these experiments, Zeigarnik [50] demonstrated that people were better at recalling the details of incomplete or interrupted tasks than tasks that had been finished.

Since the advent of the computer revolution, research has focused on investigating the impact that interruptions have on task performance and productivity. This shift was probably spurred on by people's annoyances with poorly designed computer notification systems that interrupted them to attend to incoming e-mails or perform software updates while trying to work on other important tasks. Experiments offer a suitable research method to address the question of whether these feelings of being annoyed by interruptions and notifications translate into systematic and observable decrements in task performance.

What Is the Aim of an Experiment?

Before we review what has been learned from interruption experiments, it is worth taking a moment to reflect on the purpose of an experiment. Experiments are designed to test a hypothesis. For example, do people work slower when interrupted compared to when they have not been interrupted? To test this hypothesis, the researcher manipulates a feature of interest (the independent variable), which in our case might be the presence or absence of an interrupting task. The researcher wants to learn whether this manipulation has an effect on an outcome measure (the dependent variable), which in our case might be how quickly a task is completed.

Experiments are designed to test the *causal* relationship between variables. To do this, the researcher will attempt to control all other extraneous variables. This is why experiments are usually conducted in a controlled setting using a fixed set of instructions and tasks given to all participants who take part in the experiment. In doing so, the researcher wants to be able to isolate whether a change in the independent variable has a reliable (i.e., statistically significant) effect on the dependent variable. If an effect exists, then it should show up time and again through the independent replication of results. As we will learn in a moment, experiments have consistently shown that interruptions negatively impact task performance.

A Typical Interruptions Experiment

In a typical interruptions experiment, the researcher will ask a participant to work on a contrived task that they have designed. For example, the participant might be asked to use a computer interface to order some tasty donuts [32]. The cover story is provided to give some context to the task that the participant has been asked to work on, and it can be easily adjusted to suit the target domain of the study. For example, naval researchers have asked participants to place orders for the construction of ships [46], and healthcare researchers have asked participants to place orders for prescription medicines [18]. Regardless of the domain, the researcher gives the participant detailed instructions on how to complete the task using the interface and plenty of opportunities to practice it before starting the main part of the experiment.

In the main part of the experiment, participants will be asked to complete a number of tasks (e.g., place ten orders for doughnuts) using the instructed procedure. While the participant is working on this task, the researcher will occasionally interrupt them and ask them to work on a secondary task instead. The secondary task might require the participant to solve some mental arithmetic problems [32] or use a mouse to track a moving cursor on the screen [39]. In these experiments, the arrival of this interrupting task is carefully controlled by the experimenter, and the participant is often given no choice but to switch from the primary task to the interrupting task. This is because the researcher wants to learn whether the interrupting task affects the quality and pace of the work produced on the primary task.

How Is Disruptiveness of an Interruption Measured?

This discussion leads us to consider how we measure the impact of an interruption on task performance. The primary measure that has been used is the time it takes a participant to resume work on the primary task after dealing with an interruption. This time-based measure is referred to in the literature as the *resumption lag* [4, 45]. The resumption lag measures the time it takes a person to re-engage with a task following an interruption. A longer resumption lag following an interruption reflects a general decrease in productivity: people are taking more time to complete a task, even when the time spent working on the interrupting task is deducted. In this way, the resumption lag is taken to reflect the time that is needlessly "wasted" as a consequence of being interrupted and later having to resume an unfinished task.

Over recent years a number of experiments have been reported that use the resumption lag measure to carefully unpack which features of an interrupting task make it disruptive. Experiments have investigated whether longer interruptions are more disruptive than shorter interruptions—finding that longer interruptions result in longer resumption lags [19, 39]. Studies have also been conducted to learn whether there are better or worse points in a task to be interrupted—shorter interruption lags are found when interruptions occur at natural breakpoints in a task, such as the completion of a subtask [2, 7]. The content of an interrupting task also matters—interruptions that are relevant to the primary task are less disruptive than interruptions that have nothing to do with the primary task [17, 21]. As we will discuss, the resumption lag has been explained by assuming that interruptions interfere with people's ability to remember what they were doing prior to the interruption.

Interruptions Cause Errors

When a person resumes a task following an interruption, it often matters whether they get it right or make a mistake. Previous research has shown that interruptions increase the likelihood of errors being made on a task, in that important components of the task are either repeated or missed [9, 32, 46]. This finding has been taken as evidence to support the idea that following an interruption people fail to remember what they were doing in a task prior to being interrupted.

It has also been informative to consider whether there is a link between how quickly a task is resumed and the likelihood that an error is made. As discussed, interruption researchers have generally considered a longer resumption lag to be a bad thing— reflecting time needless wasted following an interruption. In contrast, Brumby et al. [9] found that longer resumption lags following an interruption were in fact *beneficial* in terms of reducing the occurrence of errors. This has important practical implications for the design of systems to encourage more reflective task resumption behavior in situations where interruptions are commonplace. Based on these findings, Brumby et al. developed and tested a post-interruption interface lockout that allowed users to look at the task interface but prohibited actions to be made. This interface lockout led to a significant reduction in resumption errors because it encouraged users to take the time to cognitively re-engage with a task before diving back into it and making a mistake.

Moving Controlled Experiments Out of the Lab

A criticism that is often leveled at the kind of interruption experiments that we've reviewed is that the controlled setting in which they are conducted bears little resemblance to people's actual work environments and how they manage the interruptions that they experience at work. In other words, our experiments can lack *ecological validity* because an important aspect of the phenomena that we are attempting to investigate is missing. This is an important concern because it means that the results of these interruption experiments might be of limited practical value or that they might not be valid at all when taken away from the controlled setting of the lab and applied to an actual work setting.

How might an interruption experiment lack ecological validity? Interruption experiments are often conducted in controlled environments in which the researcher actively works to remove unwanted distractions and interruptions (e.g., participants will be asked to turn off their phone and give their complete attention to the researcher's task). The reason for this is that the experimenter wants to carefully control the nature and the timing of any interruptions so as to learn how they affect performance. Ironically, this desire for control presents a major threat to the ecological validity of the experiment. This is because most of the everyday interruptions that we experience are not forced but are instead *discretionary*. For example, an e-mail notification might appear on a screen, but we can choose whether to act on it or ignore it. By using enforced interruptions that participants have to attend to, interruption experiments can fail to capture this important aspect of the phenomena that they are attempting to study in the lab.

To overcome concerns about low ecological validity, Gould et al. [18] has taken an approach that relaxes experimental control over the environment in which participants work to study how naturally occurring interruptions affect performance. To do this, Gould et al. used an online crowdsourcing platform, Amazon's Mechanical Turk, to host an interruptions experiment. Just like in a regular interruptions experiment, participants were asked to use a browser-based task interface to place orders for prescription medicines. But unlike a traditional lab experiment, participants worked on this task in their regular everyday environment: an office, a coffee shop, or their home. These are naturalistic environments that are filled with everyday interruptions and distractions. In addition, workers on crowdsourcing platforms, like Amazon's Mechanical Turk, often work on multiple tasks at the same time; the environment is designed to encourage workers to complete as many tasks as possible so as to maximize their pay. This means that a competing (interrupting) task is often present, vying for the participant's attention.

By running an interruptions experiment on a crowdsourcing platform, Gould et al. [18] found that workers switched to other tasks once every five minutes. This was revealed by window switching events and pauses in progression through the task. These interruptions were not inserted by the experimenter but were naturally occurring and at the discretion of the participant. Interestingly, this rate of interruptions corresponds to that seen in observational studies [16]. While these interruptions tended to be quite brief (around 30 seconds on average), Gould et al. found that they were sufficient to negatively impact performance on the primary task: participants who interrupted more often were considerably slower at completing the task, even after accounting for the time spent not working on the task. We know this only because the primary task interface was under the control of the researchers; this was not a naturalistic observation study.

Gould et al.'s study provides a bridge between controlled experiments and observation studies; it provides evidence that the disruptiveness of interruptions can be readily detected out in the field and that it is not an artificial product of the controlled setting used in interruption experiments.

Summary: Controlled Experiments

By conducting controlled experiments, researchers have been able to establish that task interruptions take time to recover from and lead to errors. Experiments offer an empirical approach for systematically testing whether the manipulation of an independent variable (e.g., the duration of a task interruption) has an effect on a dependent variable (e.g., the duration of the post-interruption resumption lag). Establishing whether the manipulation of an independent variable has an effect on the dependent variable is of both practical and theoretical value.

In practical terms, knowledge is developed about what makes an interruption disruptive, allowing practical intervention to be developed and tested. For example, Brumby et al. [9] established that when people made faster task resumptions, they were more likely to make an error. Learning about this prompted the development of an interface lockout mechanism that stopped users from resuming a task quickly following an interruption, reducing task errors.

In theoretical terms, experiments support the development of theories that seek to *explain* why longer interruptions result in a longer resumption lag. What is the mechanism that causes this? How can it be explained? In the next section, we turn our attention to reviewing efforts to develop theory using cognitive models.

Cognitive Models

Once findings have been made in experiments, the data and results can be used to develop theories about human behavior and thought. Cognitive models can be used to formalize the cumulative knowledge that is gained from experiments into formal theories (e.g., mathematical equations) that can generate predictions for future situations. For example, a mathematical model can be used to predict the likelihood that an error will be made on a task based on the duration of an interruption [4, 7]. Stated differently, cognitive models help to explain why and how interruptions are disruptive.

What Are Cognitive Models?

An important characteristic of cognitive models is that they generate an *exact prediction* (i.e., generate a number) as an *outcome* (e.g., likelihood of an error), given an *input* (e.g., time away from the main task), and a *formal description* of how input is *transformed* into output (i.e., a computer program that captures theory of the process of forgetting). Other more conceptual theories of interruptions [6] or multitasking [49] also provide insight into human behavior and thought but typically tend to miss at least one of these three components (output, input, or transformation step) or describe them in less formal terms, such that the details that are needed to give an exact prediction are not available.

The value of cognitive models lies in their ability to predict aspects of human behavior and thought *in detail*. Cognitive modeling aims to unravel human thought by uncovering the details and making those details open for scientific debate [40]. As an example, take the Memory for Goals theory of forgetting [4], which has been applied to explain the results of interruption experiments. The model can be used to make a prediction for how quickly tasks will be resumed after an interruption. To do so, the model uses a mathematical function, derived from psychological theory, to determine how quickly a person will be able to recall what they were doing prior to dealing with an interruption based on the strength of this memory. The value of the model is that it gives a prediction for how quickly someone will resume a task (i.e., the resumption lag). Moreover, the general theory of memory retrieval that underpins this model helps explain *why* these resumption lags occur (namely, because of forgetting).

Since the inception of the basic Memory for Goals theory, the theory has been refined in many ways. Examples include the prediction of errors due to interruptions [46], the prediction of task switching performance [3], and the prediction of concurrent multitasking performance [7]. The initial modeling effort was crucial in this regard: by specifying a theory (of forgetting) in detail, it allowed researchers to make predictions regarding how memory impacts other settings, which could then be tested. In the end, these new experiments led to further refinements of the theory and to an even broader understanding of the cognitive mechanisms involved in recovering from an interruption.

Although the value of cognitive models lies in the details, this is also its Achilles' heel. If a model is to be used to make predictions for a new task, then a researcher or practitioner needs to be able to specify those details ahead of time. To then specify those details, they also need to have a detailed understanding of the modeling framework and how these details should be specified within it. This is not feasible for every researcher and practitioner.

Fortunately, building on a long tradition in human-computer interaction research [10], more and more tools are being made to allow for predictions in applied settings, including dynamic settings such as driving [8, 43]. Moreover, in some cases not all details might be needed to make a prediction. For example, based on the mathematical equations behind Memory for Goals theory, recent work by Fong, Hettinger, and Ratwani [15] was able to predict the likelihood that emergency physicians resumed their original task after an interruption on their everyday emergency ward.

What Can Cognitive Models Predict About the Impact of Interruptions on Productivity?

One of the main insights to come from modeling work using the Memory for Goals theory is that the longer an interruption, the more likely it is that errors are to occur, including forgetting to resume the task altogether (and for specific cases, the models can give even more specific and exact predictions). Therefore, the implication of this work is that there is value in avoiding being interrupted.

Models can also be used to inform our understanding of discretionary self-interruptions. Previous studies have found that people often choose to interrupt themselves, switching between different activities every few minutes [16, 18]. For example, an information worker who is focusing on a particular work activity will still likely choose to monitor and check their e-mail regularly, switching back and forth between application windows. How often should the person switch between these two different activities?

In our own research, we have used cognitive models to examine how the demands of a task affect the benefit of different switching strategies (i.e., how long to focus on one task before switching back to another task). We studied this in the context of a dual-task experiment in which participants had to control a dynamic task while performing a text-entry task [13, 26, 27]. We used a cognitive model to identify the best possible strategy for dividing attention between these two tasks and then compared this to what people actually chose to do in the experiments. Across several studies, we found that people were very quick at locating the best possible strategy for dividing their time between tasks. We learn from this work that people are actually pretty good at multitasking, when the relative importance of each task is made clear to them. Cognitive modeling was a vital step in this work as it was used to identify the best possible switching strategy; without this, it would not have been possible to objectively benchmark how well people were multitasking.

Summary: Cognitive Models

Cognitive models develop our understanding of why and how interruptions are disruptive. They do this by instantiating theory using mathematical models and simulations. This puts into practice the ideas we have for what is causing an interruption to impact performance. Through this line of research, Memory for Goals has emerged as an important theory. The core idea is that when dealing with an interruption, people forget what it is they were working on. Resuming a task therefore involves remembering what one was doing before the interruption. By casting this as a memory retrieval process, the Memory for Goals theory is able to draw on general theories about the nature of human memory. In practical terms, cognitive models can be used to both explain existing data and make predictions about what will happen in novel situations or settings.

Observational Studies

Whereas controlled experiments and cognitive models enable a focus on testing specific variables while controlling other factors, observational studies (also referred to as *in-situ* studies) offer ecological validity. For example, in the laboratory, the effects of interruptions may focus on a single interruption type from a single task. In a real-world environment, people generally work on multiple tasks, receiving interruptions from a range of sources. In-situ studies can serve to uncover reasons for people's behavior (i.e., the "why" of people's practices). It is a trade-off, however, of generalizability with ecological validity. Observational studies can be very labor-intensive, limiting the scope and scale of study. Yet, with the current revolution in sensor technologies and wearables, in-situ studies are beginning to leverage these technologies for researchers to conduct observational studies at a larger scale. Nevertheless, sensors still introduce limitations on what can be observed and how the data can be interpreted.

Observational Studies of the Workplace

Most in-situ studies of interruptions have been conducted in the workplace. Workplaces can be dynamic places, and interruptions can be triggered from a number of sources involving people (colleagues, phone calls, ambient conversations), and computer and smartphone notifications (e.g. e-mail, social media, text messaging). However, interruptions can also originate from within an individual (e.g., due to mind-wandering, [37]).

Constant interruptions and the consequent fragmentation of work are a way of life for many information workers [12, 33, 38]. By closely monitoring workers in-situ, it was found that people switched activities (conversations, work on computer applications, phone calls) about every three minutes on average. At a less-granular level, when activities were clustered into tasks, or "working spheres," these were found to be interrupted or switched about every 11 minutes [16]. There is a relationship of length of time on task and interruptions: the longer time spent in a working sphere, the longer is the interrupting event. It has been proposed that when interruptions are used as breaks, then such longer interruptions might be due to replenishing one's mental resources [47].

In a work environment, observations found that people self-interrupt almost as often as experiencing interruptions by an external source such as a phone call or colleague entering the office [16, 33]. When these field studies were done, more than a decade ago now, most self-interruptions were found to be associated with people initiating in-person interactions. Most external interruptions were also due to verbal-based interruptions from other people rather than due to notification mechanisms from their e-mail or voicemail. In more recent years, social media has become popular in the workplace, and it is likely that the main triggers of self and external interruptions in the present-day workplace may be different.

Benefits and Detriments of Interruptions

Interruptions may be beneficial or detrimental. In a workplace diary study, Czerwinski et al. [12] showed how the work context of information workers continuously changes because of interruptions. A study of corporate managers showed that while interruptions can disrupt tasks, managers appreciate the usefulness of interruptions as it provides the opportunity to get useful work-related information [20]. While social media and online micro-breaks may provide numerous benefits in the workplace, field studies have shown that they create challenges due to switching contexts.

Generally, interruptions that disrupt concentration in a task, especially when they occur at a point that is not a natural breaking point for a task, can be detrimental [24]. External interruptions cause information workers to enter into a "chain of distraction" where stages of preparation, diversion, resumption, and recovery take time away from an ongoing task [22]. When notifications from smart phones were turned off for a week, people reported higher levels of attention [31]. A large cost in switching tasks on the computer is that it has been associated with higher stress [34]. Yet, people are able to adjust their work practices to manage constant face-to-face interruptions [42], as well as to manage interruptions from computer-mediated communication [48].

Interruptions in the workplace can also provide benefits. Longer interruptions (or work breaks), such as taking a walk in nature during work hours, have been shown to increase focus and creativity at work [1]. Observational studies have identified that people use a variety of social media and news sites to take breaks to refresh and to stimulate themselves [29]. However, a growing number of workplaces have policies that regulate the use of social media at work [41], which can impact the ability of people to take a mental break at work.

Stress, Individual Differences, and Interruptions

A few field studies have examined the relationship of stress and interruptions. In a study that focused specifically on the role of e-mail interruptions, Kushlev and Dunn [30] found that limiting the amount of checking e-mail significantly reduced stress. Another field study in the workplace found that cutting off e-mail (and consequently reducing both internal and external interruptions) significantly reduced stress [36]. Cutting off smartphone notifications also significantly reduced inattention and symptoms of hyperactivity [31]. On the other hand, when e-mail notifications were turned off, another field study showed that some individuals increased their self-interruptions to check e-mail due to the lack of awareness of incoming e-mails [23]. It is theorized that people who multitask more and who are susceptible to interruptions may have lower ability to filter out irrelevant stimuli [11]. Other individual differences have been observed, such as the personality trait of higher neuroticism with higher task switching [35].

Productivity

Field studies suggest that higher frequency of task switching is associated with lower perceived productivity [34, 38]. Several explanations have been proposed for this relationship, including the depletion of cognitive resources used in attending to interruptions, the redundancy of work when reorienting back to the task [34], and that a polychronic workstyle may be contrary to what most people prefer [5].

Strategies for Dealing with Interruptions

Observational studies reveal that people use strategies to manage interruptions. Whereas most people prefer monochronic work (finishing one task through to completion [5]), the demands of the workplace result in polychronic work (i.e., the consequent switching of attention to different tasks). Because of the expectation of working in an environment with interruptions, some people have been observed to develop strategies to adapt to the unpredictability of the working environment. Participants can externalize their memory of task information, for example in the form of artifacts such as sticky notes, the e-mail inbox (e-mails sent to oneself), or electronic planners, often updated throughout the day [16]. The challenge with conventional electronic planners is that they are generally not designed at a level of granularity to help people recover from interruptions from a partially completed task.

Technological solutions have also been implemented in the field to detect when people are interruptible, with the intent to minimize interruptions at inopportune times. Promising techniques tested in the field have shown that it is possible to predict when people are in cognitive states where they can be interrupted that can minimize interruptions, reduce stress, and thus minimize cognitive resources needed to reorient back to a task [14, 25, 51, 52].

Summary: Observational Studies

Observational studies document the kinds of interruptions that people experience in their actual workplace. These studies are resource intensive to conduct and so often focus in on a small number of participants, giving a detailed and rich account of a particular work setting. We have learned from observational studies that workplace interruptions are extremely commonplace. Some of these interruptions reflect the fragmented nature of work: people work on different tasks and activities through the day, and this requires constant switching between them. People also seek out interactions with others—either by having conversations with colleagues or by communicating through social networking sites and e-mail. Consistent with the results from interruption experiments, observational studies also reveal that frequent interruptions result in feelings of reduced productivity. However, regular breaks from work are also necessary, and people return from breaks feeling energized and ready to resume their work.

Key Insights

We have given a brief overview of three prominent and complementary research methods that have been used to study interruptions: controlled experiments, cognitive models, and observational studies. Across these three research approaches a consistent pattern of insights emerges to help us understand how interruptions affect productivity.

The key insights are as follows:

- Interruptions can take time from which to recover from and can lead to errors.

- Shorter interruptions are less disruptive than longer interruptions.

- Interruptions delivered during a natural break in a task are less disruptive.

- Interruptions that are relevant to the current task are less disruptive.

- Resuming a task too quickly can lead to errors being made.

- All of these characteristics of the resumption lag can be explained by an underlying memory retrieval process.

- People self-interrupt almost as often as being interrupted by external sources.

- People often work on multiple tasks at the same time, and self-interruptions are important for keeping up with these different activities.

- Interruptions can cause stress, particularly e-mail interruptions.

- Interruptions can provide an opportunity for a break to refresh, and people take longer breaks after working on a task for longer.

Key Ideas

This chapter has offered a practical and reflective account of the complementary benefits and challenges of conducting research using each of the following three methods. The main points to reflect on are these:

- Controlled experiments are designed to test a specific hypothesis, but there are challenges with designing the experiment so that it has ecological validity.

- Cognitive models offer a theoretical framework for explaining why and how things happen (e.g., how interruptions affect productivity), but these models can be complex and difficult to develop.

- Observational studies offer a rich description of situated activity, but these studies are resource intensive and can produce an overwhelming amount of data of which to make sense.

Acknowledgments

This work was supported by the UK Engineering and Physical Sciences Research Council grants EP/G059063/1 and EP/L504889/1, by a European Commission Marie Sklodowska-Curie Fellowship H2020-MSCA-IF-2015 grant 705010, and by the U.S. National Science Foundation under grant #1704889.

References

[1] Abdullah, S., Czerwinski, M., Mark, G., & Johns, P. (2016). Shining (blue) light on creative ability. In Proceedings of the 2016 ACM International Joint Conference on Pervasive and Ubiquitous Computing (UbiComp '16). ACM, New York, NY, USA, 793-804. DOI: https://doi.org/10.1145/2971648.2971751.

[2] Adamczyk, P. D., & Bailey, B. P. (2004). If not now, when?: the effects of interruption at different moments within task execution. In Proceedings of the SIGCHI Conference on Human Factors in Computing Systems (CHI '04). ACM, New York, NY, USA, 271-278. DOI: https://doi.org/10.1145/985692.985727.

[3]   Altmann, E., & Gray, W. D. (2008). An integrated model of cognitive control in task switching. Psychological Review, 115, 602–639. DOI: https://doi.org/10.1037/0033-295X.115.3.602.

[4]   Altmann, E., & Trafton, J. G. (2002). Memory for goals: an activation-based model. Cognitive Science, 26, 39–83. DOI: https://doi.org/10.1207/s15516709cog2601_2.

[5]   Bluedorn, A. C., Kaufman, C. F. and Lane, P. M. (1992). How many things do you like to do at once? An introduction to monochronic and polychronic time. The Executive, 6(4), 17-26. DOI: http://www.jstor.org/stable/4165091.

[6]   Boehm-Davis, D. A., & Remington, R. W. (2009). Reducing the disruptive effects of interruption: a cognitive framework for analysing the costs and benefits of intervention strategies. Accident Analysis & Prevention, 41, 1124–1129. DOI: https://doi.org/10.1016/j.aap.2009.06.029.

[7]   Borst, J. P., Taatgen, N. A., & van Rijn, H. (2015). What makes interruptions disruptive?: a process-model account of the effects of the problem state bottleneck on task interruption and resumption. In Proceedings of the 33rd Annual ACM Conference on Human Factors in Computing Systems (CHI '15). ACM, New York, NY, USA, 2971-2980. DOI: https://doi.org/10.1145/2702123.2702156.

[8]   Brumby, D. P., Janssen, C. P., Kujala, T., & Salvucci, D. D. (2018). Computational models of user multitasking. In A. Oulasvirta, P. Kristensson, X. Bi, & A. Howes (eds.) Computational Interaction Design. Oxford, UK: Oxford University Press.

[9]   Brumby, D.P., Cox, A.L., Back, J., & Gould, S.J.J. (2013). Recovering from an interruption: investigating speed-accuracy tradeoffs in task resumption strategy. Journal of Experimental Psychology: Applied, 19, 95-107. DOI: https://doi.org/10.1037/a0032696.

[10]   Card, S. K., Moran, T., & Newell, A. (1983). The Psychology of Human-Computer Interaction. Hillsdale, NJ: Lawrence Erlbaum Associates.

[11] Carrier, L. M., Rosen, L. D., Cheever, N. A., & Lim, A. F. (2015).
      Causes, effects, and practicalities of everyday multitasking.
      Developmental Review, 35, 64-78. DOI: `https://doi.`
      `org/10.1016/j.dr.2014.12.005`.

[12] Czerwinski, M., Horvitz, E., & Wilhite, S. (2004). A diary study of
      task switching and interruptions. In Proceedings of the SIGCHI
      Conference on Human Factors in Computing Systems (CHI
      '04). ACM, New York, NY, USA, 175-182. DOI: `https://doi.`
      `org/10.1145/985692.985715`.

[13] Farmer, G. D., Janssen, C. P., Nguyen, A. T. and Brumby, D. P.
      (2017). Dividing attention between tasks: testing whether explicit
      payoff functions elicit optimal dual-task performance. Cognitive
      Science. DOI: `https://doi.org/10.1111/cogs.12513`.

[14] Fogarty, J., Hudson, S. E., Atkeson, C. G., Avrahami, D.,
      Forlizzi, J., Kiesler, S., Lee, J. C., & Yang, J. (2005). Predicting
      human interruptibility with sensors. ACM Transactions on
      Computer- Human Interaction, 12, 119-146. DOI: `https://doi.`
      `org/10.1145/1057237.1057243`.

[15] Fong, A., Hettinger, A. Z., & Ratwani, R. M. (2017). A predictive
      model of emergency physician task resumption following
      interruptions. In Proceedings of the 2017 CHI Conference
      on Human Factors in Computing Systems (CHI '17).
      ACM, New York, NY, USA, 2405-2410. DOI: `https://doi.`
      `org/10.1145/3025453.3025700`.

[16] González, V. M., & Mark, G. J. (2004). "Constant, constant, multi-
      tasking craziness": managing multiple working spheres. In
      Proceedings of the SIGCHI Conference on Human Factors in
      Computing Systems (CHI '04). ACM, New York, NY, USA, 113-120.
      DOI: `https://doi.org/10.1145/985692.985707`.

[17] Gould, S. J. J., Brumby, D. P., & Cox, A. L. (2013). What does it
      mean for an interruption to be relevant? An investigation of
      relevance as a memory effect. In Proceedings of the Human
      Factors and Ergonomics Society Annual Meeting, 57, 149–153.
      DOI: `https://doi.org/10.1177/1541931213571034`.

[18]   Gould, S. J. J., Cox, A. L., & Brumby, D. P. (2016). Diminished
       control in crowdsourcing: an investigation of crowdworker
       multitasking behavior. ACM Transactions on Computer-
       Human Interaction, 23, Article 19. DOI: `https://doi.`
       `org/10.1145/2928269`.

[19]   Hodgetts, H. M., & Jones, D. M. (2006). Interruption of the Tower
       of London task: Support for a goal activation approach. Journal of
       Experimental Psychology: General, 135, 103-115. DOI: `https://`
       `doi.org/10.1037/0096-3445.135.1.103`.

[20]   Hudson, J. M., Christensen, J., Kellogg, W. A., & Erickson, T.
       (2002). "I'd be overwhelmed, but it's just one more thing to
       do": availability and interruption in research management. In
       Proceedings of the SIGCHI Conference on Human Factors in
       Computing Systems (CHI '02). ACM, New York, NY, USA, 97-104.
       DOI: `https://doi.org/10.1145/503376.503394`.

[21]   Iqbal, S. T., & Bailey, B. P. (2008). Effects of intelligent notification
       management on users and their tasks. In Proceedings of the
       SIGCHI Conference on Human Factors in Computing Systems
       (CHI '08). ACM, New York, NY, USA, 93-102. DOI: `https://doi.`
       `org/10.1145/1357054.1357070`.

[22]   Iqbal, S. T., & Horvitz, E. (2007). Disruption and recovery
       of computing tasks: field study, analysis, and directions. In
       Proceedings of the SIGCHI Conference on Human Factors in
       Computing Systems (CHI '07). ACM, New York, NY, USA, 677-686.
       DOI: `https://doi.org/10.1145/1240624.12407302007`.

[23]   Iqbal, S. T., & Horvitz, E. (2010). Notifications and awareness: a
       field study of alert usage and preferences. In Proceedings of the
       2010 ACM conference on Computer supported cooperative work
       (CSCW '10). ACM, New York, NY, USA, 27-30. DOI: `https://doi.`
       `org/10.1145/1718918.1718926`.

[24]   Iqbal, S. T., Adamczyk, P. D., Zheng, X. S., & Bailey, B. P. (2005).
       Towards an index of opportunity: understanding changes in
       mental workload during task execution. In Proceedings of the

SIGCHI Conference on Human Factors in Computing Systems
(CHI '05). ACM, New York, NY, USA, 311-320. DOI: https://doi.
org/10.1145/1054972.1055016.

[25] Iqbal, S.T., & Bailey, B.P. (2010). Oasis: A framework for linking
      notification delivery to the perceptual structure of goal-directed
      tasks. ACM Transactions on Computer-Human Interaction, 17,
      Article 15. DOI: https://doi.org/10.1145/1879831.1879833.

[26] Janssen, C. P., & Brumby, D. P. (2015). Strategic adaptation to
      task characteristics, incentives, and individual differences in
      dual-tasking. PLoS ONE, 10(7), e0130009. DOI: https://doi.
      org/10.1371/journal.pone.0130009.

[27] Janssen, C. P., Brumby, D. P., Dowell, J., Chater, N., & Howes,
      A. (2011). Identifying optimum performance trade-offs using
      a cognitively bounded rational analysis model of discretionary
      task interleaving. Topics in Cognitive Science, 3, 123–139. DOI:
      https://doi.org/10.1111/j.1756-8765.2010.01125.x.

[28] Janssen, C. P., Gould, S. J., Li, S. Y. W., Brumby, D. P., & Cox, A. L.
      (2015). Integrating knowledge of multitasking and Interruptions
      across different perspectives and research methods. International
      Journal of Human-Computer Studies, 79, 1–5. DOI: https://doi.
      org/10.1016/j.ijhcs.2015.03.002.

[29] Jin, J., & Dabbish, L. (2009). Self-interruption on the computer: a
      typology of discretionary task interleaving. In Proceedings of the
      SIGCHI Conference on Human Factors in Computing Systems
      (CHI '09). ACM, New York, NY, USA, 1799-1808. DOI: https://
      doi.org/10.1145/1518701.1518979.

[30] Kushlev, K., & Dunn, E.W. (2015). Checking e-mail less frequently
      reduces stress. Computers in Human Behavior, 43, 220-228. DOI:
      https://doi.org/10.1016/j.chb.2014.11.005.

[31] Kushlev, K., Proulx, J., & Dunn, E.W. (2016). "Silence Your
      Phones": smartphone notifications increase inattention and
      hyperactivity symptoms. In Proceedings of the 2016 CHI
      Conference on Human Factors in Computing Systems

(CHI '16). ACM, New York, NY, USA, 1011-1020. DOI: https://doi.org/10.1145/2858036.2858359.

[32]   Li, S. Y. W., Blandford, A., Cairns, P., & Young, R. M. (2008). The effect of interruptions on postcompletion and other procedural errors: an account based on the activation-based goal memory model. Journal of Experimental Psychology: Applied, 14, 314 –328. DOI: https://doi.org/10.1037/a0014397.

[33]   Mark, G., González, V., & Harris, J. (2005). No task left behind?: examining the nature of fragmented work. In Proceedings of the SIGCHI Conference on Human Factors in Computing Systems (CHI '05). ACM, New York, NY, USA, 321-330. DOI: https://doi.org/10.1145/1054972.1055017.

[34]   Mark, G., Iqbal, S. T., Czerwinski, M., & Johns, P. (2015). Focused, aroused, but so distractible: temporal perspectives on multitasking and communications. In Proceedings of the 18th ACM Conference on Computer Supported Cooperative Work & Social Computing (CSCW '15). ACM, New York, NY, USA, 903-916. DOI: https://doi.org/10.1145/2675133.2675221.

[35]   Mark, G., Iqbal, S., Czerwinski, M., Johns, P., & Sano, A. (2016). Neurotics can't focus: an in situ study of online multitasking in the workplace. In Proceedings of the 2016 CHI Conference on Human Factors in Computing Systems (CHI '16). ACM, New York, NY, USA, 1739-1744. DOI: https://doi.org/10.1145/2858036.2858202.

[36]   Mark, G., Voida, S., & Cardello, A. (2012). "A pace not dictated by electrons": an empirical study of work without e-mail. In Proceedings of the SIGCHI Conference on Human Factors in Computing Systems (CHI '12). ACM, New York, NY, USA, 555-564. DOI: https://doi.org/10.1145/2207676.2207754.

[37]   Mason, M. F., Norton, M. I., Van Horn, J. D., Wegner, D. M., Grafton, S. T., & Macrae, C. N. (2007). Wandering minds: the default network and stimulus-independent thought. Science, 315(5810), 393-395. DOI: https://doi.org/10.1126/science.1131295.

[38] Meyer, A. N., Barton, L. E., Murphy, G. C., Zimmerman, T., & Fritz, T. (2017). The work life of developers: activities, switches and perceived productivity. IEEE Transactions on Software Engineering, 43(12), 1178–1193. DOI: https://doi.org/10.1109/TSE.2017.2656886.

[39] Monk, C. A., Trafton, J. G., & Boehm-Davis, D. A. (2008). The effect of interruption duration and demand on resuming suspended goals. Journal of Experimental Psychology: Applied, 14, 299-313. DOI: https://doi.org/10.1037/a0014402.

[40] Newell, A. (1990). Unified Theories of Cognition. Cambridge, MA: Harvard University Press.

[41] Olmstead, K., Lampe, C., & Ellison, N. (2016). Social media and the workplace. Pew Research Center. Retrieved from http://www.pewinternet.org/2016/06/22/social-media-and-the-workplace/.

[42] Rouncefield, M., Hughes, J. A, Rodden, T., & Viller, S. (1994). Working with "constant interruption": CSCW and the small office. In Proceedings of the 1994 ACM conference on Computer supported cooperative work (CSCW '94). ACM, New York, NY, USA, 275-286. DOI: https://doi.org/10.1145/192844.193028.

[43] Salvucci, D. D. (2009). Rapid prototyping and evaluation of in-vehicle interfaces. Transactions on Computer-Human Interaction, 16, Article 9. DOI: https://doi.org/10.1145/1534903.1534906.

[44] Salvucci, D. D., & Taatgen, N. A. (2011). The Multitasking Mind. New York, NY: Oxford University Press.

[45] Trafton, J. G., & Monk, C. M. (2008). Task interruptions. In D. A. Boehm-Davis (Ed.), Reviews of human factors and ergonomics (Vol. 3, pp. 111–126). Santa Monica, CA: Human Factors and Ergonomics Society.

[46] Trafton, J. G., Altmann, E. M., & Ratwani, R. M. (2011). A memory for goals model of sequence errors. Cognitive Systems Research, 12, 134–143. DOI: https://doi.org/10.1016/j.cogsys.2010.07.010.

[47]   Trougakos, J. P., Beal, D. J., Green, S. G., & Weiss, H. M. (2008).
        Making the break count: an episodic examination of recovery
        activities, emotional experiences, and positive affective displays.
        Academy of Management Journal, 51, 131-146. DOI: https://
        doi.org/10.5465/amj.2008.30764063.

[48]   Webster, J., & Ho, H. (1997). Audience engagement in multi-media
        presentations. SIGMIS Database 28, 63-77. DOI: https://doi.
        org/10.1145/264701.264706.

[49]   Wickens, C. D. (2008). Multiple resources and mental workload.
        Human Factors, 50, 449- 455. DOI: https://doi.org/10.1518/00
        1872008X288394.

[50]   Zeigarnik, B. (1927). Das Behalten erledigter und unerledigter
        Handlungen. Psychologische Forschung, 9, 1-85. Translated in
        English as: Zeigarnik, B. (1967). On finished and unfinished tasks.
        In W. D. Ellis (Ed.), A sourcebook of Gestalt psychology, New York:
        Humanities press.

[51]   Züger, M., & Fritz, T. (2015). Interruptibility of software
        developers and its prediction using psycho-physiological
        sensors. In Proceedings of the 33rd Annual ACM Conference
        on Human Factors in Computing Systems (CHI '15).
        ACM, New York, NY, USA, 2981-2990. DOI: https://doi.
        org/10.1145/2702123.2702593.

[52]   Züger, M., Corley, C., Meyer, A. N., Li, B., Fritz, T., Shepherd, D.,
        Augustine, V., Francis, P., Kraft, N., & Snipes, W. (2017). Reducing
        Interruptions at Work: A Large-Scale Field Study of FlowLight. In
        Proceedings of the 2017 CHI Conference on Human Factors in
        Computing Systems (CHI '17). ACM, New York, NY, USA, 61–72.
        DOI: https://doi.org/10.1145/3025453.3025662.

CHAPTER 10

Happiness and the Productivity of Software Engineers

Daniel Graziotin, University of Stuttgart, Germany

Fabian Fagerholm, Blekinge Institute of Technology, Sweden and University of Helsinki, Finland

Software companies nowadays often aim for flourishing happiness among developers. Perks, playground rooms, free breakfast, remote office options, sports facilities near the companies...there are several ways to make software developers happy. The rationale is that of a return on investment: happy developers are supposedly more productive and, hopefully, also retained.

But is it the case that *happy software engineers = more productive software engineers*[1]? Moreover, are perks the way to go to make developers happy? Are developers happy at all? These questions are important to ask both from the perspective of productivity and from the perspective of sustainable software development and well-being in the workplace.

This chapter provides an overview of our studies on the happiness of software developers. You will learn why it is important to make software developers happy, how happy they really are, what makes them unhappy, and what is expected for their productivity while developing software.

---

[1]In our studies, we consider a software developer to be "a person concerned with any aspect of the software construction process (such as research, analysis, design, programming, testing, or management activities), for any purpose including work, study, hobby, or passion." [4, page 326]. We also interchange the terms *software developer* and *software engineer* so that we do not repeat ourselves too many times.

© The Author(s) 2019
C. Sadowski and T. Zimmermann (eds.), *Rethinking Productivity in Software Engineering*,
https://doi.org/10.1007/978-1-4842-4221-6_10

Why the Industry Should Strive for Happy Developers

We could think that happiness is a personal issue that individual developers are responsible for on their own time. In this line of thinking, software companies should focus on maximizing the output they get from each developer. However, to get productive output from a human, we must first invest. As humans, software developers' productivity depends on their skills and knowledge—but to access those, we need to create favorable conditions that allow the human potential to be realized. As noted in Chapter 5, developer satisfaction is important for productivity because reduced satisfaction can incur future costs; it follows that companies should be interested in the general well-being of their software developers. Furthermore, we believe we should simply strive to create better working environments, teams, processes, and, therefore, products.

What Is Happiness, and How Do We Measure It?

This is a very deep question that ancient and modern philosophers have aimed to answer in more than one book. However, present-day research does give us concrete insight into happiness and ways to measure it. We define happiness (as many others do) as a sequence of experiential episodes. Being happy corresponds to frequent positive experiences, which lead to experiencing positive emotions. Being unhappy corresponds to the reverse: frequent negative experiences leading to negative emotions. Happiness is the difference or balance between positive and negative experiences. This balance is sometimes called *affect balance*.

The Scale of Positive and Negative Experience (SPANE, [8]) is a recent but valid and reliable way to assess the affect balance (happiness) of individuals. Respondents are asked to report on their affect, expressed with adjectives that individuals recognize as describing emotions or moods, from the past four weeks. This provides a balance between the sampling adequacy of affect and the accuracy of human memory to recall experiences and reduce ambiguity. The combination of the scoring of the various items yields an affect balance (SPANE-B) score, which ranges from -24 (extremely unhappy) to +24 (extremely happy), where 0 is to be considered a neutral score of happiness.

Scientific Grounds of Happy and Productive Developers

While it is intuitive that happiness is beneficial for productivity and well-being, these ideas are also supported by scientific research. We have previously shown that happy developers solve problems better [1], that there is a relationship between affect and how developers assess their own productivity [2], and that software developers themselves are calling for research in this area [5]. We have also presented a theory that provides an explanation of how affect impacts programming performance [3]: events trigger affects in programmers. These affects might earn importance and priority to a developer's cognitive system, and we call them *attractors*. Together with affects, attractors drive or disturb programmers' focus, which impacts their performance. On a larger scale, our studies show that affect is an important component of performance in software teams and organizations [11]. Affect is linked to group identity—the feeling of belonging to the group—affecting cohesion and social atmosphere, which in turn are key factors for team performance and retention of team members.

We will now consider four important and ambitious questions.

- How happy are software developers overall?

- What makes them (un)happy?

- What happens when they are (un)happy?

- Are happy developers more productive?

Answering these questions is challenging. We spent a year designing a comprehensive study [4, 6] to address them. We needed data from as many software developers as possible. We also needed as much diversity as possible in terms of age, gender, geographical location, working status, and other background factors. We designed and piloted a questionnaire in such a way that the results could be generalizable (with a certain error tolerance) to the entire population of software developers. Our questionnaire had demographic questions, SPANE, and open-ended questions asking about developers' feelings of happiness and unhappiness when developing software. We asked them to describe a concrete recent software development experience, what could have caused them to experience their feelings in that situation, and if their software development was influenced by these feelings in any way, and, if so, how.

We obtained 1,318 complete and valid responses to all our questions.

How Happy Are Software Developers?

In Figure 10-1, you can see how happy our 1,318 participants were.

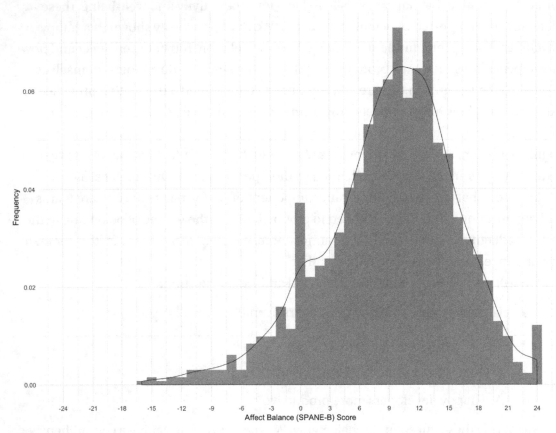

Figure 10-1. *Distribution of happiness of software developers (SPANE-B score)*

Our participants had a SPANE-B average score of 9.05, and we estimated the true mean happiness score of software developers to be between 8.69 and 9.43 with a 95 percent confidence interval. In other words, most software developers are moderately happy.

We compared our results with similar studies (Italian workers, U.S. college students, Singapore university students, Chinese employees, South African students, and Japanese college students). All results from other studies reported a mean SPANE-B score higher than 0 but lower than in our study. Software developers are indeed a *slightly happy* group—and they are happier than what we would expect based on knowledge about various other groups of the human population. This is good news, indeed, but there is room for improvement nonetheless. Some developers have a negative SPANE-B score, and there were many examples in the open responses about episodes of unhappiness that could be avoided.

What Makes Developers Unhappy?

Our analysis of the responses of our 1,318 participants uncovered 219 causes of unhappiness, which were mentioned 2,280 times in the responses [4]. We present here a brief summary of the results and the top three categories of things that make developers unhappy.

The causes of unhappiness that are controllable by managers and team leaders are mentioned four times as often as those being personal and therefore beyond direct managerial control. We also expected the majority of the causes to be related to human aspects and relationships. However, most of them came from technical factors related to the artifact (software product, tests, requirements and design document, architecture, etc.) and the process. This highlights the importance of strategic architecture and workforce coordination.

Being stuck in problem-solving and time pressure are the two most frequent causes of unhappiness, which corroborates the importance of recent research that attempts to understand these issues. We recognize that it is in software development's nature to be basically problem-solving under deadlines: we cannot avoid problem-solving in software development. However, developers *feel bad* when they are stuck and under pressure, and several detrimental consequences do happen (see the rest of this chapter). This is where researchers and managers should intervene to reduce the detrimental effects of time pressure and getting stuck. Psychological grit could be an important characteristic to train among software developers. Another could be how to switch your mind-set to get unstuck.

The third most frequent cause of unhappiness is to work with bad code and, more specifically, with bad code practices. Developers are unhappy when they produce bad code, but they suffer tremendously when they meet bad code that could have been avoided in the first place. As our participants stated, bad code can be a result of management decisions aiming to save time and effort in the short term. Similar negative effects were mentioned regarding third persons (such as colleagues, team leaders, or customers) who make developers feel inadequate with their work, forced repetitive mundane tasks, and imposed limitations on development. Many of the negative consequences can be avoided by rotating tasks, by making better decisions, and by actually listening to developers. Several top causes are related to perceptions of inadequacy of the self and others, validating recent research activities related to interventions that improve the affect of developers [3].

Finally, we see that factors related to information needs in terms of software quality and software construction are strong contributors to unhappiness among developers. Chapter 24 shows an example of how current software tools may overload developers with information and illustrates how problems related to information flow could be solved for individual developers, teams, and organizations. More research is needed on producing tools and methods that make communication and knowledge management in software teams easier and that help effortlessly store, retrieve, and comprehend information in all stages of the software development life cycle.

What Happens When Developers Are Happy (or Unhappy)?

We classified the answers to our open-ended questions and found dozens of causes and consequences of happiness and unhappiness while developing software [4, 6]. Developers in our study reported a variety of consequences of being unhappy. We have summarized these consequences in Figure 10-2. There is a pictogram for each major consequence, and they are divided into internal and external consequences. The internal consequences, pictured inside the mind of the developer, are directed toward developers themselves and have a personal impact. The external consequences are ones that have an effect outside the individual developer. They might impact a project, the development process, or a software artifact.

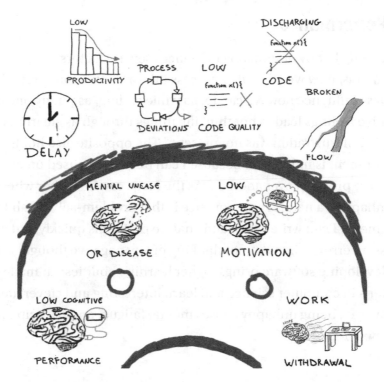

Figure 10-2. *Consequences of unhappiness while developing software. Available as CC-BY from Graziotin et al. [16]*

As you can see, developers reported several productivity-related consequences—and some even explicitly reported experiencing lower productivity. Other consequences include delays, process deviations, low code quality, throwing away code, and breaking the process flow in projects. These external effects are direct impacts on productivity and performance. Internal consequences, such as low motivation and reduced cognitive performance, indirectly affect productivity as well. Work withdrawal and mental unease, or, in the worst case, signs of disorders, are among the gravest consequences mentioned that impact developers personally.

For the purposes of this chapter, it is worth going into more detail on the consequences of happiness and unhappiness, because several of them are productivity-related and productivity was the most populated category of consequences. We are reporting them in an order that favors narrative, not by frequency of occurrence.

Cognitive Performance

We found that being happy or unhappy influences several factors related to cognitive performance, that is, how we efficiently process information in our brain. Happiness and unhappiness influence how we can focus while coding, as put by one participant: "[...] The negative feelings lead to not thinking things through as clearly as I would have if the feeling of frustration was not present." The opposite also holds true: "My software development is influenced because I can be more focused on my tasks and trying to solve one problem over another." As the focus can be higher when happy (or lower when unhappy), a natural consequence is that problem-solving abilities are influenced: "I mean, I can write codes and analyze problems quickly and with lesser or no unnecessary errors when I'm not thinking of any negative thoughts." Being happy while developing software brings higher learning abilities: "It made me want to pursue a master's in computer science and learn interesting and clever ideas to solve problems." However, being unhappy causes mental fatigue, and participants reported "getting frustrated and sloppy."

Flow

Participants mentioned how being unhappy caused breaks in their flow. *Flow* is a state of intense attention and concentration resulting from task-related skills and challenges being in balance (see more about that in Chapter 23). Unhappiness causes interruptions in developers' flow, resulting in adverse effects on the process. As put by a participant, "Things like that [of unhappiness] often cause long delays or cause one getting out of the flow, making it difficult to pick up the work again where one has left off." When happy, developers can enter a state of sustained flow. They feel full of energy and with strong focus. In such a state, they are "unaware of time passing." They can "continue to code without any more errors for the rest of the day" and "just knock out lines of code all day," with "dancing fingers." Flow is related to mindfulness, which is discussed in Chapter 25.

Motivation and Withdrawal

Motivation was often mentioned by our participants. They were clear in stating that unhappiness leads to low motivation for developing software: "[The unhappiness] has left me feeling very stupid, and as a result I have no leadership skills, no desire to participate, and feel like I'm being forced to code to live as a kind of punishment." The participants also stated that increased motivation occurred when they were happy.

Unhappiness and happiness are causes of work withdrawal and work engagement, respectively. Work withdrawal is a destructive consequence of unhappiness, and it emerged often among the responses. Work withdrawal is a family of behaviors that is defined as employees' attempts to remove themselves, either temporarily or permanently, from daily work tasks. We found varying degrees of work withdrawal, ranging from switching to another task ("[...] You spend like two hours investigating on Google for a similar issue and how it was resolved, you find nothing, and desperation kicks in.") to considering quitting developing software ("I really start to doubt myself and question whether I'm fit to be a software developer in the first place.") or even quitting the job. High work engagement and perseverance, on the other hand, were reported to occur when respondents were happy. This means, for example, pushing forward with a task: "I think I was more motivated to work harder the next few hours." This is slightly different from motivation, which is more about the energy directed to acting toward a goal. Work engagement is committing to the act of moving toward a goal.

Happiness and Unhappiness, and How They Relate to the Productivity of Developers

Finally, participants directly mentioned how unhappiness hinders their productivity. We grouped all responses related to performance and productivity losses. The responses within this category ranged from simple and clear ("productivity drops" and "[Negative experience] definitely makes me work slower") to more articulated ("[Unhappiness] made it harder or impossible to come up with solutions or with good solutions."). Unhappiness also causes delays in executing process activities: "In both cases [negative experiences] the emotional toll on me caused delays to the project." Of course, participants reported that happiness leads to high productivity: "When I have this [happy] feeling, I can just code for hours and hours," "I felt that my productivity grew while I was happy," and "The better my mood, the more productive I am." Here are more details on that by one participant: "I become productive, focused, and enjoy what I'm doing without wasting hours looking here and there in the code to know how things are hooked up together." An interesting aspect is that, when happy, developers tend to take on undesired tasks: "I think that when I'm in this happy state, I am more productive. The happier I am, the more likely I'll be able to accomplish tasks that I've been avoiding." On the other hand, unhappy developers could be so unproductive that they become destructive. We found some instances of participants who destroyed the task-related codebase ("I deleted the code that I was writing because I was a bit angry")

117

up to deleting entire projects ("I have deleted entire projects to start over with code that didn't seem to be going in a wrong direction."). Another intriguing aspect is about long-term considerations of being happy: "I find that when I feel [happy], I'm actually more productive going into the next task, and I make better choices in general for the maintenance of the code long-term. [...] I'm more likely to comment code thoroughly."

Are Happy Developers More Productive?

But are happy developers *really* more productive? Whenever science attempts to show if a factor X causes an outcome Y, researchers design *controlled* experiments. Controlled experiments attempt to keep every possible factor constant (A, B, C, ...) except for the factors (X) that should cause a change to the outcome Y. You can find more about controlled experiments in Chapter 9. Whenever this control is not possible, we call these studies *quasi-experiments*.

Here is the issue with research on happiness: it is challenging to control the happiness (or the mood, the emotions) of people. One of the reasons is that a perfectly controlled experiment would need to be quite unethical to make the unhappy control group truly unhappy. The effects of asking participants to remember sad events, or showing depressing photographs, is negligible. Still, we set up two quasi-experiments to observe some correlations.

One of these studies [1] has received considerable media attention. We tested a hypothesis regarding a difference of intellectual (cognitive-driven) performance in terms of the analytical (logical, mathematical) problem-solving of software engineers according to how happy they were. We also wanted to perform a study where all the tools and measurements came from psychology research and were validated. So, we designed a quasi-experiment in a laboratory, where 42 BSc and MSc students of computer science had their happiness measured and then conducted a task resembling algorithmic design. For measuring happiness, we opted for SPANE (explained previously).

The analytic task was similar to algorithm design and execution. We decided to administer the Tower of London test (also known as Shallice test) to our participants. The Tower of London test resembles the Tower of Hanoi game. The test comprises two boards with stacks and several colored beads. There are usually three stacks per board, and each stack can accommodate only a limited number of beads. The first board presents predefined stacked beads. The participants received the second board, which has the same beads as the first board but stacked in a different configuration. The participants have to re-create the configuration of the first board by unstacking one bead at a time and moving it to another stack. The Psychology Experiment Building Language (PEBL) is an open source language and a suite of neuropsychology tests [13, 14]. The Tower of London test is among them.

PEBL was able to collect the measures that let us calculate a score for the analytic performance. We compared the scores obtained in both tasks with the happiness of developers. The results showed that the happiest software developers outperformed the other developers in terms of analytic performance. We estimated the performance increase to be about 6 percent. The performance increase was not negligible, and we confirmed it by measuring Cohen's d statistic. Cohen's d is a number usually ranging from 0 to 2, which represents the magnitude of the effect size of a difference of means. Our Cohen's d for the difference between the two groups mean was 0.91—a large effect given that we did not obtain extreme cases of happiness and unhappiness. The margins could even be higher than that.

In another study [2], we did something more esoteric. We aimed to continue using psychology theory and measurement instruments for understanding the linkage between the real-time affect (let's say happiness) raised by a software development task and the productivity related to the task itself. Eight software developers (four students and four from software companies) worked on their real-world software project. The task length was 90 minutes (as it is about the typical length for a programming task). Each ten minutes, the developers filled a questionnaire formed by the Self-Assessment Manikin (SAM) and an item for self-assessing the productivity.

SAM is a scale for assessing an emotional state or reaction. SAM is peculiar because it is a validated way to measure the affect raised by a stimulus (like an object, or a situation) and it is picture-based (no words). SAM is simply three rows of puppets with different face expressions and body language. Therefore, it is quick for a participant to fill SAM, especially if implemented on a tablet (only three touches). We analyzed how developers felt during the task and how they self-assessed themselves in terms of productivity. Self-assessment is not a very objective way of measuring productivity, but it has been demonstrated that individuals are actually good at self-assessing themselves if they are observed alone [15]. The results have shown that high pleasure with the programming task and the sensation of having adequate skills are positively correlated with the productivity. This correlation holds over time. We also found that there are strong variations of affect in 90 minutes of time. Happy software developers are indeed more productive.

Potential Impacts of Happiness on Other Outcomes

Happiness influences so many things besides productivity, most of which are still related to development performance. Here we list three of them.

Unhappiness causes glitches in communication and a disorganized process: "Miscommunication and disorganization made it very difficult to meet deadlines." But happy developers can also mean more collaborative team members, leading to increased collaboration. Often, we saw a repeating pattern of willingness to share knowledge ("I'm very curious, and I like to teach people what I learned") and to join an effort to solve a problem ("We never hold back on putting our brains together to tackle a difficult problem or plan a new feature"), even when not related to the task at hand or the current responsibilities ("I was more willing to help them with a problem they were having at work.").

Being happy or unhappy influences not only the productivity of the code writing process but also the quality of the resulting code. Participants reported that "Eventually [due to negative experiences], code quality cannot be assured. So this will make my code messy, and more bug can be found in it," but also mentioned making the code less performant, or "As a result, my code becomes sloppier." Sometimes, being unhappy results in discharging quality practices ("[...] so I cannot follow the standard design pattern") as a way to cope with the negative experiences. Yet, being happy improves the quality of code. A participant told a small story about their work: "I was building an interface to make two applications talk. It was an exciting challenge, and my happy and positive feelings made me go above and beyond to not only make it functional but I made the UX nice too. I wanted the whole package to look polished and not just functional." When happy, developers tend to make less mistakes, see solutions to problems more easily, and make new connections to improve the quality of the code. A participant told us this: "When I'm in a good mood and I feel somehow positive, the code I write seems to be very neat and clean. I mean, I can write code and analyze problems quickly and with lesser or no unnecessary errors." As a result, the code is cleaner, more readable, better commented and tested, and with less errors and bugs.

The last factor we would like to report is mostly related to unhappiness, and it is quite an important one. It is about mental unease and mental disorder. We created this category to collect those consequences that threaten mental health. Participants reported that unhappiness while developing software is a cause of anxiety ("These kinds of situations make me feel panicky."), stress ("[The] only reason [for] my failure [is] due [to] burnout."), self-doubt ("If I feel particularly lost on a certain task, I may sometimes begin to question my overall ability to be a good programmer."), and sadness and feeling depressed ("[...] feels like a black fog of depression surrounds you and the project."). In addition, we found mentions of feelings of being judged, frustration, and lack of confidence in one's ability.

What Does the Future Hold?

In 1971, Gerald Weinberg's book *The psychology of programming* [12] drew attention to the fact that software development is a human endeavor, and the humans doing it—the developers—are individuals with feelings. To this day, we still have more to understand about the human factor in software development. Software development productivity is still often managed as if it were about delivering code on an assembly line (see, e.g., Chapter 11). On the other hand, many companies do understand the importance of happy developers, invest in their well-being, and consider it to be worthwhile.

As we have shown, the link between happiness and productivity in software development is real. It is possible to quantify the happiness of software developers, and there are distinct patterns in the causes and consequences of their happiness.

What if we could include happiness as a factor in software development productivity management? In the future, an increasing number of people will work with digital products and services and perform tasks that are, in effect, software development. It would be worth investing in their happiness. It is important that we learn more about the relationship between well-being and software development performance. Rigorous research and educating practitioners on the research results are keys to improve the field. Besides sharp technical skills, we would like to give future software developers an understanding of the social and psychological factors that influence their own work.

Further Reading

In this chapter, we reported on several studies on the happiness of software engineers. Some of these studies [1, 2, 3, 5, 11] were self-contained and independent. Other studies [4, 6] are part of an ongoing project that we described in the section "Scientific Grounds of Happy and Productive Developers."

At the time of writing of this chapter, we still have to uncover all the categories, including those about what makes developers happy. We invite readers to inspect our open science repository [10], where we add new papers and results as we uncover them. The repository contains the entire taxonomy of what makes developers unhappy.

Key Ideas

Here are the key ideas from this chapter:

- Science says the industry should strive for happy developers.

- The overall happiness of software developers is slightly positive. Yet, many are still unhappy.

- The causes of unhappiness among software engineers are numerous and complex.

- Happiness and unhappiness bring a plethora of benefits and detriments to software development processes, people, and products.

References

[1]   Graziotin, D., Wang, X., and Abrahamsson, P. 2014. Happy software developers solve problems better: psychological measurements in empirical software engineering. PeerJ. 2, e289. DOI=10.7717/peerj.289. Available: https://doi.org/10.7717/peerj.289.

[2]   Graziotin, D., Wang, X., and Abrahamsson, P. 2015. Do feelings matter? On the correlation of affects and the self-assessed productivity in software engineering. Journal of Software: Evolution and Process. 27, 7, 467–487. DOI=10.1002/smr.1673. Available: https://arxiv.org/abs/1408.1293.

[3]   Graziotin, D., Wang, X., and Abrahamsson, P. 2015. How do you feel, developer? An explanatory theory of the impact of affects on programming performance. PeerJ Computer Science. 1, e18. DOI=10.7717/peerj-cs.18. Available: https://doi.org/10.7717/peerj-cs.18.

[4]   Graziotin, D., Fagerholm, F., Wang, X., and Abrahamsson, P. 2017. On the Unhappiness of Software Developers. 21st International Conference on Evaluation and Assessment in Software Engineering. 21st International Conference on Evaluation and Assessment in Software Engineering, 324–333. DOI=10.1145/3084226.3084242. Available: https://arxiv.org/abs/1703.04993.

[5]   Graziotin, D., Wang, X., and Abrahamsson, P. 2014. Software
Developers, Moods, Emotions, and Performance. IEEE Software. 31,
4, 24–27. DOI=10.1109/MS.2014.94. Available: `https://arxiv.org/
abs/1405.4422`.

[6]   Graziotin, D., Fagerholm, F., Wang, X., & Abrahamsson, P.
(2018). What happens when software developers are (un)happy.
Journal of Systems and Software, 140, 32-47. DOI=10.1016/j.
jss.2018.02.041. Available: `https://doi.org/10.1016/j.
jss.2018.02.041`

[7]   Zelenski, J. M., Murphy, S. A., and Jenkins, D. A. 2008. The Happy-
Productive Worker Thesis Revisited. Journal of Happiness Studies.
9, 4, 521–537. DOI=10.1007/s10902-008-9087-4.

[8]   Diener, E., Wirtz, D., Tov, W., Kim-Prieto, C., Choi, D.-w., Oishi, S.,
and Biswas-Diener, R. 2010. New Well-being Measures: Short Scales
to Assess Flourishing and Positive and Negative Feelings. Social
Indicators Research. 97, 2, 143-156. DOI=10.1007/s11205-009-9493-y.

[9]   Bradley, M. M. and Lang, P. J. 1994. Measuring emotion: The
self-assessment manikin and the semantic differential. Journal
of Behavior Therapy and Experimental Psychiatry. 25, 1, 49-59.
DOI=10.1016/0005-7916(94)90063-9.

[10]   Graziotin, D., Fagerholm, F., Wang, X., and Abrahamsson, P. 2017.
Online appendix: the happiness of software developers. Figshare.
Available: `https://doi.org/10.6084/m9.figshare.c.3355707`.

[11]   Fagerholm, F., Ikonen, M., Kettunen, P., Münch, J., Roto, V.,
Abrahamsson, P. 2015. Performance Alignment Work: How
software developers experience the continuous adaptation of team
performance in Lean and Agile environments. Information and
Software Technology. 64, 132–147. DOI=10.1016/j.infsof.2015.01.010.

[12]   Weinberg, G. M. (1971). Psychology of Computer Programming
(1 ed.). New York, NY, USA: Van Nostrand Reinhold Company.

[13]   Piper, B. J., Mueller, S. T., Talebzadeh, S., Ki, M. J. 2016. Evaluation of the
validity of the Psychology Experiment Building Language tests of vigilance,
auditory memory, and decision making. PeerJ. 4, e1772. DOI=10.7717/
peerj.1772. Available: `https://doi.org/10.7717/peerj.1772`.

[14]   Piper, B. J., Mueller, S. T., Geerken, A. R, Dixon, K. L., Kroliczak,
        G., Olsen, R. H. J., Miller, J. K. 2015. Reliability and validity of
        neurobehavioral function on the Psychology Experimental Building
        Language test battery in young adults. PeerJ. 3, e1460. DOI=10.7717/
        peerj.1460. Available: https://doi.org/10.7717/peerj.1460.

[15]   Miner, A. G., Glomb, T. M., 2010. State mood, task performance,
        and behavior at work: A within-persons approach. Organizational
        Behavior and Human Decision Processes. 112, 1, 43–57.
        DOI=10.1016/j.obhdp.2009.11.009.

[16]   Graziotin, Daniel; Fagerholm, Fabian; Wang, Xiaofeng;
        Abrahamsson, Pekka (2017): Slides for the consequences
        of unhappiness while developing software. https://doi.
        org/10.6084/m9.figshare.4869038.v3.

CHAPTER 11

Dark Agile: Perceiving People As Assets, Not Humans

Pernille Bjørn, University of Copenhagen, Denmark

Revisiting the Agile Manifesto

The agile principles for software engineering were developed as a reaction against structuring software engineering processes in strict stepwise and sequential ways. The idea that it was possible to create a clearly predefined scope prior to the actual software engineering activities was questioned—and the agile methodology was an attempt to rephrase the basic nature of software engineering. The agile understanding of software engineering is that the fundamental nature of software means that we cannot predetermine scope, goals, and objectives up front. Instead, goals, scope, and objectives are transformed throughout the software development process. This setup requires participants (developers and clients) to balance and negotiate resources and priorities, and this is what drives agile development. Agile development is not one thing but can instead be seen as a set of principles that guide the organization of work and can be implemented in different ways. The main principles provided by the agile manifesto (http://agilemanifesto.org) are as follows:

- Individuals and interaction over processes and tools

- Working software over comprehensive documentation

© The Author(s) 2019
C. Sadowski and T. Zimmermann (eds.), *Rethinking Productivity in Software Engineering*,
https://doi.org/10.1007/978-1-4842-4221-6_11

- Customer collaboration over contract negotiation

- Responding to change over following a plan

These agile principles are based upon the main idea of providing the power over software engineering to the people—the software team. Instead of letting software developers be controlled from the outside, the software teams are to be empowered to find and prioritize their own work. The software team is to be a self-organized team, and the client or customer is to be part of the team supporting the prioritizing of tasks based upon available resources. When we, in computer science departments at Danish universities, teach computer science students about software engineering, we talk about the benefits of agile development and the problems with the waterfall model. We explain how the waterfall model does not take into account the iterative and creative process of developing software. Furthermore, if you visit any kind of Danish IT company and talk to the developers and ask them about methods, they will tell you how the waterfall model does not work and how agile methodologies provide better quality within an appropriate time frame. Agile is seen as a positive perspective on software engineering in Denmark.

However, the story about agile is quite different when we change perspective from Scandinavia and turn to India.

Agile in Global Outsourcing Setups

Based upon a long-term research project called Next-Generation Tools and Processes for Global Software Development (NexGSD; nexsgsd.org), we have studied how global software development takes place in different places around the world. Concretely, we went to observe and interview software developers in the Philippines about their experiences working with software developers in Denmark [4, 5, 7], and we also went to India, more concretely Bangalore, Mumbai, and Chennai, to observe and interview software developers about their experiences collaborating with software teams and vendors located in Northern Europe and the United States [6, 8, 11, 12]. Throughout all these empirical studies, we began to notice the consequences of implementing agile principles such as scrum methodologies in global outsourcing setups. We witnessed a transformation in the way global software development was organized between 2011, when we started the project, until 2014, where all the organizations we studied went from waterfall models toward agile models [1, 2].

So, what does this mean? Let's take a closer look at the experience of agile development seen from a software developer working out of India in one of our empirical case studies between Bangalore, India, and Phoenix, United States [3].

Global software development can at a high level be organized as outsourcing or off-shoring. Outsourcing is when you move work from one internal location toward an external partner, who then does the work for you. Differently, global off-shoring is when work is moved to a different location, but still within the same company—like IBM USA working with IBM India. In our empirical cases, we are looking at global out-sourcing, which means that work is moved from either the United States or Denmark to a different geographical location and a different organizational setting.

In outsourcing setups, it is important to note that the power remains with the client. This mean the client chooses which company is doing the work, and deciding to move work to other outsourcing vendors (still in the same region of the world) is always an option. In one of our cases, the U.S. client put together a global agile team comprised of experts from different IT vendor companies in India and then one representative from the client was the project owner. This meant that the team members, even being in the same team, were simultaneously in competition. The client was able to exchange specific members with new people if particular individuals were not performing well accordingly to the client. This multivendor setup created a high-performance team, which despite being geographically distributed was highly productive. The global agile setup raised the competition among the team members, and from a productivity perspective, this was a huge success. But how did the agile principles—concretely manifested in the scrum methodology—impact the global outsourcing team?

Tracking Work to Increase Productivity

One of the main processes in scrum is that members of the team specify what they are currently working on, directly linked to specific numbers of hours. How many hours specific tasks might take is up to the team members, who negotiate the resources required during planning. In this way, each team member is tasked with assignments to be accomplished and finished within detailed time frames. In India, the workday of software developers is ten hours. In all software projects, some hours will be spent on other activities than directly on the project. Therefore, the hours that are tracked are eight hours a day. This means that each day, each team member is committing to produce software tasks resembling the work of eight hours. Thus, regardless of what might happen, each team member must produce the task assignment. Even if their child gets sick and they need to leave the office, they cannot. They have to stay on task and complete the task as planned or else their client might move the task to a competing IT-vendor company (still in India). Interestingly, the software developers working in Bangalore explained to us how they prefer waterfall over agile. Waterfall had less time pressure since they had a specific target—and longer deadlines, which made it possible to pick up a sick child if needed, rather than being constantly pushed by short deadlines.

Daily Stand-Up Meeting to Monitor Productivity

Besides agile allowing clients to constantly track the productivity of each individual team member, global agile also forced team members to participate in daily stand-up meetings. While the stand-up meeting alone was not problematic, the time of day for the meeting was. Because of the time difference between the East Coast in the United States and India, the time for stand-up meetings were set to late evening (10 p.m.) Indian time. This was regardless of the day of the week—so all days including Friday, there were stand-up meetings in the evening. This meant that team members involved in global agile outsourcing were forced to work out of sync locally to accommodate global work. Working out of sync locally is problematic in terms of family life or social events, especially in situations where the software developers had their families in villages far away. Several developers we spoke with moved to the electronic city of Bangalore during the week and then traveled back on the weekends. The stand-up meetings made it difficult to travel home Friday evening. Furthermore, the tenure of the projects changed from being four- or five-month-long projects to being more than a year. This provided constant pressure on the software developers; there was no time for breaks or vacations. The high level of productivity for the extended time led to a stressful environment.

Stressful Work Environment

Over the three years we conducted interviews, it became apparent that, while the global agile team had high productivity and was the preferred IT vendor for the customer, the software developers working in the global agile setting felt "more pressure, more time pressure, stress" and the experience of agile methodology was that it "is very stressful, at the tester level." It is important to note that while it can be expected that people in higher positions working in global projects be available at odd times and work many hours, the people working under pressure in this situation were the developers and testers working in low-level positions. The way global agile was implemented meant that the customer pressured the team on speed constantly—so even though agile principles stipulate that the ideal sprint size is two to three weeks, the customer pushed it down to one week. Analyzing, designing, implementing, and testing workable deliveries within five days of work is hard, especially for the testers. As a delivery manager explained to us: "Yes, for the techies, or for the technical department, it is a very stressful, stressful methodology I would say because the expectation is too high from the customer's side."

Cost of Productivity

There is no doubt that the IT vendor we studied was highly productive in terms of speed and quality, delivered good quality work on time, and was the customers' preferred IT vendor, even in the competitive multivendor setup. As the preferred IT vendor, they gained more tasks, especially in situations where other vendors were not able to deliver. Now the question is, what was the cost of this high productivity?

Financially, global agile is more expensive than waterfall methods for the customer: when talking with the IT vendor, it was clear that they were able to produce the same kind of products much cheaper under the waterfall methodology. The argument for global agile as a way to save costs, which are often a fundamental problem in global software development [10], was not on the agenda. When we asked the IT vendor why they were using agile principles in the first place, they explained that it was a request from the customers: the customers wanted the vendor to use scrum. Let's take a step back and reflect on this request from the customers. When you, as a company, are hired to deliver a service or a product, negotiations about the price, timeline, and collaboration are to be expected. Clients direct requests for how the vendor is to use specific methods are less obvious. So, why did the client request this? Despite it being a more expensive methodology for the client, they gained direct access to highly qualified people, who all had proportionally high salaries (though the IT vendor then had difficulty including and training new people to work on the projects).

What about the human costs of this high productivity? What happens to people when agile goes global? If we return to the principles in the agile manifesto, we find that the principles of "working software over comprehensive documentation," "customer collaboration over contract negotiation," and "responding to change over following a plan"

129

are all very pertinent in the global agile outsourcing setting as well. In our case, there was close collaboration with the customer, the scope and objectives were a moveable target, and there was a constant focus on working software deliveries. However, if we look at the first principle of "individuals and interaction over processes and tools," we see a shift. The processes and tools created to structure the agile delivery were used to micromanage the software developers' work in all the small details. We can view the global agile principles in our case as an algorithmic machine, with specific input and output features. The input measures are the numbers, the hours, and the deliverables deadlines, which are then used to push people to maximize their efforts. Given the tools and processes of agile, the remote client is able to monitor and control every little aspect of the work done by the software developers. Sure, global agile is very productive. If the only criteria for success is high-quality work done fast, global agile is attractive.

Nevertheless, there is a dark side to global agile, since in the case of scrum comes tools and processes that can be used to micromanage software developers. Focusing only on productivity, we risk losing sight of individuals and the "mushy stuff" that is at the core of the agile ideals. According to Jim Highsmith for the Agile Alliance, "At the core, I believe agile methodologists are really about the 'mushy' stuff about delivering good products to customers by operating in an environment that does more than talk about 'people as our most important asset' but actually 'acts' as if people were the most important and lose the word 'asset'" (`http://agilemanifesto.org/history.html`).

I that we must consider the conditions for work created by the constant focus on productivity introduced and controlled by agile tools and processes. This risk of the "global agile algorithmic machine" is that it turns people into assets, resources, and numbers—and we lose sight of individual developers. While waterfall methodologies have been criticized for heavily regulating work and introducing micromanagement, our empirical observations point to how the global agile methodology can also be used for micromanagement and strong regulation of software developers.

Global agile provides good conditions for high productivity in software engineering but also these risks:

- Perceiving people as assets, not human beings

- Creating stressful work environments in continuous work cycles

- Supporting clients in micromanagement from afar

- Making developers and testers work out of sync with their local time zones

What we risk losing is the focus on the software developers and the self-organization and empowerment that are supposed to be introduced with agile methodologies. Software engineering organized by global agile methodologies in highly competitive multivendor settings risks resembling the assembly line in factory work. Is this really what we want the future of software engineering to look like?

Open Questions for Productivity in Software Engineering

I am not arguing that global agile is problematic per se. Clearly, in all the NexGSD empirical studies, closely coupled collaboration was essential to get that collaboration to function across sites, and the agile principles enable and stipulate closely coupled collaboration. However, I am arguing that "being a software developer involved in global outsourcing" means different things depending on where you physically are located in the world. Software developers at low-level positions working in Bangalore, India, have different conditions for work than software developers working in Ballerup, Denmark [9]. This means that they will experience the implementation of global agile in different ways. Software engineers located in Denmark have a privileged position in the global setup. For software engineers located in India, the way global agile techniques, tools, and processes shapes work do not provide the same conditions for self-organization and empowerment. Moreover, it means that when we are designing software tools and processes to support global work, we should take into consideration the different conditions and not just focus on productivity. Fast delivery and high-quality code should not be our main measurements; instead, we should start to develop measurements that are more nuanced and take into consideration work conditions. We must think about how artifacts such as "burndown charts" reflect only partial aspects of productivity [10], and we should ask, what is not represented in such artifacts? What are artifacts and tools neglecting to make visible? Finally, we need to consider how to ensure that we do not lose our human values when we think about how we design tools and processes and create good work conditions for all, no matter where in the world they are placed. People work more and more in the global setting; and as life and work starts to blend due to us bringing home our laptops and continuing checking e-mail in the evenings and on weekends, we need to prepare long-term strategies for dealing with the pressure of productivity—even for low-level software developers and testers working in India.

When software developers complain that they have to attend a meeting at 10 p.m. and are not able to leave work to pick up sick children, they are not complaining about agile development per se. Instead, they are complaining about the lack of power and decision-making within the organizational setup. Agile development works well for software developers in Scandinavia, Northern Europe, and United States because the software teams are powerful and privileged. When clients demand agile development from software developers elsewhere, those developers are not empowered. Instead, the power to choose and organize their work is taken away from them. The following are important questions we must ask:

- What kind of productivity and values do we want software engineering to reflect?

- How do we ensure that these values are manifested in our productivity measurements shaping software engineering processes and tools?

- How can we design software engineering practices and technologies to support productivity without losing human values?

Key Ideas

The following are the key ideas from this chapter:

- Global agile software development has several risks: perceiving people as assets, not humans; creating a stressful work environment; micromanagement; and making engineers work out of sync with local time zones.

- Productivity measurement should be about more than speed and quality.

Acknowledgments

This chapter is based upon the academic research paper co-authored by Pernille Bjørn, Anne-Marie Søderberg, and S. Krishna titled "Translocality in Global Software Development: The Dark Side of Global Agile" and published in the journal of Human-Computer Interaction [3]. Further, the work referred to is part of several subprojects in the NexGSD research project (`nexgsd.org`), which was financially supported by the National Council for Strategic Research, Ministry of Science, Innovation, and Higher Education in Denmark.

References

[1]   Bjørn, P. (2016). "New fundamentals for CSCW research: From distance to politics." Interactions (ACM SIGCHI) 23(3): 50–53.

[2]   Bjørn, P., M. Esbensen, R. E. Jensen and S. Matthiesen (2014). "Does distance still matter? Revisiting the CSCW fundamentals on distributed collaboration." ACM Transaction Computer Human Interaction (ToChi) 21(5): 1–27.

[3]   Bjørn, P., A.-M. Søderberg and S. Krishna (2017). "Translocality in Global Software Development: The Dark Side of Global Agile." Human-Computer Interaction 10.1080/07370024.2017.1398092.

[4]   Christensen, L. and P. Bjørn (2014). Documentscape: Intertextuallity, sequentiality and autonomy at work. ACM CHI Conference on Human Factors in Computing Systems Toronto, ON, Canada, ACM.

[5]   Christensen, L. R., R. E. Jensen and P. Bjørn (2014). Relation work in collocated and distributed collaboration. COOP: 11th International Conference on Design of Cooperative Systems. Nice, France, Springer.

[6]   Esbensen, M. and P. Bjørn (2014). Routine and standardization in Global software development. GROUP. Sanible Island, Florida, USA, ACM.

[7]   Jensen, R. E. and B. Nardi (2014). The rhetoric of culture as an act of closure in cross- national software development department. European Conference of Information System (ECIS). Tel Aviv, AIS.

[8]   Matthiesen, S. and P. Bjørn (2015). Why replacing legacy systems is so hard in global software development: An information infrastructure perspective. CSCW. Vancouver, Canada, ACM.

[9]   Matthiesen, S. and P. Bjørn (2016). Let's look outside the office: Analytical lens unpacking collaborative relationships in global work. COOP2016. Trento, Italy, Springer.

[10] Matthiesen, S. and P. Bjørn (2017). "When distribution of tasks and skills are fundamentally problematic: A failure story from global software outsourcing." PACM on Human-Computer Interaction: Online first 2018 ACM Conference on Computer-supported Cooperative Woek and Social Computing 1(2, Article 74): 16.

[11] Matthiesen, S., P. Bjørn and L. M. Petersen (2014). "Figure Out How to Code with the Hands of Others": Recognizing Cultural Blind Spots in Global Software Development. Computer Supported Cooperative Work (CSCW). Baltimore, USA, ACM.

[12] Søderberg, A.-M., S. Krishna and P. Bjørn (2013). "Global Software Development: Commitment, Trust and Cultural Sensitivity in Strategic Partnerships." Journal of International Management 19(4): 347–361.

PART IV

Measuring Productivity in Practice

CHAPTER 12

Developers' Diverging Perceptions of Productivity

André N. Meyer, University of Zurich, Switzerland

Gail C. Murphy, University of British Columbia, Canada

Thomas Fritz, University of Zurich, Switzerland

Thomas Zimmermann, Microsoft Research, USA

Quantifying Productivity: Measuring vs. Perceptions

To overcome the ever-growing demand for software, software development organizations strive to enhance the productivity of their developers. But what does productivity mean in the context of software development? A substantial amount of work on developer productivity has been undertaken over the past four decades. The majority of this work considered productivity from a *top-down perspective* (the manager view) in terms of the artifacts and code created per unit of time. Common examples of such productivity measures are the lines of source code modified per hour, the resolution time for modification requests, or function points created per month. These productivity measures focus on a single, output-oriented factor for quantifying productivity and do not take into account developers' individual work roles, practices, and other factors that might affect their productivity, such as work fragmentation, the tools used, or the work/office environment. For example, a lead developer who spends a big part of work supporting co-workers with their inquiries might develop less code in the process

© The Author(s) 2019

C. Sadowski and T. Zimmermann (eds.), *Rethinking Productivity in Software Engineering*,
https://doi.org/10.1007/978-1-4842-4221-6_12

and would thus be considered less productive when using traditional, top-down measurements compared to developers who focus solely on coding.

Another approach to quantify productivity is *bottom-up*, starting at the productivity of individual software developers to then also learn more about quantifying productivity more broadly. By investigating developers' individual productivity, it is possible to better understand individual work habits and patterns, how they relate to productivity perceptions, and also which factors are most relevant for a developer's productivity.

Studying Software Developers' Productivity Perceptions

There are various ways to investigate productivity from the bottom up. In this chapter, we describe three studies that we conducted using a variety of methods, from very detailed observations to two-week field studies using a monitoring application.

- First, to gather insights into what developers' considered productive and unproductive work, we conducted an online survey with 389 professional software developers, followed by observations and follow-up interviews with 11 developers to corroborate some of the findings of the survey [1].

- To better understand activities developers pursue at work, the fragmentation of their work, and how these activities relate to self-reported productivity, we conducted a two-week field study with 20 professional software developers. For this study, we deployed a monitoring application that logged developers' computer interaction and collected self-reports on their productivity every 90 minutes [2].

- To analyze and compare the situations when developers feel productive, we conducted a further online survey with 413 professional software developers [3].

The remainder of this chapter highlights the most prominent findings. Detailed descriptions of the studies and findings can be found in the corresponding papers.

The Cost of Context Switching

Developers reported that they usually feel most productive when they make progress on tasks and when they have only a few context switches and interruptions. However, observing developers' workdays revealed that they constantly switch contexts, often multiple times an hour. For example, developers switched tasks on average 13 times an hour and spent just about 6 minutes on a task before switching to another one. An example of a task switch is a developer who is switching from implementing a feature to answering e-mails that are unrelated to the previous task. Similarly, when we looked at how much time developers spend on activities–actions they usually pursue at work (e.g., writing code, running tests, or writing an e-mail)–we found out that they usually remain in an activity only between 20 seconds and 2 minutes before switching to another one. This high number of task and activity switches and the high variety of activities and tasks developers pursue each day illustrate the high fragmentation of a developer's work.

Surprisingly, many developers still felt productive despite the high number of context switches. The follow-up interviews with the developers revealed that the cost of context switches varies. The cost or "harm" of a context switch depends on several factors: the duration of the switch, the reason for the switch, and the focus on the current task that is interrupted. A short switch from the IDE to respond to a Slack message is usually less costly than being interrupted from a task by a co-worker and discussing a topic unrelated to the main task for half an hour. Also, short context switches, such as writing a quick e-mail while waiting for a build to complete, do not usually harm productivity, as self-reported by our participants.

Interruptions from co-workers are one of the most often mentioned reasons for costly context switches, especially when they happen at an inopportune moment, such as when a developer is focused on a challenging problem. Chapter 23 presents one possible solution of how developers and other knowledge workers can reduce the number of costly interruptions by visualizing their current focus to the team.

A Productive Workday in a Developer's Life

Investigating how developers organize their time at work and what activities they pursue revealed notable differences. During an average workday of 8.4 hours, developers spend about half of their time, on average 4.3 hours, actively working on their computer. Surprisingly, they spend only about one-fourth of their total work time with coding-related activities and another fourth of their time with collaborative activities such as meetings, e-mails, and instant messaging. There are also big differences across companies, for example how much time their developers spend reading or writing e-mails. At one of the observed companies, developers spent less than one minute with e-mail each workday, compared to developers at another company where they spent more than an hour.

Relating the activities developers pursue at work with how productive they feel during these activities revealed that productivity is highly individual and differs greatly across developers. The majority of developers reported coding as the most productive activity, as coding allows them to make progress on the tasks that are most important to them. With most other activities, there was no clear consensus about whether an activity is generally productive or not. Meetings were the most controversial activity: more than half of the developers considered meetings as unproductive, especially when they lack goals, have no outcome, or there are too many attendees; the other half of developers considered meetings to be productive. E-mails are considered to be a less productive activity by many developers. However, no single activity is considered exclusively productive or unproductive by all developers. Coding, for instance, was not always considered to be a productive activity, for example when the developer was blocked on a task. This suggests that measures or models that attempt to quantify productivity should take individual differences, such as the context of a developer's workday, into account, and attempt to capture a developer's work more holistically rather than reducing them to a single activity and one outcome measure.

Developers Expect Different Measures for Quantifying Productivity

When we asked developers about how they would like to quantify their productivity, the majority wanted to assess their productivity based on the number of completed tasks but also combine it with other measures. These additional measures include output-related measures, such as the lines of code, number of commits, number of bugs found or fixed, and e-mails sent, but they also include higher-level measures, such as how focused they were during their work, if they were working "in the flow" (or "the zone"), and if they felt they had made any significant progress. Across all measures that developers were asked about, there was no single measure or combination of multiple measures that were consistently rated higher by most developers. This result indicates that there are a variety of aspects that impact the productivity of developers and their feeling of productivity differently. For example, on days when a developer spends a lot of time working on development task, a measure of the number of work items completed or check-ins made may be appropriate. However, the same measure on days a developer spends most of the time in meetings or helping co-workers would result in a low productivity and high frustration for the developer. Furthermore, the findings suggest that it is difficult to broadly measure productivity without defining specific objectives. We will have to find ways to do measure productivity more holistically, by not only leveraging output measures, but also considering developers' individual abilities, work habits, contributions to the team, and more. Chapters 2 and 3 discuss this further and argue that productivity should be considered not only from the perspective of individuals but also for teams and organizations.

Characterizing Software Developers by Perceptions of Productivity

The differences in how developers feel about productivity makes it also more challenging to determine meaningful actions that could help increase productivity on a team or organizational level. One way to better understand differences and commonalities in developers' perceptions of productivity is to investigate if we can find patterns or group developers with similar perceptions. Analyzing productivity ratings from hourly self-reports during three workweeks, we found that developers can roughly be categorized into three groups that are similar to the circadian rhythm: morning person, afternoon person, and low-at-lunch person, as visualized in Figure 12-1. The curved regression line in the three figures shows the overall pattern of what part of the day an individual developer typically felt more or less productive with the shaded area showing the confidence range. Morning people were rare in our sample, with only 20 percent of all participants. The biggest group were afternoon people (40 percent), who may be those who are industrious later in the day or who feel more productive as a result of having the majority of their workday behind them. These results suggest that while developers have diverse perceived productivity patterns, individuals do appear to follow their own habitual patterns each day.

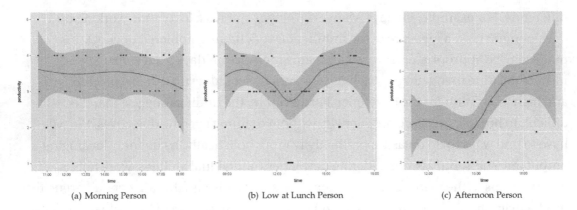

(a) Morning Person   (b) Low at Lunch Person   (c) Afternoon Person

Figure 12-1. *Three types of developers and their perceptions of productivity over the course of a workday*

In another effort to group developers with similar perceptions of productivity together, we asked participants to describe productive and unproductive workdays, rate their agreement with a list of factors that might affect productivity, and rate the interestingness of a list of productivity measures at work. We found that developers can be clustered into six groups: social, lone, focused, balanced, leading, and goal-oriented.

- The *social developers* feel productive when helping co-workers, collaborating, and doing code reviews. To get things done, they come early to work or work late and try to focus on a single task.

- The *lone developers* avoid disruptions such as noise, e-mail, meetings, and code reviews. They feel most productive when they have little to no social interactions and when they can work on solving problems, fixing bugs, or coding features in quiet and without interruptions. To reflect about work, they are mostly interested in knowing the frequency and duration of interruptions they encountered. Note that this group of developers is almost the opposite of the first group (the social developer) in how productive they feel when encountering social interactions.

- The *focused developers* feel most productive when they are working efficiently and concentrated on a single task at a time. They feel unproductive when they are wasting time and spend too much time on a task because they are stuck or working slowly. They are interested in knowing the number of interruptions and length of focused time.

142

- The *balanced developers* are less affected by disruptions. They feel unproductive when tasks are unclear or irrelevant, when they are unfamiliar with a task, or when tasks are causing overhead.

- The *leading developers* are more comfortable with meetings and e-mails and feel less productive with coding activities than other developers. They feel more productive when they can write and design things, such as specifications. They do not like broken builds and blocking tasks, preventing them (or the team) from doing productive work.

- The *goal-oriented developers* feel productive when they complete or make progress on tasks. They feel less productive when they multitask, are goal-less, or are stuck. They are more open to meetings and e-mails compared to the other groups if they help them achieve their goals. In contrast to focused developers, goal-oriented developers care more about actually getting stuff done (i.e., crossing items off the task-list), while focused developers care more about working efficiently.

Each developer can belong to one or more of these groups. The six groups and their characteristics highlight differences in developers' productivity perceptions and show that their ideal workdays, tasks, and work environments often look differently. We can further use these findings to tailor process improvements and tools to the different types of developers, as discussed in the next section.

Opportunities for Improving Developer Productivity

Developers and development teams might benefit from these findings in various ways. On the individual level, we could build self-monitoring tools that allow developers to increase their awareness about productive and unproductive behaviors and use the insights they gain to set well-founded goals for self-improvements at work (see Chapter 22).

These approaches should provide a variety of measures and support developers in getting insights into individual aspects of their work, such as identifying productive or unproductive work habits or identifying external or internal factors that have the biggest impact on their productivity. In addition to self-monitoring that has been shown to motivate positive behavior changes in other fields (e.g., physical activity and health), supporting developers with setting goals to improve themselves at work through actionable insights might be a next step toward fostering productivity. Maybe one day, we can further build virtual assistants, such as Alexa for Developers, that recommend (or automatically take) actions, depending on the goals of developers or based on the productivity patterns/roles/clusters of developers. For example, such a virtual assistant could block out notifications from e-mail, Slack, and Skype during coding sessions to avoid disruptions for the "lone developer" but allow them for the "social developer." Or they could recommend the "focused developer" to come to work early to have a few hours of uninterrupted work time or suggest the "balanced developer" to take a break to avoid boredom and tiredness.

By knowing the trends of developers' perceived productivity and the activities they consider as particularly productive/unproductive, it might be possible to schedule the tasks and activities developers must perform in a way that best fits their work patterns. For example, if a developer is a morning person and considers coding particularly productive and meetings as impeding productivity, blocking calendar time in the morning for coding tasks and automatically assigning afternoon hours for meeting requests may allow the developer to best employ their capabilities over the whole day. Or, it could remind developers to reserve slots for unplanned work or interruptions at times where they usually happen.

Our studies also revealed that interruptions, one specific type of a context switch, are one of the biggest impediments to productive work. Productivity could potentially be improved on the team level by enhancing the coordination and communication between co-workers, depending on their preferences, availabilities, and current focus. For example, on the team level, quiet, less interruption-prone offices could be provided to the "lone developers" and "focused developers," and "social developers" who feel more comfortable with discussions every now and then could be seated in open space offices. Alternatively, interruptions at inopportune moments could be reduced by visualizing the developer's current focus and concentration to other developers using an external cue. Hence, at times when the developer is "in the flow" or is usually most productive, expensive interruptions could be postponed to a more opportune moment (see Chapter 23).

Key Ideas

The following are the key ideas from this chapter:

- Different software developers experience productivity differently, which is why they do not agree on how to measure productivity.

- Most developers follow their own habitual patterns each day and are most productive either in the morning, during the day (and not at lunch), or in the afternoon.

- Measuring developer productivity should not only include output measures but also include measures inherent to developers' abilities, workdays, work environments, and more.

References

[1]   André N Meyer, Thomas Fritz, Gail C Murphy, and Thomas Zimmermann. 2014. Software Developers' Perceptions of Productivity. In Proceedings of the 22Nd ACM SIGSOFT International Symposium on Foundations of Software Engineering, 19–29.

[2]   André N Meyer, Laura E Barton, Gail C Murphy, Thomas Zimmermann, and Thomas Fritz. 2017. The Work Life of Developers: Activities, Switches and Perceived Productivity. Transactions of Software Engineering (2017), 1–15.

[3]   André N Meyer, Thomas Zimmermann, and Thomas Fritz. 2017. Characterizing Software Developers by Perceptions of Productivity. In Empirical Software Engineering and Measurement (ESEM), 2017 International Symposium on.

CHAPTER 13

Human-Centered Methods to Boost Productivity

Brad A. Myers, Carnegie Mellon University, USA

Amy J. Ko, University of Washington, USA

Thomas D. LaToza, George Mason University, USA

YoungSeok Yoon, Google, Korea

Since programming is a human activity, we can look to fields that have already developed methods to better understand the details of human interactions with technologies. In particular, the field of human-computer interaction (HCI) has dozens, if not hundreds, of methods that have been validated for answering a wide range of questions about human behaviors [4]. (And many of these methods, in turn, have been adapted from methods used in psychology, ethnography, sociology, etc.) For example, in our research, we have documented our use of at least ten different human-centered methods across all the phases of software development [11], almost all of which have impacts on programmer productivity.

Why would one want to use these methods? Even though productivity may be hard to quantify, as discussed in many previous chapters of this book, it is indisputable that problems exist with the languages, APIs, and tools that programmers use, and we should strive to fix these problems. Further, there are more ways to understand productivity than just metrics. HCI methods can help better understand programmers' real *requirements and problems*, help *design* better ways to address those challenges, and then help *evaluate* whether the design actually works for programmers. Involving real programmers in these investigations reveals real data that makes it possible to identify and fix productivity bottlenecks.

© The Author(s) 2019

C. Sadowski and T. Zimmermann (eds.), *Rethinking Productivity in Software Engineering*,
https://doi.org/10.1007/978-1-4842-4221-6_13

For example, a method called *contextual inquiry* (CI) [1] is commonly used to understand barriers *in context*. In a CI, the experimenter observes developers performing their real work where it actually happens and makes special note of *breakdowns* that occur. For example, in one of our projects, we wondered what key barriers developers face when fixing defects, so we asked developers at Microsoft to work on their own tasks while we watched and took notes about the issues that arose [7]. A key problem for 90 percent of the longest tasks was understanding the *control flow* through code in widely separated methods, which the existing tools did not adequately reveal. CIs are a good way to gather qualitative data and insights into developers' real issues. However, they do not provide quantitative statistics, owing to the small sample size. Also, a CI can be time-consuming, especially if it is difficult to recruit representative developers to observe. However, it is one of the best ways to identify what is *really* happening in the field that affects the programmers' productivity.

Another useful method to understand productivity barriers is doing *exploratory lab user studies* [14]. Here, the experimenter assigns specific tasks to developers and observes what happens. The key difference from a CI is that here the participants perform tasks provided by the experimenter instead of their own tasks, so there is less realism. However, the experimenter can see whether the participants use different approaches to the same task. For example, we collected a detailed data set at the keystroke level of multiple experienced developers performing the same maintenance tasks in Java [5]. We discovered that the developers spent about one-third of their time navigating around the code base, often using manual scrolling. This highlights an important advantage of these observational techniques—when we asked the participants about barriers when performing these tasks, no one mentioned scrolling because it did not rise to the level of salience. However, it became obvious to us that this was a barrier to the programmers' productivity when we analyzed the logs of what the developers actually did. Knowing about such problems is the first step to inventing solutions. And these kinds of studies can also provide numeric data, which can later be used to measure the difference that a new tool or other intervention makes.

Neither of these methods can be used to evaluate *how often* an observed barrier occurs, which might be important for calculating the overall impact on productivity. For this, we have used *surveys* [16] and *corpus data mining* [9]. For example, after we observed in our CIs that understanding control flow was important, we performed a survey to count how often developers have questions about control flow and how hard those questions are to answer [7]. The developers reported asking such questions on average about nine times a day, and most felt that at least one such question was hard to answer. In a different study, we felt that programmers were wasting significant time trying to *backtrack* (return code to a previous state) while editing code. We had observed that this seemed to be error-prone as changes often had to be undone in multiple places. Therefore, we analyzed 1,460 hours of fine-grained code-editing logs from 21 developers, collected during their regular work [18]. We detected 15,095 backtracking instances, for an average rate of 10.3 per hour.

Once such productivity barriers have been identified, an intervention might be designed, such as a new programming process, language, API, or tool. We have used a variety of methods during the design process to help ensure that the intervention will actually help. *Natural-programming elicitation* is a way to understand how programmers think about a task and what vocabulary and concepts they use so the intervention can be closer to the users' thoughts [10]. One method for doing natural-programming elicitation is to give target programmers a "blank paper" participatory design task, where we describe the desired functionality and have the programmers design how that functionality should be provided. The trick is to ask the question in a way that does not bias the answers, so we often use pictures or samples of the *results*, without providing any vocabulary, architecture, or concepts.

Rapid prototyping [15] allows quick and simple prototypes of the intervention to be tried, often just drawn on paper, which helps to refine good ideas and eliminate bad ones. Sometimes it might be too expensive to create the real intervention before being able to test it. In these cases, we have used another recommended human-centered method called *iterative design* using *prototypes* [14]. Typically, the first step employs *low-fidelity prototypes*, which means that the actual interventions are simulated. For many of our tools, we have used *paper prototypes*, which are quickly created using drawing tools or even just pen and paper. For example, when trying to help developers understand the interprocedural control flow of code, we used a Macintosh drawing program called OmniGraffle to draw mock-ups of a possible new visualization and printed them on paper. We then asked developers to pretend to perform tasks with them. We discovered that the initial visualization concepts were too complex to understand yet lacked information important to the developers [7]. For example, a key requirement was to preserve the order in which methods are invoked, which was not shown (and is not shown by other static visualizations of call graphs, either). In the final visualization, the lines coming out of a method show the order of invocation, as shown in Figure 13-1.

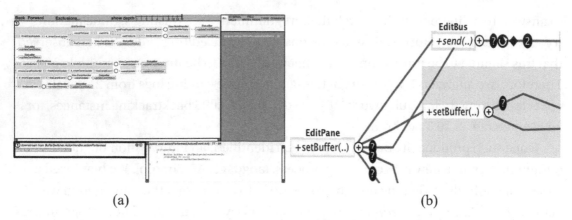

(a)   (b)

Figure 13-1. *(a) A paper prototype of the visualization drawn with the Omnigraffle drawing tool revealed that the order of method calls was crucial to visualize, as is shown in the final version of the tool (b), which is called Reacher [7]. The method* EditPane.setBuffer(..) *makes five method calls (the five lines exiting* setBuffer *shown in order from top to bottom, with the first and third being calls to* EditBus.send(..)*). Lines with "?" icons show calls that are conditional (and thus may or may not happen at runtime). Other icons on lines include a circular arrow to show calls inside of loops, diamonds to show overloaded methods, and numbers to show that multiple calls have been collapsed.*

No matter what kind of intervention it is, the creator might want to evaluate how well programmers can use it and whether it actually improves productivity in practice. For example, our observations about backtracking difficulties motivated us to create Azurite, a plug-in for the Eclipse code editor that provides more flexible selective undo, in which developers can undo past edits without necessarily undoing more recent ones [19]. But how can we know if the new intervention can actually be used? There are three main methods we have used to *evaluate* interventions: expert analyses, think-aloud usability evaluations, and formal A/B testing.

In expert analyses, people who are experienced with usability methods perform the analysis by inspection. For example, *heuristic evaluation* [13] employs ten guidelines to evaluate an interface. We used this method to evaluate some APIs and found that the really long function names violated the guideline of error prevention because the names could be easily confused with each other, wasting the programmer's time [12]. Another expert-analysis method is called *cognitive walkthrough* [8]. It involves carefully going through tasks using the interface and noting where users will need new knowledge to be able to take the next step. Using both of these methods, we helped a company iteratively improve a developer tool [3].

Another set of methods is empirical and involves testing the interventions with the target users. The first result of these evaluations is an understanding of what participants actually do, to see how the intervention works. In addition, we recommend using a *think-aloud study* [2], in which the participants continuously articulate their goals, confusion, and other thoughts. This provides the experimenter with rich data about *why* users perform the way they do so problems can be found and fixed. As with other usability evaluations, the principle is that if one participant has a problem, others will likely have it too, so it should be fixed if possible. Research shows that a few representative users can find a great percentage of the problems [14]. In our research, when we have evidence of usefulness from early needs analysis through CI and surveys, it is often sufficient to show usability of tools through think-alouds with five or six people. However, the evaluations should not involve participants who are associated with the tool because they will know too much about how the tool should work.

Unlike expert analyses and think-aloud usability evaluations, which are informal, *A/B testing* uses formal, statistically valid experiments [6]. This is the key way to demonstrate that one intervention is *better* than another, or better than the status quo, with respect to some measure. For example, we tested our Azurite plugin for selective undo in Eclipse against using regular Eclipse, and developers using Azurite were twice as fast [19]. Such formal measures can be useful proxies for the productivity gains that an intervention might bring. The resulting numbers might also help convince developers and managers to try new interventions and change developers' behaviors because they might find having numbers more persuasive than just the creator's claims about the intervention. However, these experiments can be difficult to design correctly and require careful attention to many possibly confounding factors [6]. In particular, it is challenging to design tasks that are sufficiently realistic yet doable in an appropriate time frame for an experiment (an hour or two).

To get a more realistic evaluation of an intervention, it may need to be measured in actual practice. We have found this to be easiest to do by instrumenting the tools to gather the desired metrics during real use, and then we can use *data mining and log analysis*. For example, we used our Fluorite logger, which is another plugin for Eclipse, to investigate how developers used the Azurite tool [17]. We found that developers often selectively undid a selected block of code, such as a whole method, restoring it to how it used to work and leaving the other code as is, which we call *regional undo*, confirming our hypothesis that this would be the most useful kind of selective undo [19].

Many other HCI methods are available that can answer additional questions that creators of interventions might have (see Table 13-1 for a summary). Large companies such as Microsoft and Google already embed user interface specialists into their teams that create developer tools (such as in Microsoft's Visual Studio group). However, even small teams can learn to use at least some of these methods. Based on our extensive use of these methods over many years, we argue that they will be useful for better understanding the many different kinds of barriers that programmers face, for creating useful and usable interventions to address those barriers, and for better evaluating the impact of the interventions. In this way, these methods will help increase the positive impact of future interventions on developers' productivity.

Table 13-1. Methods We Have Used (Adapted from [11])

Method	Cite	Software Development Activities Supported	Key Benefits	Challenges and Limitations
Contextual inquiry	[1]	Requirements and problem analysis.	Experimenters gain insight into day-to-day activities and challenges. Experimenters gain high-quality data on the developer's intent.	Contextual inquiry is time-consuming.
Exploratory lab user studies	[14]	Requirements and problem analysis.	Focusing on the activity of interest is easier. Experimenters can compare participants doing the same tasks. Numerical data can be collected.	The experimental setting might differ from the real-world context.
Surveys	[16]	Requirements and problem analysis. Evaluation and testing.	Surveys provide quantitative data. There are many participants. Surveys are (relatively) fast.	The data is self-reported and is subject to bias and participant awareness.
Data mining (including corpus studies and log analysis)	[9]	Requirements and problem analysis. Evaluation and testing.	Data mining provides large quantities of data. Experimenters can see patterns that emerge only with large corpuses.	Inferring or reconstructing the developer's intent is difficult. Data mining requires careful filtering.
Natural-programming elicitation	[10]	Requirements and problem analysis. Design.	Experimenters gain insight into developer expectations.	The experimental setting might differ from the real-world context.

(continued)

153

Table 13-1. (*continued*)

Method	Cite	Software Development Activities Supported	Key Benefits	Challenges and Limitations
Rapid prototyping	[15]	Design	Experimenters can gather feedback at low cost before committing to high-cost development.	Rapid prototyping has lower fidelity than the final tool, limiting what problems might be revealed.
Heuristic evaluations	[13]	Requirements and problem analysis. Design. Evaluation and testing.	Evaluations are fast. They do not require participants.	Evaluations reveal only some types of usability issues.
Cognitive walk-throughs	[8]	Design. Evaluation and testing.	Walk-throughs are fast. They do not require participants.	Walk-throughs reveal only some types of usability issues.
Think-aloud usability evaluations	[2]	Requirements and problem analysis. Design. Evaluation and testing.	Evaluations reveal usability problems and the developer's intent.	The experimental setting might differ from the real-world context. Evaluations require appropriate participants. Task design is difficult.
A/B testing	[6]	Evaluation and testing	Testing provides direct evidence that a new tool or technique benefits developers.	The experimental setting might differ from the real-world context. Testing requires appropriate participants. Task design is difficult.

Key Ideas

The following are the key ideas from the chapter:

- There are many methods used in human-computer interaction research that can also be used to study what hinders and improves software developer productivity, to help design interventions that increase productivity, and to then evaluate and improve their impact.

- The ten methods listed in this chapter have proven useful at various phases of the process.

References

[1] H. Beyer and K. Holtzblatt. *Contextual Design: Defining Custom-Centered Systems*. San Francisco, CA, Morgan Kaufmann Publishers, Inc. 1998.

[2] Chi, M. T. (1997). Quantifying qualitative analyses of verbal data: A practical guide. The journal of the learning sciences, 6(3), 271–315.

[3] Andrew Faulring, Brad A. Myers, Yaad Oren and Keren Rotenberg. "A Case Study of Using HCI Methods to Improve Tools for Programmers," *Cooperative and Human Aspects of Software Engineering (CHASE'2012)*, An ICSE 2012 Workshop, Zurich, Switzerland, June 2, 2012. 37–39.

[4] Julie A. Jacko. (Ed.). (2012). Human computer interaction handbook: Fundamentals, evolving technologies, and emerging applications. CRC press.

[5] Amy J. Ko, Brad A. Myers, Michael Coblenz and Htet Htet Aung. "An Exploratory Study of How Developers Seek, Relate, and Collect Relevant Information during Software Maintenance Tasks," *IEEE Transactions on Software Engineering*. Dec, 2006. 33(12). pp. 971–987.

[6]   Ko, A. J., Latoza, T. D., & Burnett, M. M. (2015). A practical guide to controlled experiments of software engineering tools with human participants. Empirical Software Engineering, 20(1), 110–141.

[7]   Thomas D. LaToza and Brad Myers. "Developers Ask Reachability Questions," *ICSE'2010: Proceedings of the International Conference on Software Engineering*, Capetown, South Africa, May 2-8, 2010. 185–194.

[8]   C. Lewis et al., "Testing a Walkthrough Methodology for TheoryBased Design of Walk-Up-and-Use Interfaces," *Proc. SIGCHI Conf. Human Factors in Computing Systems (CHI 90)*, 1990, pp. 235–242.

[9]   Menzies, T., Williams, L., & Zimmermann, T. (2016). Perspectives on Data Science for Software Engineering. Morgan Kaufmann.

[10] Brad A. Myers, John F. Pane and Amy J. Ko. "Natural Programming Languages and Environments," *Communications of the ACM*. Sept, 2004. 47(9). pp. 47–52.

[11] Brad A. Myers, Amy J. Ko, Thomas D. LaToza, and YoungSeok Yoon. "Programmers Are Users Too: Human-Centered Methods for Improving Programming Tools," *IEEE Computer*, vol. 49, issue 7, July, 2016, pp. 44–52.

[12] Brad A. Myers and Jeffrey Stylos. "Improving API Usability," *Communications of the ACM*. July, 2016. 59(6). pp. 62–69.

[13] J. Nielsen and R. Molich. "Heuristic evaluation of user interfaces," Proc. ACM CHI'90 Conf, see also: http://www.useit.com/papers/heuristic/heuristic_list.html. Seattle, WA, 1–5 April, 1990. pp. 249–256.

[14] Jakob Nielsen. *Usability Engineering*. Boston, Academic Press. 1993.

[15] Marc Rettig. "Prototyping for Tiny Fingers," Comm. ACM. 1994. vol. 37, no. 4. pp. 21–27.

[16] Rossi, P. H., Wright, J. D., & Anderson, A. B. (Eds.). (2013). Handbook of survey research. Academic Press.

[17] YoungSeok Yoon and Brad A. Myers. "An Exploratory Study of Backtracking Strategies Used by Developers," *Cooperative and Human Aspects of Software Engineering (CHASE'2012)*, An ICSE 2012 Workshop, Zurich, Switzerland, June 2, 2012. 138–144.

[18] YoungSeok Yoon and Brad A. Myers. "A Longitudinal Study of Programmers' Backtracking," *IEEE Symposium on Visual Languages and Human-Centric Computing (VL/HCC'14)*, Melbourne, Australia, 28 July–1 August, 2014. 101–108.

[19] YoungSeok Yoon and Brad A. Myers. "Supporting Selective Undo in a Code Editor," *37th International Conference on Software Engineering (ICSE 2015)*, Florence, Italy, May 16–24, 2015. 223–233 (volume 1).

CHAPTER 14

Using Biometric Sensors to Measure Productivity

Marieke van Vugt, University of Groningen, The Netherlands

Operationalizing Productivity for Measurement

If we want to be productive, it would be great if we could track productivity in some way, such that it is possible to determine what factors help and hinder productivity. Biometric sensors may be helpful for such productivity tracking. But what does being productive mean? A simplistic notion of productivity is being able to pay attention without getting distracted. Indeed, to be productive in simple tasks such as filling out routine forms, one needs to carefully monitor one's goals and ensure not to get distracted. On the other hand, for more complex tasks such as developing a new software architecture or implementing a complex function, one also needs creativity and outside-the-box thinking, which is incompatible with a singular focus. In other words, aspects of productivity such as creativity depend not on concentration but on its opposite: mind-wandering [1], which is a process of task-unrelated thinking. How would that work? Mind-wandering, when it involves thinking about other things while you are engaged in a task such as writing a computer program can help you to access new information that brings an alternative perspective on what you are doing. This means that when the contents of mind-wandering are monitored and are not too engrossing, it can in fact be very useful. Moreover, this also means that a singular focus does not always indicate productivity because, for example, being very concentrated on a single stupid task such as writing the same line of code over and over again is not very productive.

© The Author(s) 2019
C. Sadowski and T. Zimmermann (eds.), *Rethinking Productivity in Software Engineering*,
https://doi.org/10.1007/978-1-4842-4221-6_14

In summary, productivity requires sometimes singular focus and sometimes distraction. What is crucial is monitoring to ensure that attention is being paid to the most relevant goals and that the degree of attentional focus is in line with those goals. The attentional focus should be neither too narrow nor too wide and should be directed to the task that is most important at that moment.

Interestingly, most current attempts at developing biometric sensors focus on measuring attentional focus. Here I argue that another (albeit more technically challenging) target could be the goal-directedness of attention. A goal-directed attention is one that does not get pulled into patterns of thoughts that are difficult to disengage from, such as, for example, rumination and worry.

In this chapter, I will first discuss biometric sensors on the basis of eye tracking and electroencephalography (EEG) that simply track attention and then preview some new potential sensors that track the broader definition of productivity that depends on focusing on the most relevant goals and not being sidetracked by thoughts that pull one away.

What the Eye Says About Focus

Arguably the simplest method to measure attention is by following the eye gaze and the width of the pupil. In laboratory studies this is measured with fancy cameras that are following the eyes, but potentially similar functions could be provided by webcams that are present on almost every computer. In our lab we have demonstrated that webcam-based eye tracking is sensitive enough to predict upcoming choices from a set of stimuli presented on the screen.

So, what can you measure with eye tracking? In one experiment investigating distraction by external stimuli, we found that when we had a participant do a memory task on the screen but showed cat videos on a flanking screen, their eyes were drawn to the video [9]. The frequency with which the eyes were drawn to the cat video depended on the difficulty of the task, such that the more visual resources a task consumed (e.g., requiring poring over a visual image very precisely), the less likely a person was distracted by the cat videos. On the other hand, the more memory resources a task required (e.g., keeping in mind a series of numbers), the more likely the person's eyes were drawn to the cat videos. In other words, video screens with moving images are a terrible idea on the work floor. In another study, we used eye tracking to examine whether a person was keeping a location on the computer screen in mind that they were trying to memorize [3]. We found that when they were distracted, as you would expect, people's eyes were less fixated on the visual locations than when they were attentive. In short, when you are doing a task where your eyes have to be located at a specific spot (such as a coding window that occupies only part of the screen), then using eye gaze can be an effective measure of your attention.

However, most of the time, your work does not require your attention to be focused on a single spot. In that case, potentially we could still use eye-based biosensors but focus instead on the size of the pupil. Already for many decades, pupil size has been associated with a state of mental effort [4] and arousal [2]. For example, when we make the task more difficult, we tend to see an increase in pupil size. In addition, when we reward people for successfully performing a difficult task, their pupil size increases even more.

Many studies have associated mind-wandering with a decreased pupil size [3, 11], so another potential marker for being on the ball and being productive would be the size of your pupil. A larger pupil would be indicative of higher productivity. In fact, we have previously used pupil size as a marker for when it would be best to interrupt the user [5]. Interruptions are generally best when a person is experiencing low workload, i.e., when he or she is somewhere between subtasks, not when he or she is trying to remember something or manipulate complex information in his mind. The study showed that we were successful in finding low-workload moments and performance was better when we interrupted on low-workload moments. This suggests that pupil size can successfully be used even on a single-trial basis and is a good candidate for measuring mental effort as an index of productivity.

Observing Attention with EEG

Another potential biomarker of productivity is EEG. EEG reflects the electrical activity emitted by the brain, as measured by electrodes on the scalp. EEG has frequently been used to track both mind-wandering and mental effort. A common finding is that when a person is mind-wandering, the brain activity evoked by a stimulus is reduced. This is thought to indicate a state in which the person is relatively disconnected from their environment with their attention more internally directed. While there has been long-standing research in the role of alpha waves—which are typically referred to as the brain's "idling waves"—in mind-wandering, that research has not demonstrated clear mappings between these brain waves and mind-wandering.

The most advanced studies in this field have started to use machine learning classifiers to predict an individual's attentional state. For example, a study by Mittner and colleagues [6] demonstrated that it was possible to predict with almost 80 percent accuracy whether a person was on-task or mind-wandering on the basis of a combination of behavioral and neural measures. These neural measures involved functional magnetic resonance imaging (fMRI). The problem with fMRI is that it is not a very suitable measure in an applied context because it requires an expensive and heavy MRI scanner in which the person has to lie down to be scanned. Moreover, MRI scanners produce a large amount of noise, making it not conducive for work. Nevertheless, recent work in our lab suggests that it is possible to achieve up to 70 percent accuracy in predicting mind-wandering using the more portable EEG. Moreover, in our study, this accuracy was achieved across two different behavioral tasks, suggesting that it can tap into a general mind-wandering measure, which is crucial for application in a work environment.

EEG has been used to measure not only mind-wandering but also mental effort. The most frequently used index of mental effort in EEG is the P3, an EEG potential that occurs roughly 300 to 800 ms after a stimulus has been shown to an individual [10]. This component is larger when a person exerts mental effort. This component is also smaller when a person is mind-wandering, suggesting that the P3 is potentially not a very unique index of mental effect. However, because this EEG component is time-locked to a discrete stimulus, it may be challenging to monitor such potentials in the office environment, unless you display periodic discrete stimuli to the individual with the purpose of measuring this P3 potential.

Taking these concerns into account, if EEG is potentially usable for monitoring distraction and productivity, then a problem to take into consideration is that despite that it is less unwieldy than MRI, an EEG system is typically still quite inconvenient and takes a lot of time to set up (usually somewhere between 15 and 45 minutes). A research-grade EEG system consists of a fabric cap in which anywhere between 32 and 256 electrodes are embedded, and for each of these electrodes, the connection with the scalp needs to be ascertained by means of an electrode gel and manual adjustments. On top of that, the cap needs to be connected to an amplifier that enhances the weak signals recorded on the scalp such that they are elevated above the noise. Only with these procedures a sufficiently clean signal can be collected. Clearly this would not be feasible for the workplace.

Luckily, recently there has been a boom in the development of low-cost EEG devices that have only between 1 and 8 sensors and that do not need extensive preparation (e.g., Emotiv and MUSE). If these electrodes were placed in the correct locations, they could potentially serve as productivity-monitoring devices. In fact, they are frequently marketed as devices that can record concentration. Despite these claims, however, I have found that when comparing a research-grade EEG system to these portable devices, that the portable EEG devices do not provide a reliable signal. Many place electrodes on the forehead, which are primarily expected to capture muscle activity instead of brain activity. Of course, muscle activity can be an index of how stressed a person is, since stress is associated with muscle tension, but it does not say much about a person's mind-wandering and distraction. For example, it is possible to be quite tense while working on a software development project while being really relaxed and browsing social media. So, at this time EEG is really only a useful measure of productivity in a laboratory setting.

Measuring Rumination

As mentioned, only measuring focus is not sufficient for productivity. In addition, a certain amount of mental flexibility and allocation of attention to relevant goals is crucial. This mental flexibility is difficult to monitor with biometric devices, but one related candidate signal is the one associated with "sticky mind-wandering"—a mind-wandering process that is very difficult to disengage from [12]. Sticky mind-wandering is a precursor of rumination (narrowly focused uncontrolled repetitive thinking that is mostly negatively balanced and self-referential [7]). For example, rumination may involve repeated thinking that "I am worthless, I am a failure," supplemented by recall of experiences, such as a poor evaluation of a piece of work you delivered. This thinking repeatedly intrudes into a person's consciousness, thereby making it difficult for them to concentrate, one of the major complaints that depressed people are suffering from. Sticky mind-wandering can take the form of recurrent worries, for example, about not being good enough, about their children, their future, and so on. These are the kinds of thoughts that are particularly harmful for productivity because they disrupt particular difficult thinking processes, which are crucial for software developers.

Recent work has started to map and experimentally manipulate these "sticky" forms of mind-wandering. We found that when people have a thought that they think is difficult to disengage from, then their task performance just prior to that moment tends to be worse and more variable in duration [12]. Other research where people were equipped with smart phones to measure their thoughts over the course of many days showed that sticky mind-wandering interfered more with ongoing activities and required more effort to inhibit. It was further suggested that a sticky form of mind-wandering is associated with reduced heart-rate variability compared to nonsticky mind-wandering [8]. In general, larger heart-rate variability is associated with increased well-being, and therefore reduced heart-rate variability is not desirable. This means that heart-rate variability is a potentially attractive target for biometric monitoring, especially because more and more low-cost heart-rate trackers are becoming available, such as those integrated in smart watches.

Moving Forward

The studies discussed here together suggest that there are several ways in which it may be possible to measure productivity biometrically. Possibilities include pupil size, heart-rate variability, and EEG, which each has its own possibilities and limitations. Nevertheless, the majority of these measures were tested in a relatively simple and artificial laboratory context, in which only a limited set of events can happen. In contrast, in the real world, many more scenarios play out, and it is not clear how these biometric measures fare in those contexts. What is needed is a better understanding of the boundary conditions under which different biometric measures can work, and potentially a combination of different measures can give a suitably accurate index of distraction, thereby potentially differentiating between helpful mind-wandering and harmful mind-wandering.

Such an index could potentially be integrated into an interception system that makes the user aware of their distraction and then reminds them of their longer-term goals. Distraction usually arises when goals with short-term rewards or instant rewards such as social media are less active in our minds than longer-term goals. Even in the case of the stickier ruminative mind-wandering, a small reminder may be enough to allow a person to step out of this thought process and redirect attention to more productive long-term goals such as writing a paper or finishing a computer program.

In short, I have discussed what it means to be productive and how we can potentially measure this. Since most jobs require more than mechanical concentration on a single thing, measurement of productivity is nontrivial. Nevertheless, scientific studies on tracking attention provide a good starting point, and they demonstrate that eye movements, pupil size, heart rate variability, and EEG all provide some useful information about a person's attentional state. On the other hand, none of these measures by themselves provides a fool-proof metric of productivity. Moreover, in many of them there are challenges to measuring it in a real-world context. For this reason, I think that the most productive use of biometric monitoring is not tracking productivity per se but rather helping the user to monitor himself or herself. The biometric sensors could be combined and in this way could help a user to become aware of potential lapses of productivity and remind them of their most important long-term goals.

Key Ideas

The following are the key ideas from this chapter:

- While some forms of productivity require targeted attentional focus, other forms of productivity require mental flexibility.

- With eye tracking, we can follow whether a person is paying attention and exert mental effort.

- The EEG can also track attention but is difficult to measure with mobile sensors.

- Rumination is an important factor to consider in productivity.

References

[1]   Baird, B., J. Smallwood, M. D. Mrazek, J. W. Y. Kam, M. J. Frank, and J. W. Schooler. 2012. "Inspired by Distraction. Mind Wandering Facilitates Creative Incubation." *Psychological Science* 23 (10):1117–22. https://doi.org/10.1177/0956797612446024.

[2]   Gilzenrat, M. S., S. Nieuwenhuis, M. Jepma, and J. D. Cohen. 2010. "Pupil Diameter Tracks Changes in Control State Predicted by the Adaptive Gain Theory of Locus Coeruleus Function." *Cognitive, Affective & Behavioral Neuroscience* 10 (2):252–69.

[3]   Huijser, S., M. K. van Vugt, and N. A. Taatgen. 2018. "The
      Wandering Self: Tracking Distracting Self-Generated Thought in
      a Cognitively Demanding Context." *Consciousness and Cognition*
      Consciousness & Cognition 58, 170-185.

[4]   Kahneman, D., and J. Beatty. 1966. "Pupil Diameter and Load
      on Memory." *Science* 154 (3756). American Association for the
      Advancement of Science:1583-5.

[5]   Katidioti, Ioanna, Jelmer P Borst, Douwe J Bierens de Haan,
      Tamara Pepping, Marieke K van Vugt, and Niels A Taatgen. 2016.
      "Interrupted by Your Pupil: An Interruption Management System
      Based on Pupil Dilation." *International Journal of Human–
      Computer Interaction* 32 (10). Taylor & Francis:791–801.

[6]   Mittner, Matthias, Wouter Boekel, Adrienne M Tucker, Brandon
      M Turner, Andrew Heathcote, and Birte U Forstmann. 2014.
      "When the Brain Takes a Break: A Model-Based Analysis of
      Mind Wandering." *The Journal of Neuroscience* 34 (49). Soc
      Neuroscience:16286–95.

[7]   Nolen-Hoeksema, S., and J. Morrow. 1991. "A Prospective Study
      of Depression and Posttraumatic Stress Symptoms After a
      Natural Disaster: The 1989 Loma Prieta Earthquake." *Journal of
      Personality and Social Psychology* 61 (1):115–21.

[8]   Ottaviani, C., B. Medea, A. Lonigro, M. Tarvainen, and
      A. Couyoumdjian. 2015. "Cognitive Rigidity Is Mirrored by
      Autonomic Inflexibility in Daily Life Perseverative Cognition."
      Biological Psychology 107. Elsevier:24–30.

[9]   Taatgen, N. A, M. K. van Vugt, J. Daamen, I. Katidioti, and
      J. P Borst. "The Resource- Availability Theory of Distraction and
      Mind-Wandering." (under review)

[10] Ullsperger, P, A-M Metz, and H-G Gille. 1988. "The P300
      Component of the Event-Related Brain Potential and Mental
      Effort." *Ergonomics* 31 (8). Taylor & Francis:1127–37.

[11]   Unsworth, Nash, and Matthew K Robison. 2016. "Pupillary
Correlates of Lapses of Sustained Attention." *Cognitive, Affective, &
Behavioral Neuroscience* 16 (4). Springer:601– 15.

[12]   van Vugt, M. K., and N. Broers. 2016. "Self-Reported Stickiness
of Mind-Wandering Affects Task Performance." *Frontiers in
Psychology* 7. Frontiers Media SA:732.

CHAPTER 15

How Team Awareness Influences Perceptions of Developer Productivity

Christoph Treude, University of Adelaide, Australia

Fernando Figueira Filho, Federal University of Rio Grande do Norte, Brazil

Introduction

In their day-to-day work, software developers perform many different activities: they use numerous tools to develop software artifacts ranging from source code and models to documentation and test cases, they use other tools to manage and coordinate their development work, and they spend a substantial amount of time communicating and exchanging knowledge with other members on their teams and the larger software development community. Making sense of this flood of activity and information is becoming harder with every new artifact created. Yet, being aware of all relevant information in a software project is crucial to enable productivity in software development.

In formal terms, awareness is defined as "an understanding of the activities of others, which provide context for your own activity." In any collaborative work environment, being aware of the work of other team members and how it can affect one's own work is crucial. Maintaining awareness ensures that individual contributions are relevant to the group's work in general. Awareness can be used to evaluate individual actions against the group's goals and progress, and it allows groups to manage the process of collaborative working [1].

© The Author(s) 2019
C. Sadowski and T. Zimmermann (eds.), *Rethinking Productivity in Software Engineering*,
https://doi.org/10.1007/978-1-4842-4221-6_15

Contributing to a software project requires a multitude of different kinds of awareness, ranging from high-level status information (e.g., What is the overall status of the project? What are the current bottlenecks?) to more fine-grained information (e.g., Who else is working on the same file right now and has uncommitted changes? Who is affected by the source code I am writing at the moment?). Awareness includes both short-term, momentary awareness (awareness of events at this particular point in time, such as the current build status) and long-term, historical awareness (awareness of past events, such as code evolution and team velocity). As the complexity of software systems grows, maintaining awareness of all relevant context is becoming increasingly challenging. To address this situation, many tools have been developed over the last decades to help developers maintain awareness of everything that goes on in a project.

Given the plethora of information available, tools that support awareness for software developers inevitably need to abstract some details and have to aggregate information. This leads to risks. The aggregation of developer activity information has the potentially unintended side effect of quantifying the developer's work, enabling productivity comparisons across developers and time. As an example, imagine a tool that aims to provide high-level information about what a developer is working on at the moment. Such a tool will likely be able to say that a developer is working on three features (by counting the open issues assigned to this developer, for example), but it might not be able to say that a developer is currently working on refactoring a database connector, fixing a bug in the persistence layer of the application, and improving the performance of a query (which would require an automated understanding of the semantics of the open issues). Of course, a tool could simply list all open issues, but this would lead to information overload.

In this chapter, we discuss this tension between awareness information and productivity measures, and we advocate for the design of tools that enable awareness without quantifying information. We also report on the findings from an empirical study in which we asked developers about how to design such tools. The study revealed that awareness can influence developers' perceptions of the productivity of their colleagues and that developers do not feel that productivity can be collapsed into a single metric. We conclude that while automated tools for making sense of everything that goes on in a software project are necessary to enable developer awareness, such tools need to focus on summarizing instead of measuring information.

Awareness and Productivity

We first illustrate the relationship between team awareness and developer productivity, using an existing categorization of awareness types as a guideline [2].

- *Collaboration awareness*: Collaboration awareness refers to the perception of group availability, i.e., whether people are in the same physical place, who is online/offline, and their virtual availability. In software development—and in many other domains—these concepts are directly related to productivity. If a member of a software development team is perceived to be unavailable, it is easy to conclude that they are not productive, whereas a team member who is always online and/or in the same physical place would be perceived as being productive.

- *Location awareness*: Location awareness refers to the geographical and physical nature of spaces, e.g., where someone is physically located. Similar to collaboration awareness, the physical location of team members can be related to perceptions of their productivity. This might be the case if co-workers who share the same office space are perceived as having more or less productivity compared to others, but it might also have cultural implications, e.g., if developers in an outsourcing location are perceived differently simply based on their location.

- *Context awareness*: Context awareness allows a group of co-workers to maintain a sense of what is going on in the virtual space. In software development projects, context awareness can, for example, refer to the context of a shared task, e.g., the progress of a development team toward the next release. If the development team is perceived as not being on track, this type of awareness can easily be used to reach conclusions about a team's lack of productivity.

- *Social awareness*: According to Antunes et al., social awareness is related to the understanding of "social practice, i.e., the others' roles and activities, or what and how the group members are contributing to a task." It is easy to see then how social awareness in a software development team is linked to developer productivity. If a team member's contributions to a task are perceived as not good enough, they will be considered as unproductive, and vice versa.

- *Workspace awareness*: Workspace awareness is defined as the up-to-the-moment understanding of another person's interaction with the shared workspace, i.e., awareness of people and how they interact with the workspace rather than just awareness of the workspace itself [3]. This type of awareness is also directly linked to productivity: if a developer's interactions with the shared workspace, e.g., the issue tracking system of a software project, are not as frequent or fruitful as expected, this developer will be seen as being unproductive.

- *Situation awareness*: Situation awareness refers to being aware of what is happening in the vicinity to understand how information, events, and one's own actions will impact goals and objectives. Applied to software development, this definition could refer to peripheral awareness of the work of other teams that are working on the same product, awareness of updates to libraries that a particular product relies on, or awareness of technology trends [4]. As with the other awareness types, this kind of awareness also links to productivity: if another team is not delivering the feature they are supposed to deliver or a critical bug in a library is not being fixed, developers can be seen as unproductive.

Enabling Awareness in Collaborative Software Development

There are many different kinds of information that developers need to be aware of in any software development project, as discussed in the previous section. However, with the flood of activity and information in a software repository, it is impossible and also often not necessary for a developer to maintain awareness of every aspect of a project. As a result, a mechanism for filtering and aggregating relevant information is needed.

Many tools such as feeds and dashboards (see Chapter 16) have been developed to help developers maintain awareness and aggregate relevant information. However, these tools often focus on quantitative instead of qualitative aspects since it is arguably easier to count the number of open issues than interpret what these issues are about, for example. In the next sections, we discuss developers' opinions on the aggregation of awareness information using both quantitative and qualitative means.

Aggregating Awareness Information into Numbers

Automated tools for extracting, aggregating, and summarizing development activity are essential to provide software teams with crucial awareness information. To investigate how to design such tools, in earlier work [5] we asked developers how they would design quantitative and qualitative aspects of such tools. We first summarize our findings with regard to the quantitative aspects, which revealed the risk of misinterpreting awareness information as productivity measures.

Our study participants stressed that no single metric, e.g., lines of code, number of tasks, etc., would truly reflect the wide range of activities a developer may take action on throughout the development life cycle of a software product. For instance, conceptual work is hardly measurable and may go unnoticed just by monitoring a metric, as shown in this example from one of our study participants: "It's difficult to measure output. Changing the architecture or doing a conceptual refactoring may have significant impact but very little evidence on the code base." Similarly, the difficulty of a task cannot be measured in lines of code.

Software projects may go through different stages in their development cycle. According to our study participants, these variabilities from project to project make it difficult to devise any uniform, one-size-fits-all measurement system that would work across different project contexts and distinct development workflows (challenges detailed in Chapter 2). Also, developers may assume different roles in a single day. For instance, interacting with customers and users was regarded by our study participants as an activity that is difficult to measure, although it is an integral part of development work: "We do systems for people in the first place."

Another problem perceived by our study participants is that measures can be gamed so that any automatic system aimed at measuring productivity would be potentially exploitable. This applies in particular to simple measures such as the number of issues or number of commits: "A poor-quality developer may be able to close more tickets than anyone else, but a high-quality developer often closes fewer tickets but of those few, almost none get reopened or result in regressions. For these reasons, metrics should seek to track quality as much as they track quantity."

Given the limited value of numbers as a means to provide developers with meaningful information, we next investigate the potential of qualitative mechanisms, in particular summarization, to improve the quality of awareness information.

Aggregating Awareness Information into Text

As we have discussed in the previous section, aggregating the work of software developers into numbers has many disadvantages. However, information in a software repository has to be aggregated to enable awareness without having to look at every artifact created, modified, or deleted. With this in mind, in our earlier work [5], we presented our study participants with the following scenario: "Assume it's Monday morning and you have just returned from a week-long vacation. One of your colleagues is giving you an update on their development activities last week." We then asked them what information they would expect to be included in such a summary. In the following paragraphs, we summarize the answers we received from developers.

Many of the events in the day-to-day work of software developers can be categorized according to whether they are expected or unexpected. Expected events comprise status updates that are generally not surprising to a software developer—such as a development task moving from open to closed—while unexpected events are unforeseen, for example the presence of a critical bug. Our participants requested that both kinds of events should be included in summaries of development activity.

Summaries of expected events in software development projects are mostly concerned with how different artifacts, such as development tasks or user stories, move through the development cycle. For example, one participant requested what they called "task state transition history—which tasks were taken, which were done, which were tested." An important dimension of expectations is planning—our participants were also interested to hear about short-term and long-term plans as well as the goals driving these plans.

Basic awareness tools for software developers typically support this kind of awareness of development artifacts and plans. For example, a burndown chart visualizes the actual work being done compared to a plan, and a kanban board shows tasks along with their current status. However, these tools are still limited in their expressiveness: A burndown chart cannot explain why a project is not on track, and it can also easily be misinterpreted as measuring productivity. In addition, it can be gamed, for example by overestimating user stories. Kanban boards can aggregate only to a certain extent—if the number of tasks or work items included in the kanban board becomes too large, it becomes hard to obtain a high-level overview of the project status from looking at the board.

If everything in a software project is progressing as expected, no particular action outside of a developer's routine might be required. However, things tend not to always go according to plan in software projects. Requirements might change, a major refactoring might be needed, or a critical bug might be discovered. In those situations, developers need to act, which explains why anything unexpected should play a major role in a summary of software development activity: "We cut our developer status meetings way down and started stand up meetings focusing on problems and new findings rather than dead-boring status. [The] only important point is when something is not on track, going faster than expected and why."

When we asked our participants about how to automatically detect such unexpected events, several examples were mentioned, in particular related to the commit history: "Commits that take particularly long might be interesting. If a developer hasn't committed anything in a while, his first commit after a long silence could be particularly interesting, for example because it took him a long time to fix a bug. Also, important commits might have unusual commit messages, for example including smileys, lots of exclamation marks, or something like that...basically something indicating that the developer was emotional about that particular commit." While developer tools that summarize expected events already exist—albeit often still focusing on numbers rather than textual content—research on what constitutes important unexpected events in a software project is still in its infancy.

Rethinking Productivity and Team Awareness

Throughout a software project's life cycle, developers generate a vast corpus of software artifacts and perform a multitude of actions; however, only a fraction of those events are relevant to one's own activity. Automated methods for aggregating and summarizing awareness information are important, as they potentially save developers from the cumbersome task of manually inspecting a large number of events—or asking others—to answer the various questions that may arise in one's development work.

Automated methods for aggregating awareness information are likely to produce quantitative over qualitative information since aggregating numbers (e.g., the number of issues per developer) is much easier than aggregating textual information (e.g., what kinds of issues a developer is working on). Unsurprisingly, measures such as lines of code and number of issues open/closed are available in most development tools, but many developers in our study found them too limited to be used as awareness information and worried that such simple numbers may act as a proxy of their productivity. In short, awareness can influence developers' perceptions of the productivity of their colleagues—and these perceptions are often not accurate if based on the awareness information that tools commonly provide.

From the perspective of who receives awareness information, numeric measures should not be provided in isolation: they should be augmented with useful information about recent changes in the project that happened according to plan, i.e., expected events, and most importantly, they should provide information about the unexpected. As we noticed, awareness tool design has given greater emphasis to the former type of information, leaving information about unexpected events to be gathered by developers themselves. Similarly, awareness tools have fed developers more information about what happened and less information about why things happened.

As empirical evidence shows, the design of automated awareness mechanisms should consider the tension between team awareness and productivity measures in collaborative software development. Developers' information needs are indirectly related to productivity aspects, yet the way information is typically presented by awareness tools (e.g., kanban boards, burndown charts) can have negative effects as they facilitate judgment on the productivity of developers. We found that the ultimate goal of developers is not associated with productivity measurement: they seek to answer questions that are impacting their own work and the expected flow of events. They want to become aware of the unexpected so that they can adapt more easily and quickly.

While tools that help developers make sense of everything that goes on in a software project are necessary to enable developer awareness, these tools currently favor quantitative information over qualitative information. To accurately represent what goes on in a software project, awareness tools need to focus on summarizing instead of measuring information and be careful when presenting numbers that could be used as an unintended proxy for productivity measures. We argue for the use of natural language and text processing techniques to automatically summarize information from a software project in textual form. Based on the findings of our study, we suggest that such tools should categorize the events in a software project according to whether they are expected or unexpected and use natural language processing to provide meaningful summaries rather than numbers and graphs that are likely to be misinterpreted as productivity measures.

Key ideas

The following are the key ideas from the chapter:

- Tools that help developers make sense of everything that goes on in a software project are necessary to enable developer awareness.

- These tools currently favor quantitative information over qualitative information but need to focus on summarizing instead of measuring information.

- Team awareness can influence developers' perceptions of their colleagues' productivity, and developers do not feel that productivity can be collapsed into a single metric.

References

[1]   Paul Dourish and Victoria Bellotti. 1992. Awareness and coordination in shared workspaces. In Proceedings of the 1992 ACM conference on Computer-supported cooperative work (CSCW '92). ACM, New York, NY, USA, 107-114. DOI=https://doi.org/10.1145/143457.143468.

[2]   Pedro Antunes, Valeria Herskovic, Sergio F. Ochoa, José A. Pino, Reviewing the quality of awareness support in collaborative applications, Journal of Systems and Software, Volume 89, 2014, Pages 146-169, ISSN 0164-1212, https://doi.org/10.1016/j.jss.2013.11.1078.

[3]   Gutwin, C. & Greenberg, S. Computer Supported Cooperative Work (CSCW) (2002) 11: 411. https://doi.org/10.1023/A:1021271517844.

[4] Leif Singer, Fernando Figueira Filho, and Margaret-Anne Storey. 2014. Software engineering at the speed of light: how developers stay current using twitter. In Proceedings of the 36th International Conference on Software Engineering (ICSE 2014). ACM, New York, NY, USA, 211-221. DOI: https://doi.org/10.1145/2568225.2568305.

[5] Christoph Treude, Fernando Figueira Filho, and Uirá Kulesza. 2015. Summarizing and measuring development activity. In Proceedings of the 2015 10th Joint Meeting on Foundations of Software Engineering (ESEC/FSE 2015). ACM, New York, NY, USA, 625-636. DOI: https://doi.org/10.1145/2786805.2786827.

CHAPTER 16

Software Engineering Dashboards: Types, Risks, and Future

Margaret-Anne Storey, University of Victoria, Canada

Christoph Treude, University of Adelaide, Australia

Introduction

The large number of artifacts created or modified in a software project and the flood of information exchanged in the process of creating a software product call for tools that aggregate this data to communicate higher-level insights to all stakeholders involved. In many projects—in software engineering as well as in other domains—dashboards are used to communicate information that may bring insights on the productivity of project activities and other aspects. Stephen Few defines a dashboard as "a visual display of the most important information needed to achieve one or more objectives which fits entirely on a single computer screen so it can be monitored at a glance" [4].

Dashboards are cognitive awareness and communication tools designed to help people visually identify trends, patterns and anomalies, reason about what they see, and help guide them toward effective decisions [3]. Their real value and one of the main reasons for their popularity is their ability to "replace hunt-and-peck data-gathering techniques with a tireless, adaptable, information flow mechanism" [9]. The goal of dashboards is to transform the raw data contained in an organization's repositories into consumable information. In software engineering, dashboards are used to provide information related to questions such as "Is this project on schedule?"

C. Sadowski and T. Zimmermann (eds.), *Rethinking Productivity in Software Engineering*,
https://doi.org/10.1007/978-1-4842-4221-6_16

and "What are the current bottlenecks?" and "What is the progress of other teams?" [7]. In this chapter, we review the different types of dashboards that are commonly used in software engineering and the risks that are associated with their use. We conclude with an overview of current trends in software engineering dashboards.

The link between productivity and dashboards becomes apparent when investigating one of the dimensions that Few proposes for the categorization of dashboards: *type of measures*. While not always intended this way, much of the quantitative data presented in developer dashboards can also be interpreted as a measure of developer productivity (discussed in more detail in Chapter 15). For example, a bar chart that shows open issues grouped by team can easily be interpreted as a chart highlighting the most productive team (i.e., the team with the least open issues). The relationship between productivity of a development team and the number of open issues is obviously much more complex, as one of our interviewees in a study on developer dashboards confirmed: "Just because one team has a lot more defects than another that doesn't necessarily mean that the quality of that component is any worse" [7]. Instead, a component might have more defects because it is more complex, because it has a user-facing role, or because it is a technically more central component that other components depend on, exposing it to more unexpected conditions.

Few also proposes a categorization of dashboards based on their *role*, in particular discussing dashboards in terms of their strategic, analytical, and operational purposes. In software projects, the use of dashboards for operational purposes is the most common. Such dashboards are dynamic and based on real-time data, supporting drilling down to specific artifacts such as critical bugs in a software project. Dashboards for strategic purposes (so called "executive dashboards") tend to avoid interactive elements and focus on snapshots rather than real-time data.

Software developers produce many textual artifacts, ranging from source code and documentation to bug reports and code reviews. Therefore, it is unsurprising that dashboards used in software projects often combine different *types of data*, i.e., qualitative and quantitative data. A bar graph showing the number of open issues grouped by team would be a simple example of quantitative data, whereas a tag cloud of the most common words used in bug reports is a simple representation of some of the qualitative data present in a software repository.

Another important dimension highlighted by Few is the *span of data*. When creating a dashboard for a software project, many considerations have to be taken into account; e.g., should the dashboard feature enterprise-wide data or just data from a single project (bearing in mind that projects tend not to be independent)? Should each developer have their own personalized dashboard, or do all dashboards from a project look the same? In addition, dashboards can cover different timespans, such as the entire lifetime of a project, the current release, or the last week. In software projects, one week is not necessarily like any other. For example, development activity during feature or code freeze is expected to be different from the activity when starting to work on features for a new release.

Dashboards in Software Engineering

Within software engineering, dashboards are used to provide information and metrics on the product under development, as well as to display information or to support the analysis of the development process. Typically, they are designed with a specific stakeholder and goal in mind, and many of these goals relate directly or implicitly to some aspect of productivity, including the product quality, work velocity, or stakeholder satisfaction (see Chapter 5).

In the following text, we present some high-level categories of dashboards (those that support individual developers, teams, projects, and communities), alluding to the stakeholders who use the dashboard and to the kinds of tasks they support within each category, as well as where those dashboards tend to be hosted.

We do not aim to be exhaustive but rather to illustrate the myriad of dashboards that are used to support software engineering productivity. Most software engineering dashboards support operational or analytical tasks, while fewer support strategic tasks. Many of these dashboards are static, but more and more, software dashboards are becoming interactive as they play an increasingly important role in how software productivity is understood, measured, and managed.

Developer Activity

Dashboards may be used to display individual developer activity and performance, such as how coding time is spent (authoring, debugging, testing, searching, etc.), how much focus time the developers have in a given time frame, the number and nature of interruptions they may face, time spent using other ancillary tools, coding behaviors (e.g., speed of correcting syntactical errors), and metrics indicating how many lines of code or features they contributed to a repository. This information, when used by the developers themselves, can assist in personal performance monitoring, as well as personal productivity improvements especially when the dashboards allow the comparison of such information over time. Such dashboards also help developers reveal bottlenecks from the project code itself (which areas they spend much of their coding time on) or from their own development process (see Chapter 22 for another example of a dashboard to increase developers' awareness about their work and productivity).

Codealike is one example of a dashboard service that integrates with a developer's IDE and supports developers in visualizing their own activities showing time spent navigating the Web (if they opt to use an additional web browser plugin), focus and interruption time, coding behavior over time, and coding effort on specific areas of the project code. WakaTime similarly produces dashboards to show metrics and insights on programming activity (such as programming language usage) and supports private leaderboards to allow developers to compete with other developers if they wish (in an effort to be more productive). RescueTime offers interactive features that allow developers to set personal goals and to alert them when they may go off track (e.g., if they spend more than two hours on Facebook, they receive an alert).

In addition to presenting personal productivity information in dashboards, many of these services go beyond that and will also send information on a regular basis to the developers (or other stakeholders) in an e-mail; they may even produce a metric to represent a productivity score (see RescueTime for an example that allows the developers to customize the productivity score), or they may further block web sites in an attempt to improve personal productivity. The primary feature of these services are the dashboards they provide, but we also see that they start to offer more features that go beyond the restrictive definition of dashboards given by Few.

Team Performance

Although many dashboards are primarily designed for developers to gain insights on their own activities and behaviors, many display or aggregate information across a team for other stakeholders, such as team leads, managers, business analysts, or researchers.

This team-level information may be used to improve the working environment, development process, or tools they use. Many services (such as Codealike) provide specific-team level dashboards showing team metrics and even ranking information across developers. Some services also provide support for teams to actively improve their performance together. However, there is concern that information captured about individual developer behaviors may be inaccurate at capturing all the activities individual developers may do and that the information may be used inappropriately.

Keeping track of and monitoring work at a team level is especially important for distributed teams. The Atlassian tool suite offers dashboards that help not only the individual developers but also the team (see `https://www.atlassian.com/blog/agile/jira-software-agile-dashboard`) to maintain awareness across the team and to regulate their work at both the individual and team levels [2]. GitHub also supports many dashboards to present project information to teams (as we will discuss). Also, for monitoring, development teams may use task boards for task tracking (such as Trello). Although such task boards are not typically referred to as dashboards, they can be used to give an overview of team performance and support team regulation.

Agile teams use many different tools for tracking project activities as they have to deal with a lot of data to help them manage and reflect on their process, in particular tracking their performance across sprints (e.g., see `https://www.klipfolio.com/blog/dashboards-agile-software-development`). In agile teams, dashboards especially may play an important role for managers. Managers, who are responsible for keeping track of all things in flight during a sprint, may rely on dashboards that visualize all open issues for a particular project to see who open issues are assigned to and what is the priority of open issues. Burndown charts, shown in dashboards, may show how the team is tracking against a predicted burndown line. Axosoft is another service to support agile teams in visually tracking their progress so that they can plan more accurately.

Teams commonly use TV monitors for displaying dashboards so that the team and managers can maintain awareness at a glance on how sprints are progressing in agile projects, while dashboard services such as the one provided by Geckoboard can be used to show project-level monitoring information on TV screens to help teams focus on key performance metrics.

Project Monitoring and Performance

For showing activity at a specific project level, GitHub, like other repository services, extensively uses dashboards to provide insights to managers, project owners, and other developers who may want to decide on the value of using, depending on or contributing to particular projects (see `https://help.github.com/categories/visualizng-repository-data-with-graphs/`). Grafana, used by the GitHub Stats monitoring project, visualizes project forks, stars, number of issues, and other project metrics over time. Bitergia also provides many dashboards for visualizing project and organization information pulling data from many diverse tools and integrations.

As many projects nowadays rely on continuous integration and deployment services, many dashboards visualize how code is moving through the pipeline, especially as new features are flighted in A/B testing experiments. Additional DevOps support may be provided by visualizing the performance of running services, tracking outages, etc. (see `https://blog.takipi.com/the-top-5-devops-dashboards-every-engineer-should-consider/`, `https://blog.newrelic.com/2017/01/18/dashboards-devops-measurement/` and `https://www.klipfolio.com/resources/dashboard-examples/devops` for some discussion on DevOps dashboards).

There are also project-level dashboards that focus particularly on customer management. Zendesk dashboards visualize how customers use specific web applications, as well as how they use their support channels for communicating with the development team, and they visualize satisfaction levels of the end users. Similarly, AppNeta creates dashboards that provide insights on end-user satisfaction with web applications over time. UserVoice also provides dashboards but goes one step further by helping to prioritize customer feedback in the form of a road map to guide future development priorities.

Community Health

Closely related to project-level dashboards, other dashboard services aim specifically at visualizing data at a community or ecosystem level. For example, the CHAOSS web site gathers and visualizes data to support the analytics of community health for open source communities such as Linux. For Linux, the foundation defines interesting health metrics such as number of licenses used among others (see `https://github.com/chaoss/metrics/blob/master/activity-metrics-list.md`).

Summary

As we can see, the landscape of dashboards that already exist (and could exist) for visualizing software development information is extremely broad and varied. They support a wide array of stakeholders and tasks and are hosted on different media. We also see some dashboards stretching the definition of a dashboard by providing additional features and services. However, we can also anticipate that the power they provide in terms of analytics introduces some risks, which we discuss next.

Risks of Using Dashboards

Despite their usefulness to turn repository data into consumable information, dashboards come with a number of risks. Indeed, just as others in our community are rethinking productivity in software engineering, we suggest that how dashboards are used should be reconsidered at the same time. In the following, we discuss these risks in the context of software engineering projects and software developer productivity.

- *Dashboards favor numbers over text*: While many of the artifacts that software developers work with are textual, such as requirement specifications, commit messages, or bug reports, presenting the content of these textual artifacts on a dashboard is not trivial. Techniques that aggregate textual information—for example, topic modeling or summarization algorithms—do not always produce perfect results, and it is therefore often easier to present numbers instead of text on a dashboard. As a result, a developer dashboard is more likely to contain information on how many issues were closed than information on which feature is the most mentioned in bug reports. To address this challenge, further advances in text processing research, especially applied to the heterogeneous artifact landscape of a software project, are needed.

- *Dashboards might not display relevant context*: The aggregation of information implies missing some of the details, which often means that not all contextual information is available. A dashboard that displays information about a critical bug fix might not contain all the caveats of this bug fix, and a dashboard that compares time spent in a browser to time spent in an IDE might not contain information about which of the activities were related to software development. In addition, no two software projects are alike. While the presentation of aggregated information on dashboards might invite users to compare between projects and companies, these comparisons are often flawed since they miss important context. To some extent, this can be addressed by making a dashboard interactive and allowing its users to drill down to more complete information.

185

- *Dashboards often don't explain*: A dashboard might be able to show that one team has fewer open issues than another team, that one component has fewer bugs than another component, or that a developer has spent more time in the IDE compared to the previous month. However, many dashboards do not provide explanations for such observations, and without explanations, this information might not be actionable. For example, a team would not know what they need to do to decrease the number of open issues they have, it might not be obvious why one component has more issues than another, and a developer might not know what they can do to improve their productivity.

- *You get what you measure*: Goodhart's law—usually cited as "When a measure becomes a target, it ceases to be a good measure"—describes another risk of the use of dashboards in software development projects. For example, if a dashboard emphasizes the number of open issues, developers will become more careful about opening new issues, e.g., by combining several smaller issues into one. Similarly, if a dashboard conceptualizes productivity as time spent in the IDE, developers might become hesitant to look up information outside of the IDE. In both examples, this was likely not the intent of the dashboard, yet decades of research on gamification have shown that humans tend to game such systems. As one of our interviewees in a previous study [8] told us: "Developers are the most capable people on Earth to game any system you create."

- *Dashboards can only be as good as the underlying data*: Many studies have found that data captured in software repositories does not always accurately reflect the development reality. For example, Aranda and Venolia [1] found that the coordination that happens around software bugs cannot solely be extracted from software repositories as it would lead to incomplete and often erroneous accounts of coordination. In a study on GitHub, Kalliamvakou et al. [5] found that almost 40 percent of all pull requests do not appear as merged, even though they actually have been merged. These are just two examples of cases where looking at repository data alone provides an inaccurate account of different aspects of software development. If a dashboard is based on such data, it is impossible for this dashboard to display accurate information.

- *Dashboards can only display data that has been tracked somewhere*: While today's software repositories are able to capture many of the actions taken by software developers, there are still many activities that are not captured. For example, a repository would not be able to capture the watercooler conversation between developers that might have provided a crucial piece of coordination for fixing a particular bug. Negotiations with clients taking place outside of the confines of a developer office would be another example of critical information that is often not appropriately captured in a software repository. Information that does not exist in a repository cannot be displayed in a dashboard, and users of dashboards have to be aware that a dashboard might not always provide the complete picture.

- *Performance-related data on dashboards can easily be misinterpreted as productivity data*: Many of the metrics that can be easily visualized on a dashboard, such as number of open issues or number of lines of code, can be interpreted as productivity measures, enabling comparisons between developers, teams, or components that ignore the many complexities of software development. As discussed in the previous chapter, developers have many reservations about such productivity measures. As a result, they will only accept dashboards that do not attempt to reduce the complexity of a developer's contribution to a single number. Stephen Few notes that analytical dashboards need subtle performance measures— until such performance measures have been established, they should not be replaced with their nonsubtle counterparts.

- *Dashboards often do not encode the actual goals well*: There can be a tension between the goals of a software development organization and the items that are surfaced in a dashboard. While the goal of an organization might be long-term value creation, dashboards often use relatively short time spans. Values such as customer satisfaction are not readily extractable from a software repository, even though they might actually align with the organization's goal much better than the number of open issues in a project or time spent in the IDE.

Rethinking Dashboards in Software Engineering

As software engineering becomes more and more data driven and the tools for creating dashboards become easier to use, we expect to see a growth in the role that dashboards play in software engineering and an increase in the number of features they provide. For individual developers, dashboards provide insights on personal productivity, while teams and projects use them for monitoring performance, and managers and community leaders use them for decision making.

We expect that artificial intelligence, natural language processing, and software bots [6] will also impact dashboard design and the features they provide in the next few years. There is certainly opportunity to automate the display of more and more insights on data but also to improve how developers and other stakeholders collaborate with one another through dashboards. Furthermore, artificial intelligence and natural language processing could be used to gather insights on how and when dashboards are used, on the impact they may have on software projects, and on how their design could be improved over time.

We may also wonder if dashboards may even partially replace other modes of information exchange (e.g., PowerPoint slides), and indeed we have observed (informally) that this is the case at some large software companies. Once these dashboards render relevant data, will some stakeholders interpret the view they show as "truth" even though the underlying data or how it is analyzed and presented may be inaccurate, biased or misleading? Do we have sufficient understanding on the significant role they may play in software engineering projects and furthermore on the ethical concerns they may introduce when they accentuate or reveal data that may be sensitive to some stakeholders?

Dashboards and the technologies to create them are likely to become ubiquitous and easier to use over time. Whether they will enhance or possibly harm and detract from productivity or whether they may just give insights on productivity remains to be seen, but care should be taken in how they are created and used. We hope this chapter brings some insights on the diverse way they may be used as well as some awareness of some of the risks as well as opportunities they may bring to our community.

Key Ideas

These are the key ideas from this chapter:

- The landscape of dashboards that exist for visualizing software development information is extremely broad and varied.

- For individual developers, dashboards provide insights on personal productivity, while teams and projects use them for monitoring performance and managers and community leaders use them for decision-making.

- The power that dashboards provide in terms of analytics introduces risks such as the misinterpretation of productivity data and the misalignment of goals.

References

[1] Jorge Aranda and Gina Venolia. 2009. The secret life of bugs: Going past the errors and omissions in software repositories. In Proceedings of the 31st International Conference on Software Engineering (ICSE '09). IEEE Computer Society, Washington, DC, USA, 298–308.

[2] Arciniegas-Mendez, M., Zagalsky, A., Storey, M. A., & Hadwin, A. F. 2017. Using the Model of Regulation to Understand Software Development Collaboration Practices and Tool Support. In CSCW (pp. 1049–1065).

[3] Brath, R. & Peters, M. (2004) Dashboard design: Why design is important. DM Direct, October 2004. Google Scholar

[4] Few, Stephen. 2006. Information dashboard design: the effective visual communication of data. Beijing: O'Reilly.

[5] Kalliamvakou, E., G. Gousios, K. Blincoe, L. Singer, D. M. German, and D. Damian. 2014. The promises and perils of mining GitHub. In Proceedings of the 11th Working Conference on Mining Software Repositories (MSR 2014). ACM, New York, NY, USA, 92–101.

[6] Storey, M. A., & Zagalsky, A. 2016. Disrupting developer
     productivity one bot at a time. In Proceedings of the 2016 24th
     ACM SIGSOFT International Symposium on Foundations of
     Software Engineering (pp. 928–931). ACM.

[7] Treude, C. and M. A. Storey 2010, "Awareness 2.0: staying aware
     of projects, developers and tasks using dashboards and feeds,"
     2010 ACM/IEEE 32nd International Conference on Software
     Engineering, Cape Town, 2010, pp. 365–374.

[8] Treude, C., F. Figueira Filho, and U. Kulesza. 2015. Summarizing
     and measuring development activity. In Proceedings of the 2015
     10th Joint Meeting on Foundations of Software Engineering
     (ESEC/FSE 2015). ACM, New York, NY, USA, 625–636.

[9] Gregory L. Hovis, "Stop Searching for InformationMonitor it with
     Dashboard Technology," DM Direct, February 2002.

CHAPTER 17

The COSMIC Method for Measuring the Work-Output Component of Productivity

Charles Symons, Common Software Measurement International Consortium (COSMIC), UK

The productivity of a software activity may be defined generally as work-output/work-input, where work-input is the effort needed to produce the work-output. In this chapter, we describe the ISO standard COSMIC method, which was designed to measure a size of the work-output from a software process. Measured sizes must be useful for both productivity measurement and for effort estimation, for most types of software.

For this chapter, we leave aside all the issues of how to interpret and exploit measurements of the productivity of software activities (e.g., the factors that affect productivity, the effect of measurements on the persons measured, etc.). Our challenge is how to measure a size of the work-output of software developers in a way that:

- Is independent of the technology used (e.g., language, platform, tools etc.), enabling productivity comparisons across different technology-sets

- Is credible and acceptable to the team or project whose performance is measured so that there is a clear connection with their total work-input, so not just, for example, the code size produced by the programmers in the team

© The Author(s) 2019
C. Sadowski and T. Zimmermann (eds.), *Rethinking Productivity in Software Engineering*,
https://doi.org/10.1007/978-1-4842-4221-6_17

- Is demonstrably useful for estimating the effort for future activities

- Does not take up too much time and effort in relation to how the results will be used (automatic measurement being the ideal)

As well as being able to measure a *delivered* size and/or a *developed* size in the case of new software, the method must be able to measure a *changed* size in the case of a maintenance or enhancement task or a *supported* size in the case of support activities.

Measurement of Functional Size

In the late 1970s, Allan Albrecht proposed a method for measuring a size of the functional requirements for a piece of software, an "amount of functionality delivered to the user." This was a nice piece of lateral thinking that led to the development of function point analysis. His method is now maintained by the International Function Point Users Group (IFPUG) and is still widely used.

Function point analysis was a big advance over counting source lines of code as a size measure since the latter are technology-dependent and cannot be estimated accurately until a software project is well advanced—too late for most project budgeting purposes. In contrast, sizes of requirements measured in units of function points are technology-independent. Hence, their use enables comparisons of productivity across different technologies, development methods, etc., and a software size can be estimated quite early in a project, as requirements-elicitation proceeds.

However, Albrecht's function point analysis has a number of disadvantages in the context of modern software development. In 1998, therefore, an international group of software measurement experts established the Common Software Measurement International Consortium (COSMIC) aiming to develop a new method for measuring functional requirements that overcomes the weaknesses of function points. Table 17-1 summarizes the key differences between Albrecht's function point analysis and the COSMIC method. (FP = function points; CFP = COSMIC function points.)

Table 17-1. *Comparison of Albrecht's FPA Method with the COSMIC Method*

Factor	Albrecht's FPA Method	COSMIC Functional Size Measurement Method
Design origin	A 1970s-era IBM effort- estimation method.	Fundamental software engineering principles.
Design applicability	Whole business applications.	Business, real-time, and infrastructure software, at any level of decomposition.
Size scale	Limited size ranges for any one process or file. For example, a single process must have a size in the range 3–7 FP.	Continuous size scale. The smallest possible size of a single process is 2 CFP, but there is no upper limit to its size.
Measurement of changes	Can only measure the size of a whole process or of a whole file that must be changed.	Can measure the size of a change to any part of a process, so the smallest size of a change is 1 CFP.
Availability	Membership subscription.	Open, free [1].

The COSMIC Method

The method's design rests on two fundamental software engineering principles that are illustrated in Figures 17-1 and 17-2. In the following, all words in italics are precisely defined COSMIC terms [2].

- Software functionality consists of *functional processes* that must respond to *events* outside the software, detected by or generated by its *functional users* (defined as the "senders or intended recipients of data"). *Functional users* may be humans, hardware devices, or other pieces of software.

- Software does only two things. It moves data (entering from its *functional users* and exiting to them across the software *boundary* and from/to *persistent storage*), and it *manipulates* data.

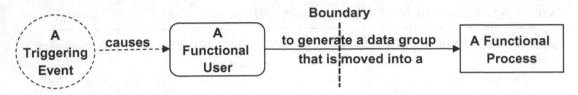

Figure 17-1. *The event/functional user/data group/functional process relationship*

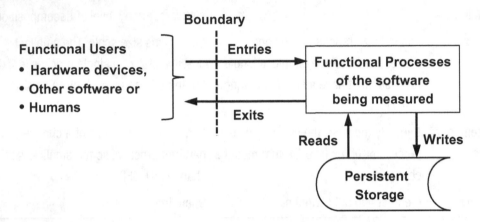

Figure 17-2. *The types of data movements of functional processes*

As there is no simple way to account for *data manipulation*, especially early in the life of a piece of software when requirements are still evolving, the COSMIC size of a *functional process* is measured by counting its *data movements*. In other words, this approach assumes that each *data movement* accounts for any associated *data manipulation*.

By definition, a *data movement* is a subprocess that moves a group of *data attributes* that all describe a single *object of interest* (think of an object-class, a relation in 3NF, or an entity-type). The unit of measurement is one *data movement*, designated as 1x COSMIC function point, or 1 CFP.

A *functional process* has a minimum size of 2 CFPs. It must have an *Entry* plus either an *Exit* or a *Write*, as the minimum outcome of its processing, but there is no maximum size. Single processes of size 60 CFP have been measured in business applications and more than 100 CFP in avionics software.

The functional size of a piece of software in CFPs is the sum of the sizes of all its *functional processes*. The size of any required change to a piece of software in CFPs is the count of its *data movements* that must be changed, regardless of whether changes must be to the *data group* moved and/or to the associated *data manipulation*.

Two examples illustrate the application of the method.

A simple functional process for a human functional user to enter data online about a new employee would have an Entry to move the new employee data, a Read of the database to check whether the employee already exists, a Write to create the new record, and an Exit to convey any validation error messages. The total size would be 4 CFP.

A functional process of a military aircraft may receive a triggering Entry from a sensor warning "missile approaching." The process will output several messages as Exits. Each Exit becomes the triggering Entry to a process in another part of the aircraft's distributed avionics system, for example, to issue warnings to the pilot to instruct the aircraft to take evasive action and other countermeasures. All communicating software components are functional users of each other; all input and output hardware devices are functional users of the software components with which they communicate.

Discussion of the COSMIC Model

In this section, we discuss various aspects of the model that might be argued to limit its practical value as a measure of work-output.

For effort estimation, we need size estimates long before we know the requirements in sufficient detail for a precise COSMIC size measurement.

When there is a new software requirement, the thought process for an estimator is usually first "how big is it?" and then "what productivity figure should I use to convert size to effort?" For example, an agile team would estimate the size of a user story in story points and use a velocity figure measured on past sprints as the productivity value. This same thought process is involved when estimating the effort to develop or change a piece of software at any level of aggregation from a single user story all the way up to a major new system. Estimators need a software size scale and a size/effort relationship, i.e., productivity data, at each relevant level. The productivity data will have been established from measurements on past, completed tasks, or projects with characteristics similar to the new challenge.

However, a sponsor of a new software development typically needs a cost estimate for budget purposes long before the requirements have been spelled out in sufficient detail for a precise COSMIC size measurement. In practice, therefore, measurements of approximate sizes of early requirements for effort estimation may be as commonly needed as are precise sizes of delivered requirements for productivity measurement.

If the COSMIC models illustrated in Figures 17-1 and 17-2 and the definitions of the various terms are to succeed, it must mean that for any given artifacts of some software to be measured, everyone will identify and agree on the same set of functional processes. (The artifacts may be early or detailed statements of requirements, designs, implemented artifacts such as screen layouts and database definitions, or working code.) Correctly identifying the functional processes is the basis for ensuring measurement repeatability.

COSMIC method publications include a guideline [1] that describes several approaches, of varying sophistication, for measuring an approximate size of early requirements. All such approaches rely on being able to identify or estimate, directly or indirectly, the number "n" of functional processes in the early requirements for the new software. As an example, the simplest way of estimating an approximate COSMIC size of such requirements is to multiply the estimated "n" by an estimated average size of one process. More sophisticated approaches to approximate sizing include identifying patterns of functional processes that are known to occur for the type of software being estimated.

An organization wanting to use any of these approaches to approximate COSMIC size measurement will need to measure some software sizes accurately and use the results to calibrate the chosen approximate sizing approach.

What about nonfunctional requirements?

A method that aims to measure a size of functional requirements might appear to intentionally ignore nonfunctional requirements (NFRs). This would be nonsense since NFRs may need a lot of effort to implement. Loosely speaking, functional requirements define what the software must do, whereas NFRs define constraints on the software and the way it is developed or, in other words, how the software must do it.

A joint COSMIC/IFPUG study developed a clear definition of NFRs and a comprehensive glossary of NFR terms [3] and divided them broadly into two main groups.

- Technical NFRs such as the programming language or hardware platform to be used, or constraints from the environment such as the number of users to be supported. These NFRs do not affect software functional size. Rather, they may be factors that you need to understand when interpreting productivity measurements and that must usually be taken into account when estimating costs for a new development.

- Quality NFRs such as requirements for usability, portability, reliability, maintainability, etc. These evolve as a project progresses, wholly or largely[1], into requirements for software functionality. The size of this functionality can be measured in the normal way, using the standard rules of the COSMIC method, or can be estimated if required for a new development.

So, sizes measured using the COSMIC method should reflect all the functionality output as a result of the work-input on the software, regardless of whether this functionality was initially stated in terms of functional or nonfunctional requirements.

What about complexity?

Productivity measurements based on functional sizes are sometimes criticized for not reflecting software complexity. In a discussion of simplicity versus complexity, Murray Gell-Mann (in "The Quark and the Jaguar") shows that crude complexity can be defined as "the length of the shortest message that will describe a system at a given level of coarse graining." According to this definition, therefore, a COSMIC size closely measures the crude complexity of the functional requirements of a software system at the level of granularity of the data movements of its functional processes.

However, as already noted, COSMIC sizes do not take into account the size or complexity of the data manipulation associated with each data movement, i.e., algorithmic complexity. Experience suggests, however, that for a large part of business, real-time and infrastructure software, the amount of data manipulation associated with each type of data movement does not vary much. I know of only one actual measurement of the number of lines of algorithm (LOA) per data movement, which was for a very large chunk of a real-time avionics system. This showed, for example, that the median number of LOA associated with one data movement was 2.5, with 99 percent of data movements having no more than 15 LOA. This one piece of evidence supports the validity of the COSMIC method design assumption for this domain that the count of data movements reasonably accounts for any associated data manipulation, except for any areas of software that are dominated by mathematical algorithms. In business, real-time, and infrastructure software, these areas are typically few and concentrated.

---

[1]An NFR for a system response time may give rise partly to the need for specific hardware or use of a particular programming language (i.e., technical NFRs) and partly for requirements for specific software functionality. The latter can be taken into account in the measure of functional size.

If the development of some software requires significant amounts of new algorithms, the effort associated with this work should probably be separated out in any productivity measurement or should be estimated separately. Developing a new algorithm is essentially a creative process for which there may be no meaningful size/effort relationship. Alternatively, the functional size associated with the algorithms may be measured, e.g., by a locally defined extension to the standard COSMIC method.

Are sizes of functional requirements still relevant in a world of component-driven software development?

This question can be expressed more generally as "Can COSMIC sizing be used, and is it still relevant in the world of modern software development, where much software is assembled from reusable components, e.g., in the IoT or for mobile apps; when agile developers don't believe in detailed documentation and their processes may involve much rework; in outsourced software contracts; etc.?"

The first obvious point to make is that if we are ever to understand software productivity and use the measurements for estimating purposes, then we need a plausible, repeatable, technology-independent measure of work-output. The COSMIC method meets this need; sizes may be measured at any point in the life of a piece of software.

It is up to each organization to determine the problem it is trying to solve and then decide for itself *how and when* to apply the COSMIC method and *how to use* the resulting measurements.

Because any one software activity could result in many types of COSMIC size measurements, the parameters of each measurement must be recorded to ensure that its meaning will be clear for future users. These parameters include the domain of the software and its layer in the architecture and distinguish, for example the following:

- Sizes of new developments from sizes of changes or enhancements

- Sizes of developed from delivered software, where the latter includes bought-in or reused software

- The level of decomposition (or of aggregation) of the software

Experience suggests that an organization should start work-output measurement on its most commonly used software processes to build confidence in using the COSMIC method and in the resulting productivity measurements, before moving on to measuring more complex situations.

In summary, the design of the COSMIC method is a compromise between taking into account all the factors we might think of as causing work-output and the practical need that measurement should be simple and not need too much effort.

Correlation of COSMIC Sizes with Development Effort

The acid test of whether the COSMIC method is of real practical use is "Do CFP sizes, as measurements of work-output, correlate well with measurements of development effort, i.e., work-input?" If the correlations are good, then productivity comparisons should be credible, and the results can be used for new effort estimation purposes with known confidence.

Happily, studies over several years show that under repeatable conditions (same type of software, same technologies, common rules for effort recording, etc.), CFP sizes correlate well with effort for a variety of business and real-time software [4]. The correlations are significantly better, according to some studies, than when using Albrecht's FP sizes.

Recent studies on agile software developments [5] also show that CFP sizes correlate with effort far better than do story point sizes at the level of sprints or iterations. (Story points may be meaningful within individual teams, but they cannot be relied upon for productivity comparisons across teams, nor for higher-level effort estimation purposes.)

Figure 17-3 shows the measurements from one such study with a Canadian supplier of security and surveillance software. In their agile process, tasks are allocated to iterations lasting from three to six weeks. The effort for each task is estimated in Planning Poker sessions in units of story points on a Fibonacci scale, which are then converted directly to work-hours. Figure 17-3 shows the actual effort versus the estimated effort for 22 tasks in nine iterations that required a total of 949 work-hours.

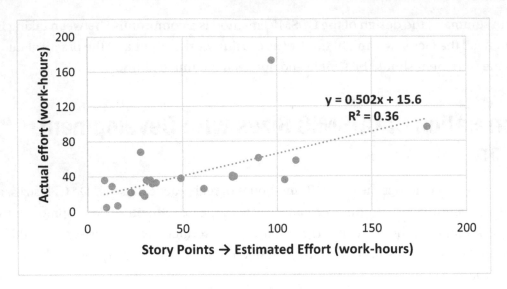

Figure 17-3. *Actual effort versus estimated effort*

The sizes of the 22 tasks were subsequently measured in units of COSMIC function points. Figure 17-4 shows the actual effort for these same 22 tasks plotted against the CFP sizes.

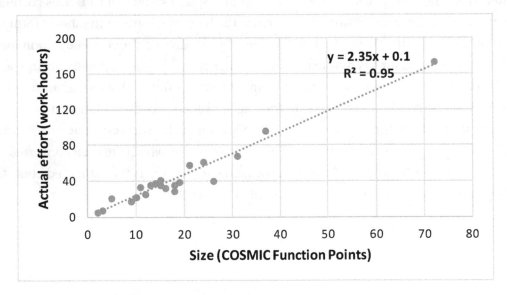

Figure 17-4. *Actual effort versus CFP sizes*

These two graphs show clearly the greatly improved correlation of task size versus effort when size is measured using COSMIC function points, rather than story points. Agile developers can substitute CFP sizes for story points to estimate or measure their work-output without any need to change their agile processes.

In addition to its uses in effort estimation, studies in the domains of embedded real-time and mobile telecoms software show that CFP sizes correlate well with the memory size needed for the corresponding code.

Organizations using the COSMIC method are now routinely exploiting these correlations to help estimate development effort from early software requirements or designs, or in agile environments.

Automated COSMIC Size Measurement

COSMIC size measurement automation is underway in three areas, in varying stages from early exploration to commercial exploitation.

a) Automated COSMIC sizing from textual requirements using natural language processing or artificial intelligence is still in the development stage. This step has great potential as it would allow early life-cycle estimating, e.g., of approximate sizes from user stories.

b) Automated COSMIC sizing from formal specifications or designs has reached the commercial exploitation stage in a few organizations. Here are two examples:

- Automatic CFP size measurement from UML models. Several Polish public-sector organizations rely on the results to help control price/performance of their software outsourcing contracts.

- Renault, the French automotive manufacturer, has implemented automatic COSMIC sizing of specifications held in the Matlab Simulink tool for the software embedded in its vehicle electronic control units [4]. CFP sizes are used to predict the development effort and the hardware memory size needed for the ECUs and to estimate the ECU execution times. The data is then used to control price/performance for the supply of ECUs and their embedded software. Other automotive manufacturers are known to be implementing these processes.

c) Automated COSMIC sizing from static and from executing Java code has been achieved with some manual input "seeding" of the code, with high accuracy.

Conclusions

The ISO-standard COSMIC method has met all its design goals and is being used around the world for measuring a functional size, i.e., work-output, for most types of software.

Measured sizes have been shown to correlate well with development effort for several types of software. The derived size/effort relationships are being used for effort estimation with, in some known cases of real-time software, great commercial benefits. The method has been recommended by the U.S. Government Accountability Office for use in software cost estimation.

The method's fundamental design principles are valid for all time. The method definition [2] is mature and has been frozen for the foreseeable future. Automatic COSMIC size measurement is already happening. As a further consequence of the universality of the method's underlying concepts, measured sizes should be easily understood and therefore acceptable to the software community whose performance is measured.

Measuring and understanding the productivity of software activities is a multifaceted topic. The COSMIC method provides a solid basis for the many needs of work-output measurement, a key component of productivity measurement.

Key Ideas

Here are the key ideas from this chapter:

- It's important for productivity measurement and estimating to have a measure for work output that can be compared across different contexts.

- COSMIC function points are such a measure.

References

[1]   All COSMIC documentation, including the references below, is available for free download from www.cosmic-sizing.org. For an introduction to the method go to https://cosmic-sizing.org/publications/introduction-to-the-cosmic-method-of-measuring-software-2/.

[2]   "The COSMIC Functional Size Measurement Method, Version 4.0.2, Measurement Manual (The COSMIC Implementation Guide for ISO/IEC 19761: 2017)," which contains the Glossary of Terms.

[3]   "Glossary of Terms for Non-Functional Requirements and Project Requirements used in software project performance measurement, benchmarking and estimating," Version 1.0, September 2015, published by COSMIC and IFPUG.

[4]   "Measurement of software size: advances made by the COSMIC community," Charles Symons, Alain Abran, Christof Ebert, Frank Vogelezang, International Workshop on Software Measurement, Berlin 2016.

[5]   "Experience of using COSMIC sizing in Agile projects," Charles Symons, Alain Abran, Onur Demirors. November 2017. https://cosmic-sizing.org/publications/experience-using-cosmic-sizing-agile-projects/

CHAPTER 18

Benchmarking: Comparing Apples to Apples

Frank Vogelezang, METRI, The Netherlands

Harold van Heeringen, METRI, The Netherlands

Introduction

For almost every organization, software development is becoming more and more important. The ability to develop and to release new functionality to the users and customers as fast as possible is often one of the main drivers to gain a competitive edge. However, in the software industry, there is a huge difference in productivity between the best and worst performers. Productivity can be a crucial element for many organizations (as well as cost efficiency, speed, and quality) to bring their competitiveness in line with their most relevant competitors.

Benchmarking is the process of comparing your organization's processes against industry leaders or industry best practices (outward focus) or comparing your own teams (inward focus). By understanding the way the best performers do things, it becomes possible to

- Understand the competitive position of the organization

- Understand the possibilities for process or product improvement

- Create a point of reference, a target to aim for

Benchmarking gives insight into best practices, with the aim to understand if and how one should improve to stay or become successful. Software development benchmarking can be done on any scale that is comparable: a sprint, a release, a project, or a portfolio.

© The Author(s) 2019

C. Sadowski and T. Zimmermann (eds.), *Rethinking Productivity in Software Engineering*,
https://doi.org/10.1007/978-1-4842-4221-6_18

The Use of Standards

Benchmarking is all about comparing. A well-known phrase is "Comparing apples to apples and oranges to oranges." One of the key challenges in the software industry is to measure productivity of completed sprints, releases, projects, or portfolios in such a way that this information can be used for processes such as estimation, project control, and benchmarking. But how can we compare *apples to apples* in an industry that is immature when it comes to productivity measurement?

The economic concept of productivity is universally defined as output/input. In the context of productivity measurement in software development, input is usually measured in effort hours spent. Although it's important to define the right scope of activities when benchmarking, it's just as important to measure the output of a sprint, release, or project in a meaningful way. To be able to benchmark productivity in an "apples to apples" way, it's crucial that the output is measured in a standardized way. An important aspect of standardization is that the measurement is repeatable, so different measurers attribute the same number to the same object. In practice, many measurement methods are being used that are not standardized. Because the output is not standardized, the same number may relate to different aspects, or the same object gets different ratings. This means that the productivity information is not comparable and therefore not useful in benchmarking. Examples of these popular, but unstandardized measurement methods are lines of code (LOC) and all variants, use case points, complexity points, IBRA points, and so on. Also, the story point, which is popular in most agile development teams, is not standardized and therefore can't be used in benchmarking across teams or organizations.

At this moment, only the standards for functional size measurement (the main ones being Nesma, COSMIC, and IFPUG) comply with demands for standardized measurement procedures and intermeasurer repeatability to produce measurement results that can be compared across domains to benchmark productivity.

Functional Size Measurement

Functional size is a measure of the amount of functionality provided by the software, derived by assigning numerical values to the user practices and procedures that the software must perform to fulfill the users' needs, independent of any technical or quality considerations. The functional size is therefore a measure of what the software must do, not how it should work. This general process is described in the ISO/IEC 14143 standard.

The COSMIC method measures the occurrences of Entries, Exits, Reads, and Writes (Figure 18-1).

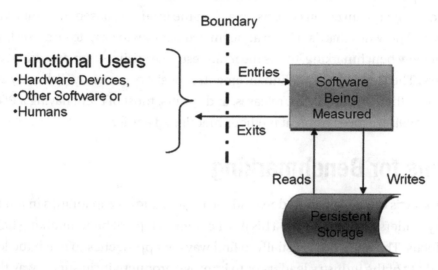

Figure 18-1. *The base functional components for the COSMIC method: Entry, Exit, Read, and Write*

COSMIC is a second-generation functional size measurement method. Most first-generation methods also assign values to data structures. This limits their use in software that processes events. See also Chapter 17 for more extensive information about functional size measurement.

To benchmark productivity across projects in a comparable way, these base parameters are now available:

- *Output*: Functional size measured in a standardized way

- *Input*: Effort hours spent for agreed activities in scope

In practice, the productivity formula (output/input) usually results in numbers of *function points per effort hour* smaller than 1. Because humans are not computers and people can more easily understand and interpret numbers greater than 1, the use of the inverse is more commonly used in software benchmarking. This inverse is called the *product delivery rate* (PDR), defined as Input/Output, or *effort hours per function point* delivered. This is an outcome-oriented way of assessing productivity. See Chapter 8 for more details on assessing productivity.

When the productivity is measured in a standardized way, for benchmarking purposes it needs to be compared to relevant peer groups in the industry. The most relevant source for peer group data is the International Software Benchmarking Standards Group (ISBSG). This not-for-profit organization collects data from the industry, based on standardized measures, and provides this data in an anonymized data set in easy-to-use Excel sheets. For productivity benchmarking, this is the main resource available for practitioners in the industry. The Development & Enhancements repository currently (February 2019) contains more than 9,000 projects, releases, and sprints, most of them having a PDR in one of the functional size measurement methods mentioned earlier.

Reasons for Benchmarking

Benchmarking is often used to understand the organization's capabilities in relation to industry leaders or competitors. This most common type of benchmarking has an outward focus. The objective is usually to find ways or approaches to reach the level of productivity of the industry leaders or to improve productivity in such a way that competitors can be outperformed.

Benchmarking can also be done with an inward focus. The most common example of this type of benchmarking is the comparison of velocity in the last sprint to the velocity in previous sprints. The objective is usually to learn from earlier sprints what can be improved to reach a higher velocity. In Chapter 3, Amy J. Ko performs a thought experiment to argue that we should focus on good management rather than productivity measurement. The effects that good management will have on productivity are true for most successful organizations we have encountered. But the only way to prove that good management brings a higher productivity is...benchmarking. And benchmarking requires measuring productivity.

Another use of benchmarking is the determination of a so-called landing zone by tendering organizations. A landing zone is a range of the minimum, average, and maximum prices that can be expected for the scope offered for tender. These ranges are based on market experience. With this use of benchmarking data, bidding companies are benchmarked in advance.

Examples of a scope that is offered for tender are

- A portfolio of applications to be maintained

- A new bespoke software solution to be developed

- A number of applications to be ported to a cloud platform

We have seen tenders that exclude bids that are outside the landing zone. How the source data for such a landing zone can be obtained is described in the section "Sources of Benchmark Data." The objective is to determine where they expect the price offers of the bidding companies will fall.

A Standard Way of Benchmarking

In 2013, the ISO published an international standard describing the industry best practice to carry out IT project performance benchmarking: ISO/IEC 29155 Information technology project performance benchmarking framework. The standard consists of five parts (Figure 18-2).

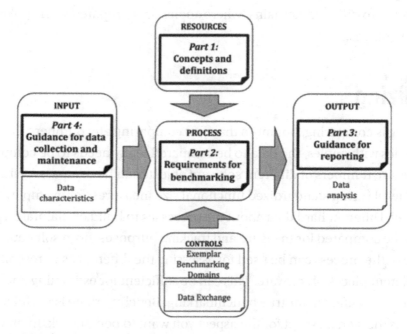

Figure 18-2. *ISO/IEC 29155 structure*

This standard can guide organizations that want to start benchmarking their IT project performance to implement an industry best practice benchmarking process in the following ways:

- By offering a standardized vocabulary of what is important in setting up a benchmark process

- By defining the requirements for a good benchmarking process

- By giving guidance on reporting, before the input part is put in place

- By giving guidance on how to collect the input data and how to maintain the benchmark process

- By defining benchmarking domains

The order of the parts of the standard is, as you can expect from an ISO-standard, deliberate. The most important aspect is that people need to know what they are talking about and need to be able to speak in the same language. The next thing is that you define *up front* what to expect from a good process. Then you need to define what you want to know. In the thought experiment by Amy J. Ko in Chapter 3, some nice examples show what can go wrong if you do not define this in the right manner. When you have done this preparation, your organization is ready to collect data and is able to make a sensible split into different domains, where apples are compared with apples and oranges with oranges.

Normalizing

Benchmarking is comparing, but more than just comparing any numbers. To really compare apples with apples, the data to be compared really needs to be comparable. In sizing, the size numbers of different software objects can be compared, either on a functional level (using standardized functional size measures, for example) or on a technical level. Different hard data about the processes to build or maintain a piece of software can be compared for measure and tracking purposes. Even soft data about the software or the process can be used for assessing the differences or resemblances between different pieces of software. This can be sufficient for estimating and planning purposes, but is insufficient for true benchmarking. Benchmarking is useful only when every aspect is the same, except for the aspect you want to benchmark. In practice, this is hardly ever the case. To have a meaningful benchmark, all aspects not under scrutiny must be made the same. This is called *normalizing*. Based on mathematical transformations or experience data, peer data can be normalized to reflect the conditions of the project that is benchmarked. Things like team size, defect density, and project duration can be made comparable. When a large data set of peer data is available, the easiest way is to select only the peer data that is intrinsically comparable and can be used without mathematical transformations. When not enough peer data is available, aspects can be normalized of which the effect is known.

For instance, the effect of team size is extensively studied. When teams of different sizes are compared, the aspects that are impacted by the team size (such as productivity, defect density, and project duration) can be normalized to reflect the size of the team that you want to benchmark.

Sources of Benchmark Data

There are multiple ways to benchmark productivity against the industry. There are several international commercial organizations worldwide that provide benchmarking services and that have collected a large amount of data through the years, examples of which are METRI, Premios, and QPMG. There are also commercial estimation models available that allow the users to benchmark their project estimates against industry knowledge bases (Galorath SEER or PRICE TruePlanning) or trendlines (QSM SLIM). Because of the confidentiality of the data, these commercial parties usually won't disclose the actual data that they use for their benchmarking services. Only the process and the results of the benchmark are usually communicated, not the actual data points used. External sources of benchmark data are particularly useful when not enough internal data is available to benchmark internal projects on an *apples to apples* basis. These external sources can be tailored to reflect the situation in the organization as well as possible.

ISBSG Repository

The only open source of productivity data is the ISBSG repository, which covers more than 100 metrics on software projects. The ISBSG is an international independent and not-for-profit organization based in Melbourne, Australia. Not-for-profit members of ISBSG are software metrics organizations from all over the world. The ISBSG grows and exploits two repositories of software data: new development projects and enhancements (currently more than 9,000 projects) and maintenance and support (more than 1,100 applications). Data is submitted by consultants and practitioners in the industry. The reward for submitting data to ISBSG is a free benchmark report comparing the realized productivity, quality, and speed against a few high-level industry peer groups.

All ISBSG data is

- Validated and rated in accordance with its quality guidelines

- Current and representative of the industry

- Independent and trusted

- Captured from a range of organization sizes and industries

As the ISBSG data can be obtained in an Excel file, it is possible to analyze and to benchmark project productivity yourself. Simply select a relevant peer group and analyze the data set using the most appropriate descriptive statistics, such as shown in the example in the section "Benchmarking in Practice."

Internal Benchmark Data Repository

If the main reason for benchmarking is for internal comparison, with the objective to improve, then the best source is always to have an internal benchmark repository. In such a repository, the cultural differences that have an impact on productivity (see Chapter 3) are not present and normalizing can be done in a reliable way. When the process to build an internal repository for benchmark data is in place, ideally this process should be used to submit this data to ISBSG as well. In this way, the organization receives a free benchmark on how they stand with regard to industry peers, and the ISBSG database is strengthened with another data point.

Benchmarking in Practice

To put all the theory in practical perspective, we end this chapter with a simplified example on how a benchmark is performed in practice. This example shows how improvements can be found by comparing with others.

An insurance company has measured the productivity of ten completed Java projects. The average PDR of these ten projects was ten hours per function point. To select a relevant peer group in the ISBSG D&E repository, the following criteria could be used:

- Data quality A or B (the best two categories in data integrity and data completeness)

- Size measurement method: Nesma or IFPUG 4+ (comparable)

- Industry sector = insurance

- Primary programming language = Java

After filtering the Excel file based on these criteria, the results can be shown in a descriptive statistics table such as Table 18-1.

Table 18-1 *Example Descriptive Statistics Table*

Statistic	PDR
Number	174
Min	3,1
10% Percentile	5,3
25% Percentile	8,2
Median	11,5
75% Percentile	15,2
90% Percentile	19,7
Max	24,8

As productivity data is not normally distributed but skewed to the right (PDR cannot be lower than 0 but has no upper limit), it is customary to use the median value for the industry average instead of the average. In this case, the average productivity of the insurance company lies between the 25th percentile and the market average (median). This may seem good, but the target may be in the best 10 percent performance in the industry. In that case, there is still a lot of room for improvement. A similar analysis can be made for other relevant metrics, such as quality (defects per FP), speed of delivery (FP per month) and cost (cost per FP). From these analyses it becomes clear on which aspect improvement is required. Comparison of the underlying data with best-in-class peers or projects reveals the differences between the benchmarked project and the best in class. These differences are input for improvement efforts.

False Incentives

Benchmarking, like any type of measurement, has a certain risk. People have a natural tendency to behave toward a better outcome of the measurement. Ill-defined measures will lead to unwanted behavior, or as Amy J. Ko puts it:

> *In pursuit of productivity, however, there can be a wide range of unintended consequences from trying to measure it. Moving faster can result in defects. Measuring productivity can warp incentives. Keeping the pace of competitors can just lead to an arms race to the bottom of software quality.*

Benchmarking needs to be done on *objects* that can be normalized to be truly comparable. In software development this means a sprint, a release, a project, or a portfolio. You should not be benchmarking individuals. Why? The simple answer is that there is no way to normalize people. More arguments against measuring productivity of individual software developers can be found in Chapter 2. Although there is sufficient evidence that there is a 10:1 difference in productivity between programmers, they are also exceedingly rare. An interesting example of what happens when you try to compare individuals is in the blog "You are not a 10x software engineer." There are unmistakably software developers who are much better than others, but this difference cannot be benchmarked in a sensible way. When you compare individuals using their output per unit of time, then the junior team members who are building a lot of simple functions might appear to be better than the brightest team member who solve the three most difficult assignments while helping the juniors and reviewing the code of the other team members. This is illustrated with facts in Chapter 1.

Summary

Benchmarking is the process of comparing your organization's processes against industry leaders or industry best practices (outward focus) or comparing your own teams (inward focus). By understanding the way the best performers do things, it becomes possible to improve. One of the key challenges in the software industry is to measure productivity of completed sprints, releases, projects, or portfolios in an *apples to apples* way so that this information can be used for processes such as estimation, project control, and benchmarking. At this moment, only the standards for functional size measurement comply with demands for standardized measurement procedures and intermeasurer repeatability to produce measurement results that can be compared across domains to benchmark productivity. Benchmarking is useful only when every aspect is the same, except for the aspect you want to benchmark. In practice, this is hardly ever the case. To have a meaningful benchmark, all aspects not under scrutiny must be made the same. This is called *normalizing*. Based on mathematical transformations or experience data, peer data can be normalized to reflect the conditions of the project that is benchmarked. There are multiple ways to benchmark productivity. The best source is always to have an internal benchmark repository. In such a repository, normalizing can be done in a reliable way. External sources of benchmark data are particularly useful when not enough internal data is available to benchmark internal projects on an apples-to-apples basis. These external sources can be tailored to reflect the situation in the organization as well as possible. Benchmarking, like any type of measurement, has a certain risk. People have a natural tendency to behave toward a better outcome of the measurement. Benchmarking needs to be done on objects that can be normalized to be truly comparable. In software development, this means a sprint, a release, a project, or a portfolio. You should not be benchmarking individuals.

Key Ideas

The following are the key ideas from this chapter:

- Benchmarking is necessary to compare productivity across teams and organizations.

- Productivity can be compared across products, but you have to compare the right thing.

- Comparison across organization makes sense only if you do it in a standardized way.

Further Reading

- Wikipedia, on: Cyclomatic complexity,
  `http://en.wikipedia.org/wiki/Cyclomatic_complexity`,
  Lines of Code (LoC),
  `http://en.wikipedia.org/wiki/Source_lines_of_code`,
  Productivity,
  `http://en.wikipedia.org/wiki/Productivity`,
  Use Case Points,
  `http://en.wikipedia.org/wiki/Use_Case_Points`.

- Nesma, on IBRA points, `http://nesma.org/themes/productivity/
  challenges-productivity-measurement`.

- Scrum alliance, on Story points, `http://scrumalliance.org/
  community/articles/2017/January/story-point-estimations-
  in-sprints`.

- ISO, on: Information Technology project Performance Benchmarking
  (ISO/IEC 29155), `http://iso.org/standard/74062.html`,
  Functional Size Measurement (ISO/IEC 14143), `http://iso.org/
  standard/38931.html`.

- ISBSG, on the source of benchmark data, `http://isbsg.org/
  project-data`.

- Amy J. Ko, on the downside of benchmarking, Chapter 3 in Caitlin
  Sadowski, Thomas Zimmermann: Rethinking Productivity in
  Software Engineering, Apress Open, 2019.

- Ciera Jaspan and Caitlin Sadowski, on the arguments against a single
  metric for measuring productivity of software developers, Chapter 2
  in Caitlin Sadowski, Thomas Zimmermann: Rethinking Productivity
  in Software Engineering, Apress Open, 2019.

- Steve McConnell, on the underlying research of the 10x Software
  Engineer, `http://construx.com/10x_Software_Development/
  Origins_of_10X_-_How_Valid_is_the_Underlying_Research_/`.

- Sean Cassidy, on the fact that you are most likely NOT a 10x Software Engineer, `http://seancassidy.me/you-are-not-a-10x-developer.html`.

- Yevgeniy Brikman, on the rarity of 10x Software Engineers, `http://ybrikman.com/writing/2013/09/29/the-10x-developer-is-not-myth/`.

- Lutz Prechelt, on why looking for the mythical 10x programmer is about asking the wrong question, Chapter 1 in Caitlin Sadowski, Thomas Zimmermann: Rethinking Productivity in Software Engineering, Apress Open, 2019.

PART V

Best Practices for Productivity

CHAPTER 19

Removing Software Development Waste to Improve Productivity

Todd Sedano, Pivotal, USA

Paul Ralph, Dalhousie University, Canada

Cécile Péraire, Carnegie Mellon University Silicon Valley, USA

Introduction

As we have seen in previous chapters, measuring the productivity of software professionals is challenging and hazardous. However, we do not need sophisticated productivity measures to recognize when time and effort are wasted. When we see software engineers rewriting code because the previous version was hastily done, their productivity is obviously suffering.

In project management, *waste* refers to any object, property, condition, activity, or process that consumes resources without benefiting any project stakeholder. Waste in a development process is analogous to friction in a physical process—reducing waste improves efficiency and productivity by definition.

However, reducing waste can be challenging. Waste is often hidden by bureaucracy, multitasking, poor prioritization, and invisible cognitive processes. People quickly acclimate to wasteful practices—*that's just how we do things here*. The actions necessary in tackling wastes are waste *prevention*, *identification*, and *removal*. Those actions require us to understand the kinds of waste present in software projects.

© The Author(s) 2019

C. Sadowski and T. Zimmermann (eds.), *Rethinking Productivity in Software Engineering*,
https://doi.org/10.1007/978-1-4842-4221-6_19

To better understand software development waste, we conducted an extended participant-observation grounded theory study at Pivotal Software. Pivotal is a large American software development organization, known for using and evolving extreme programming [1]. Pivotal builds software products and provides agile transformation services for its clients.

Grounded theory is a research method for systematically generating scientific explanations from empirical data. Participant-observation is a type of data collection in which the researcher takes part in the project to gain an insider's perspective. We observed Pivotal teams working on agile transformation projects with engineers from Pivotal's clients in various domains. The study involved two years and five months of participant-observation, 33 intensive open-ended interviews, and one year's worth of retrospection data. It is the first empirical study of waste in software development. For more information about the research method, see Sedano et al. [7].

Taxonomy of Software Development Waste

During the study, we observed nine types of waste (Figure 19-1). This section explains each waste type and associated tensions that complicate reducing the waste.

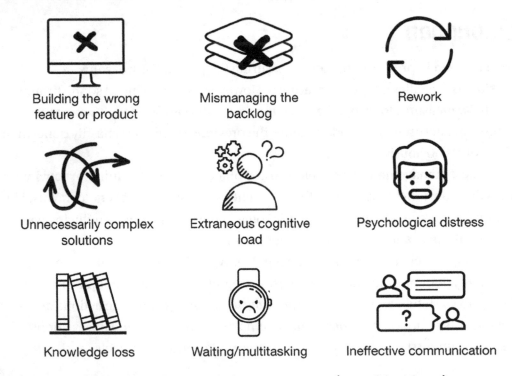

Figure 19-1. *Types of Software Development Waste (© Todd Sedano)*

Building the Wrong Feature or Product

The cost of building a feature or product that does not address user or business needs.

One of the most serious types of waste is building features that no one wants or needs. A more extreme version is building an entire product that no one wants or needs.

For example, on one Pivotal team, three engineers spent three years building a system without ever talking to potential users. The delivered system did not fulfill the users' needs. After spending nine months trying to alter the system to meet user's needs, management scrapped the project. Another example involved building a healthcare relationship management system. During user-centered design, the team ignored user feedback. After a year of trying to find people who would use the delivered system, they ran out of money.

We observed two main causes of "building the wrong feature or product":

- *Ignoring user desiderata*: This includes not doing user research, validation, or testing; ignoring user feedback; and working on features with low user value.

- *Ignoring business desiderata*: This includes not involving a business stakeholder, slow stakeholder feedback, and unclear product priorities.

Techniques for avoiding or reducing this waste include:

- Usability testing

- Feature validation

- Frequent releases

- Participatory design

Building the wrong features or products appears related to a specific tension: user versus business needs. In other words, sometimes users' needs conflict with business needs. For example, for one mobile application, the marketing organization insisted on including the company news feed. Users did not want the news feed and perceived it as spam, lowering their opinion of the mobile application.

Mismanaging the Backlog

The cost of duplicating work, expediting lower value user features, or delaying necessary bug fixes.

One kind of prioritization problem specific to agile software development is *backlog inversion*. In principle, all of the stories are kept in a prioritized backlog such that whatever is on top of the backlog is what the product manager (or equivalent) wants done next. In practice, however, some product managers only prioritize the top *n* stories, after which is a jumble of medium-priority, low-priority, and outdated stories. Backlog inversion occurs when the team gets ahead of the product manager and starts working on story *n+1*.

For instance, on Monday, the product manager examines the backlog and re-prioritizes the next seven stories. The team finishes those seven stories and begins working on stories eight, nine, and ten. Since these stories have not been prioritized recently, the team might unknowingly be working on low-priority stories.

Mismanaging the backlog includes all the waste associated with poor prioritization. We observed numerous causes of "mismanaging the backlog" waste:

- Backlog inversion
- Working on too many features simultaneously
- Duplicated work
- Not enough ready stories
- Imbalance between feature work and bug fixing
- Delaying testing or critical bug fixing
- Capricious thrashing (see below)

Solutions for avoiding or reducing this waste include:

- Prioritizing the backlog several times a week
- Minimizing work in progress by finishing features before starting new ones
- Updating the backlog with current work in progress
- Writing enough stories to stay ahead of development
- Routinely working on bug fixes while doing feature development
- Receiving feedback from users before making changes

This waste is also related to a tension: intransigence versus capricious trashing. Responding to change quickly is a core tenet of agile development and often thought of as the opposite of refusing to change. However, responding to change is more like a middle ground between intransigence (unreasonably refusing to change) and thrashing (changing features too often, especially arbitrarily alternating between equally good alternatives). As an example of trashing, on one project, the launch was delayed while the business fiddled with the sequence and number of steps in the user registration process.

Rework

The cost of altering delivered work that should have been done correctly but was not.

Not all rework is waste. Wasteful rework refers to the cost of altering delivered work *that should have been done correctly but was not.* Reworking a product because of unforeseeable or unpredictable circumstances is not waste.

For example, one enterprise team had been shipping Python code while accumulating technical debt over time. The code became so unmanageable that they decided to re-write it in Go from scratch. We see the entire rewrite as rework because ignoring technical debt impairs the understandability and modifiability of software over time, and the team could have avoided the rework by refactoring the original Python code before it became unmanageable.

We observed the following causes of "rework" waste:

- Technical debt, that is, technical work delayed by taking shortcuts to save time and meet deadlines.

- Ambiguous story definition, including ambiguous acceptance criteria and mock-ups.

- Rejected stories, that is, when a product manager rejects a story implementation because it does not satisfy the acceptance criteria.

- Defects, including poor testing strategy and not performing root-cause analysis on defects.

Solutions for avoiding or reducing this waste include:

- Continuous refactoring

- Reviewing acceptance criteria before beginning a story

- Verifying acceptance criteria before finishing a story

- Improving testing strategy and root-cause analysis on bugs

Refactoring code to handle new features is not waste. A team cannot anticipate and predict future work to be done. Instead, we recommend teams focus on aligning their code with their current understanding of the system features and code design. A team that routinely refactors its code reduces onboarding developer costs and increases its ability to deliver new functionality. Clean code has additional benefits: it is easier to understand, easier to modify, and has fewer defects. Refactoring code to support new functionality is part of the inherent cost of the new functionality. In contrast, rushing a feature introduces technical debt, which leads to rework and extraneous cognitive load.

Rework waste is related to a ubiquitous tension between doing things well and doing things quickly. A recent study of decision-making during programming found that this tension affects many developer actions, including whether to refactor problematic code and whether to implement the first approach that comes to mind or research better ones [5].

Unnecessarily Complicated or Complex Solutions

The cost of creating a more complicated solution than necessary; a missed opportunity to simplify features, user interface, or code.

Unnecessary complexity is intrinsically wasteful and harmful [3]. The more complicated a system is, the more difficult it is to learn, use, maintain, extend, and debug.

Unnecessary feature complexity wastes users' time as they struggle to understand how to use the system and achieve their objectives. For instance, one product required the user to fill in form fields not related to the task at hand. Implementing and maintaining those unnecessary fields is a waste of developer time and an opportunity to introduce defects.

We observed the following causes of "unnecessarily complicated or complex solutions" waste:

- Unnecessary feature complexity from the user's perspective. This includes overly complex user interactions and business processes.

- Unnecessary technical complexity from the team's perspective. This includes duplicating code, lack of interaction design reuse, and overly complex technical design.

Solutions for avoiding or reducing this waste include:

- Prefer simpler designs for user interaction

- Prefer simpler designs for software code

- Consider whether each proposed feature is worth the additional complexity it will introduce

We observed the following tension in relation to this waste: big design up-front versus incremental design. Up-front designs can be based on incorrect or out-of-date assumptions, leading to expensive rework especially in rapidly changing circumstances. However, rushing into implementation can produce ineffective emergent designs, also leading to rework. Despite the emphasis on responsiveness in agile development, designers struggle to backtrack on important decisions and features [2].

The logic of avoiding rework underlies disagreement over big design up-front versus incremental design—proponents of both approaches feel that they are reducing rework. However, on the observed projects, no amount of up-front consideration appears sufficient to predict user feedback and product direction. Therefore, the observed teams preferred to incrementally deliver functionality and delay integrating with technologies until a feature required it.

Extraneous Cognitive Load

The costs of unnecessary mental effort.

Human beings have limited working memory and mental resources. Technically, cognitive load refers to how much working memory a task requires. Here, however, we are using extraneous cognitive load more generally to mean the costs of making something unnecessarily mentally taxing.

For example, one project used five separate test suites that each worked differently. Running the tests, detecting failures, and rerunning just a failed test required learning five different systems. This was unnecessarily cognitively taxing in two senses: developers had to learn the five systems initially, and developers had to remember how all five systems worked and avoid confusing them.

We observed the following causes of "extraneous cognitive load" waste:

- Technical debt

- Complex or large stories

- Inefficient tools and problematic APIs, libraries, and frameworks

- Unnecessary context switching

- Inefficient development flow

- Poorly organized code

Solutions for avoiding or reducing this waste include:

- Refactor code that is difficult to understand

- Decompose large, complex stories into smaller, simpler stories

- Replace hard-to-use libraries

- Work on one task at a time until it is completed; avoid "blocking" tasks (i.e., putting a task on hold to work on something else)

- Improve the development flow including better scripts and tools

Psychological Distress

The costs of burdening the team with unhelpful stress.

Stress can be beneficial ("eustress") or harmful ("distress"). For instance, a little pressure from knowing that the client has high expectations can motivate a team to deliver a better product. Contrastingly, worrying about a sick family member, being yelled at by an angry client, or thinking you might lose your job can reduce performance.

Psychological distress can be either harmful stress or just too much stress. How much stress is too much depends on the person, but everyone has a limit after which more stress lowers performance. Both distress or extreme stress are distracting and draining. Stress can make people feel anxious, overwhelmed, and unmotivated. Therefore, we see psychological distress as intrinsically wasteful.

For example, we observed stress resulting from snarky remarks about other teams or other developers on mailing lists, including "Wow! 22 commits with zero pull requests there." Another example was a countdown to a release date written on an office whiteboard. The team felt that over-emphasizing the deadline was increasing stress and leading to poor technical decisions. Eventually, the countdown was erased from the whiteboard.

Different people find different experiences distressing. However, some common distress-inducing experiences we have observed include:

- Low team morale

- Rush mode

- Interpersonal or team conflict

- Inter-team conflict

A wealth of research investigates the nature, causes, and effects of stress. A full treatment of stress in software engineering would fill a large book. The present study, in contrast, supports only a few basic recommendations for detecting and reducing stress.

- In our experience, detecting distress is not difficult—simply asking team members, "How are things going?" is usually sufficient.

- Stress related to deadlines can sometimes be mitigated by reducing scope or extending the deadline.

- Stress related to interpersonal conflict can be mitigated by facilitated mediation.

Knowledge Loss

The cost of re-acquiring information that the team once knew.

A team can lose knowledge when a person with unique knowledge leaves, when an artifact containing unique knowledge is lost, or when the knowledge is sequestered within one person, group or system. Regardless of how the knowledge was lost, the cost of re-acquiring it is a type of waste.

We observed the following causes of "knowledge loss" waste:

- Team churn (that is, staff rotating on and off a team)

- Knowledge silos (that is, where important information is sequestered within one person, group or system)

229

In Sedano et al. [6], we propose several practices for encouraging knowledge sharing and continuity including continuous pair programming, overlapping pair rotation, and knowledge pollination (e.g., stand-up meetings). Although we have not observed it directly, code review may also help knowledge sharing and prevent knowledge loss.

This waste is related to the tension between sharing knowledge through interaction vs. documentation. One of the key insights of the agile literature is that sharing knowledge face-to-face is usually more effective than sharing knowledge through written documents. Indeed, often documentation quickly becomes outdated and unreliable.

Waiting/Multitasking

The cost of idle time, often hidden by multitasking.

When something goes wrong in a manufacturing plant, we can sometimes see people waiting around. If the boxing team runs out of boxes, they might just stand idle until more boxes arrive. This is obviously waste.

Waiting waste is less obvious among software professionals because waiting is often hidden by multitasking. For example, if the integration process takes an hour, programmers tend to switch to some other, lower-priority work while waiting for integration.

We observed the following causes of "waiting/multitasking" waste:

- Slow or unreliable tests

- Missing information, people, or equipment

- Product managers taking too long to provide needed information

- Context switching between tasks

Solutions for avoiding or reducing this waste include:

- Expose waiting time by limiting work in progress

- For short waits, take breaks (e.g., play table tennis) instead of task switching

- For longer waits, use waiting time to work on the cause of the wait (e.g., shorten a long build)

Multitasking introduces waste in two ways. First, multitasking involves a mental transition to the new task, which can be quite time-consuming, especially if the new task is cognitively demanding. Second, multitasking creates dilemmas when the original high-priority task becomes available again. Do developers finish the second lower-priority task (delaying higher priority work) or immediately switch back to the original task (leaving work-in-progress)?

Engineers remaining idle for more than a few minutes is typically viewed negatively. Thus, engineers tend to prefer context-switching over waiting despite the drawbacks described above.

Ineffective Communication

The cost of incomplete, incorrect, misleading, inefficient, or absent communication among project stakeholders.

Ineffective communication is intrinsically wasteful. For example, a product manager notices a bug and adds it to the backlog but does not explain how to reproduce it. The team ends up sleuthing—either experimenting with different possible combinations or asking the product manager for additional details. As another example, a developer changes key configuration information that affects all other developers on the team. Instead of telling everyone that they need to pull the latest code, the developer posts about the change via asynchronous communication (e.g., Slack). Some developers do not see this communication and wonder why their code stops working. They waste time trying to figure out the solution when the answer was already known within the team.

We observed the following causes of "ineffective communication" waste:

- Teams that are too large.

- Asynchronous communication, which is especially problematic for distributed teams, distributed stakeholders, and when the team depends on other teams or opaque processes outside the team.

- One person or a few people dominating the conversation or not listening.

- Inefficient meetings including lack of focus during meetings, skipping retros, not discussing blockers each day, and meetings running over (e.g. long stand-ups).

Like stress, copious research has investigated communication effectiveness, and a complete account is beyond the scope of this chapter. However, we can make some simple recommendations.

- Synchronous (especially face-to-face) communication seems more effective for most people, most of the time.

- Conversational turn-taking, where participants take turns speaking one at a time, leads to better shared understanding.

- More powerful participants (e.g., white male project manager) interrupting less powerful participants (e.g., nonwhite female junior developer) has a chilling effect on diversity of thought and quality of group decision-making. Other participants can mitigate interruptions by returning to the interrupted speaker by, for example, saying "Can we come back to what Alexis was saying about...."

Ineffective communication might lead to the other types of waste. For instance, ineffective communication resulting in delays might lead to the waiting waste. Ineffective communication resulting in misunderstanding user or business needs might lead to building the wrong feature or product, or misunderstanding the existing solution might lead to building an overly complex solution and extraneous cognitive load. Ineffective communication resulting in poor decision-making might lead to mismanaging the backlog. Ineffective communication resulting in technical mistakes might lead to defects and rework. Ineffective communication resulting in misunderstandings among team members might lead to conflicts and psychological distress. These are just a few examples highlighting the importance of effective communication and how poor communication can generate waste.

Additional Wastes in Pre-agile Projects

Since Pivotal is lean and agile, it has already eliminated some common types of waste. Professionals using waterfall, plan-driven, or other pre-agile approaches may experience waste from unnecessary bureaucracy. Some bureaucracy is necessary to govern (especially large) organizations. However, much bureaucracy is simply pointless, and some is actively harmful. Examples include:

- *Overplanning*: This involves estimating budgets, schedules, phases, milestones, or tasks at a level of detail that is not supported by the information at hand or the stability of the project environment. When a plan requires copious guesses and assumptions, it is a fantasy, not a plan. Overplanning not only wastes the planner's time but also engenders psychological distress when reality departs from the plan.

- *Overspecifying*: This involves specifying requirements or design at a level of detail that is not supported by the information at hand. Overspecifying is a common problem in projects with large, up-front requirements and design phases. Warning signs include copious optional, low-priority, or low-confidence requirements; developing an elaborate architecture while stakeholders are still arguing about the goals of the project; fleshing out features that will not be built for months, if ever. Overspecification is not only a waste of time, it can constrain developers, obscure better solutions, and reduce creativity.

- *Performance metrics*: Perhaps the main theme to emerge from the study of performance measurement is that measuring performance reduces performance. All metrics can be gamed, and gaming metrics is distracting and time-consuming. Measuring people just motivates them to engage in metric-optimizing theatrics, which are usually less efficient than what they were doing before the metrics. Attempts to quantify performance are therefore not just wasteful but often counterproductive, especially where bonuses are tied to the measurements [4].

- *Pointless documentation*: Some documentation is necessary—even critical—when it helps achieve a specific goal. However, some projects have binders full of documentation that will not be read before growing out-of-date, if ever. Pointless documentation is a form of *ineffective communication* waste.

- *Process waste*: Processes can be wasteful when they generate pointless documentation (reports, forms, formal requests), pointless meetings (like large company or department-wide meetings, not team meetings), pointless approvals (due to not trusting the people who do the work), and handoffs.

- *Handoffs*: Organizations that divide projects into phases and have different teams involved in different phases of the same project experience handoff waste. Handoff waste is the cost (in knowledge, time, resources, and momentum) of passing a project from one team to another. Handoffs contribute to other wastes including knowledge loss, ineffective communication, and waiting.

When following pre-agile practices, two general strategies may help reduce waste. First, hunt for slow-feedback loops, as shortening feedback loops often helps to reduce waste. Second, actively remove the policies responsible for the waste. One problem with bureaucracy is that, once a policy is made, following the policy becomes the bureaucrat's goal, regardless of the organizational goals the policy was written to support. Waste is the inevitable byproduct of optimal actions for achieving organizational goals diverging from the actions prescribed by flawed or outdated policies.

Discussion

The above discussion may appear to suggest that all problems are types of waste, but that is not the case. This section discusses what is special about waste, and gives more suggestions for removing waste.

Not All Problems Are Wastes

It is tempting but incorrect to label anything that goes wrong on a project as waste. Human beings make mistakes. A developer may accidentally push code before running the test suite. Our knowledge is limited. A product manager may write an impractical user story because he or she does not know of some particular limitation. We forget. A developer might forget that adding a new type to the system necessitates modifying a configuration file. Whether we conceptualize these sorts of errors as waste is a matter of opinion, but focusing on them is unhelpful because they are often unpredictable.

It is better to focus on *systemic* waste: waste that affects a wide variety of projects in consistent, predictable, and preventable ways.

Similarly, it is important to distinguish foreseeable errors from actions that only seem like errors in hindsight. Suppose that users clearly indicate that a particular feature is not desirable, but we build it anyway, and sure enough, no one uses the feature. Obviously, this is waste. In contrast, suppose users are clamoring for a feature, so we build it, but it's quickly abandoned as users realize it does not really work for them. This is not an error; it's learning. Sometimes, building a feature, prioritizing the wrong thing, refactoring, and communicating badly are the only ways of learning what is actually needed. The concept of waste should not be misused to demonize incremental development and learning.

Reducing Waste

Reducing waste is often straightforward. The countdown on the whiteboard is stressing out the team? Erase it. Five separate test suites take forever to run? Integrate them. Building a feature no one has asked for? Stop. User interface is too complex? Simplify it. Not enough knowledge sharing among programmers? Pair-program. The official approval process is inefficient? Change it. Sometimes this is easier said than done, but it's not rocket science either.

The problem is that waste is often hidden. Rework is hidden in "new features" and "bug fixes." Building the wrong features is hidden by lack of good feedback. Knowledge loss is hidden by not realizing the organization used to know this information. We hide distress to avoid looking weak. Bureaucracy hides waste behind an official policy. That is why this chapter describes all different sorts of waste—waste is easier to identify if you know what to look for.

Once we have identified some waste, there are three broad approaches for reducing it: prevention, incremental improvement, and "garbage day":

- *Prevention*: This involves creating systems that impede waste. User research impedes "building the wrong feature" waste. Continuous refactoring impedes "rework" waste. Pair programming, peer code review, and overlapping pair rotation impede "knowledge loss" [6]. Daily stand-ups impede "inefficient communication" waste.

- *Incremental improvement*: Waste reduction can be approached as a continuous improvement practice, running parallel to feature development. Waste reduction can be discussed in retrospective meetings, and one or two waste reduction tasks can be included in the backlog each week. This is a good approach for most teams, since suspending development for weeks to remove waste is not tenable in most organizations and could reduce team morale and customer satisfaction.

- *Focused waste reduction: garbage day/trash pickup day*: Some companies set aside special periods where employees are free to work autonomously. For example, Pivotal has a "hack day" during which employees can work on a theme or whatever they want. Organizations can implement a similar set period ("garbage day") in which employees tackle some source of waste, for instance, speeding up the integration process, removing redundant tests, simplifying an overcomplicated process, or just meeting with co-workers to share siloed knowledge.

A related question is, "If we have identified several different kinds of waste, what should we tackle first?" We observed teams prioritizing waste removal using the following procedure:

1. Individually list several wastes.

2. Plot each waste on a graph like Figure 19-2.

3. Prioritize wastes beginning with the best ratio of easy to remove and high impact (e.g., W1) and working your way down to wastes that are harder to remove and have less impact (e.g., W8).

4. Add waste reduction to the backlog (as chores) and prioritize these chores as time permits.

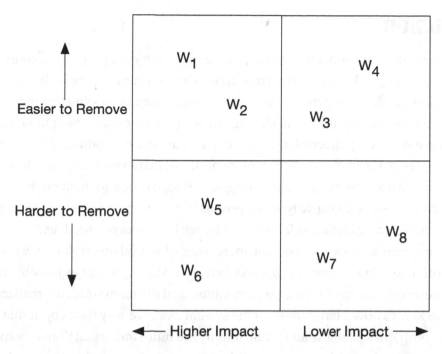

Figure 19-2. *Prioritizing waste removal*

Of course, eliminating some (low impact, hard-to-remove) wastes may not be worth the cost. For example, having a distributed team most often contributes to ineffective communication waste, but it might be the most practical solution when experts with rare skills are distributed across the globe. Eliminating waste should be and typically is a secondary goal. Waste elimination should not displace the primary goal of delivering a quality product.

Here, we recommend prioritizing wastes based on our best guesses as to their impact. Precisely quantifying the impact of each waste is impractical. How would you quantify the inefficiencies of overburdening developers with unhelpful stress and the impact on their health, or the impact of knowledge loss, when the team does not even know what knowledge is being lost? Quantifying waste might be a good PhD project but is likely not worth the trouble for most professional teams.

Conclusion

In summary, software *waste* refers to project elements (objects, properties, conditions, activities, or processes) that consume resources without producing benefits. Wastes are like friction in the development process. An important step in tackling this friction is waste awareness and identification. During our study, we identified nine main types of waste in agile software projects: building the wrong feature or product, mismanaging the backlog, rework, unnecessarily complex solutions, extraneous cognitive load, psychological distress, waiting/multitasking, knowledge loss, and ineffective communication. For each waste type, we proposed some suggestions to reduce the waste. Reducing wastes removes friction and hence improves productivity.

Software professionals have become increasingly focused on productivity (or *velocity*), often leading to increasingly risky behavior. Moving as fast as possible is great until someone quits, gets sick, or goes on vacation and the team suddenly realizes that no one else knows how a large chunk of the system works or why it was built that way. For many companies, stability and predictability are more important than raw speed. Most firms need software teams that steadily deliver value, week after week and month after month, despite unexpected problems, disruptions, and challenges.

Eliminating waste is just one way to forge more resilient, disruption-proof teams. This work on waste is part of a larger study of sustainability and collaboration in software projects. In Sedano et al. [6], we propose a theory of sustainable software development that extends and refines our understanding of extreme programming with new, sustainability-focused principles, policies, and practices. The principles include engendering a positive attitude toward team disruption, encouraging knowledge sharing and continuity, and caring about code quality. The policies include team code ownership, shared schedule, and avoiding technical debt. The practices include continuous pair programming, overlapping pair rotation, knowledge pollination, test-driven development, and continuous refactoring.

Based on our experiences, none of the results presented in this chapter appears unique to Pivotal Software or extreme programming. However, our research method does not support statistical generalization to contexts beyond the observed teams at Pivotal Software. Therefore, researchers and professionals should adapt our findings and recommendations to their own contexts, case by case.

Key Ideas

The following are the key ideas from this chapter:

- There are several different types of preventable "wastes" that occur during software development and represent lost productivity.
- While it may be hard to define and measure productivity, identifying/reducing waste is an effective way to become more productive.

References

[1]   Kent Beck and Cynthia Andres. Extreme Programming Explained: Embrace Change (2nd Edition). Addison-Wesley Professional, 2004.

[2]   Nigel Cross. Design cognition: results from protocol and other empirical studies of design activity. In Design knowing and learning: Cognition in design education. C. Eastman, W.C. Newstetter, and M. McCracken, eds. Elsevier Science. 79–103. 2001.

[3]   John Maeda. The Laws of Simplicity. MIT Press. 2006.

[4]   Jerry Muller. The Tyranny of Metrics. Princeton University Press. 2018.

[5]   Paul Ralph and Ewan Tempero. Characteristics of decision-making during coding. In Proceedings of the International Conference on Evaluation and Assessment in Software Engineering, 2016.

[6]   Todd Sedano, Paul Ralph, and Cécile Péraire. Sustainable software development through overlapping pair rotation. In Proceedings of the International Symposium on Empirical Software Engineering and Measurement, 2016.

[7]   Todd Sedano, Paul Ralph, and Cécile Péraire. Software development waste. In Proceedings of the 2017 International Conference on Software Engineering, 2017.

CHAPTER 20

Organizational Maturity: The Elephant Affecting Productivity

Bill Curtis, CAST Software, USA

The maturity of an organization's software development environment impacts the productivity of its developers and their teams [5]. Consequently, organizational attributes should be measured and factored into estimates of cost, schedule, and quality. This chapter presents an evolutionary model of organizational maturity, how the model can guide productivity and quality improvements, and how its practices can be adapted to evolving development methods.

Background

While working on improving software development at IBM in the 1980s, Watts Humphrey took Phil Crosby's course on quality management that included a maturity model for improving quality practices [1]. Crosby's model listed five stages of improvement through which a collection of quality practices should progress. While traveling home, Humphrey realized that Crosby's model would not work because it resembled approaches used for decades with little sustainable success. He realized past improvement efforts died when managers and developers sacrificed improved practices under the duress of unachievable development schedules. Until he fixed the primary problems facing projects, productivity improvements and quality practices had little chance to succeed.

© The Author(s) 2019
C. Sadowski and T. Zimmermann (eds.), *Rethinking Productivity in Software Engineering*,
https://doi.org/10.1007/978-1-4842-4221-6_20

241

During the late 1980s, Humphrey developed an initial formulation of his Process Maturity Framework [6] in the Software Engineering Institute at Carnegie Mellon University. In the early 1990s Mark Paulk, Charles Weber, and I transformed this framework into the Capability Maturity Model for Software (CMM) [10]. Since then the CMM has guided successful productivity and quality improvement programs in many software organizations globally. An organization's maturity level is appraised in process assessments led by authorized lead assessors.

Analyzing data from CMM-based improvement programs in 14 companies, James Herbsleb and his colleagues [5] found a median annual productivity improvement of 35 percent, ranging from 9 percent to 67 percent across companies. Accompanying this improvement was a median 22 percent increase in defects found prior to testing, a median reduction of 39 percent in field incidents, and a median reduction in delivery time of 19 percent. Based on cost savings during development, these improvement programs achieved a median return on investment of 5 to 1. How were these results achieved?

The Process Maturity Framework

The Process Maturity Framework has evolved over the past 30 years while sustaining its basic structure. As described in Table 20-1, this framework consists of five maturity levels, each representing a plateau of organizational capability in software development on which more advanced practices can be built. Humphrey believed that to improve productivity, impediments to sound development practices should be removed in a specific order. For instance, level 1 describes organizations with inconsistent or missing development practices. Too often crisis-driven projects rely on heroic efforts from developers who work nights and weekends to meet ridiculous schedules. Until project commitments and baselines can be stabilized, developers are trapped into working too fast, making mistakes, and having little time to correct them.

Table 20-1. *Process Maturity Framework*

Maturity Level	Attributes
Level 5 – Innovating *CMMI – Optimizing*	• Performance gaps needing innovative improvements identified • Innovative technologies and practices continually investigated • Experiments conducted to evaluate innovation effectiveness • Successful innovations deployed as standard practices
Level 4 – Optimized *CMMI – Quantitatively Managed*	• Projects managed using in-process measures and statistics • Causes of variation are managed to improve predictability • Root causes of quality problems are analyzed and eliminated • Standardized processes enable reuse and lean practices
Level 3 – Standardized *CMMI – Defined*	• Development processes standardized from successful practices • Standard processes and measures tailored to project conditions • Project artifacts and measures are retained, and lessons shared • Organization-wide training is implemented
Level 2 – Stabilized *CMMI – Managed*	• Managers balance commitments with resources and schedule • Changes to requirements and product baselines are managed • Measures are implemented for planning and managing projects • Developers can repeat sound practices in stable environments
Level 1 – Inconsistent *CMMI – Initial*	• Development practices are inconsistent and often missing • Commitments are often not balanced with resources and time • Poor control over changes to requirements or product baselines • Many projects depend on unsustainable heroic effort

The path to improvement begins when project managers or team leaders stabilize the project environment by planning and controlling commitments, in addition to establishing baseline and change controls on requirements and deliverable products. Only when development schedules are achievable and product baselines stable can developers work in an orderly, professional manner. Achieving level 2 does not force consistent methods and practices across the organization. Rather, each project adopts the practices and measures needed to create achievable plans and rebalance commitments when the inevitable requirements or project changes occur. When unachievable commitments are demanded by higher management or customers, level 2 managers and team leaders learn to say "no" or diplomatically negotiate altered and achievable commitments.

Once projects are stable, the standard development processes and measures that characterize level 3 can be synthesized across the organization from practices and measures that have proven successful on projects. Implementation guidelines are developed from past experience to tailor practices for different project conditions. Standard practices transform a team/project culture at level 2 into an organizational culture at level 3 that enables an economy of scale. CMM lead assessors often report that standard processes are most frequently defended by developers because they improved productivity and quality and made transitioning between projects much easier.

Once standardized processes and measures have been implemented, projects can use more granular in-process measures to manage the performance of development practices and the quality of their products across the development cycle. Process analytics that characterize level 4 are used to optimize performance, reduce variation, enable earlier adjustments to unexpected issues, and improve prediction of project outcomes. Standardized development practices establish a foundation on which other productivity improvements such as component reuse and lean practices can be implemented [7].

Even when optimized to their full capability, processes may not achieve the productivity and quality levels required in a competitive environment or for demanding requirements. Consequently, organization must identify and evaluate innovations in technology, processes, workforce practices, etc., that can dramatically improve productivity and quality outcomes beyond existing performance levels. At level 5, the organization moves into a continuous innovation loop driven by specific targets for improvement that will change over time.

The Process Maturity Framework can be applied to individual processes—the so-called continuous approach. However, this framework is most effective when applied as a unique guidebook for organizational change and development. If the organization does not change, individual best practices typically will not survive the stress of crisis-driven challenges. This approach is consistent with observations on organizational systems in exceptionally successful businesses described in Jim Collin's books *Built to Last* and *Good to Great*.

The Impact of Maturity on Productivity and Quality

One of the earliest and best empirical studies of a maturity-based process improvement program was reported by Raytheon [2, 4, 8]. Raytheon's time reporting system collected data in effort categories drawn from a cost of quality model designed to show how improvements in product quality increased productivity and reduced costs. This model divided effort into four categories:

- Original design and development work

- Rework to correct defects and retest the system

- Effort devoted to first-run testing and other quality assurance activities

- Effort in training, improvement, and process assurance to prevent quality problems

Over the course of their improvement program (Table 20-2), Raytheon reported that the percentage of original development work increased from only a third of the effort at level 1 to just over half at level 2, two-thirds at level 3, and three-quarters at level 4. At the same time, rework was cut in half at level 2 and declined by a factor of almost 7 at level 4. As they achieved level 4, Raytheon reported that productivity had grown by a factor of 4 from the level 1 baseline.

Table 20-2. *Raytheon's Distribution of Work Effort by CMM Level*

Year	CMM Level	Percent of total effort				Productivity growth
		Original work	Rework	First-run tests	Prevention	
1988	1	34%	41%	15%	7%	baseline
1990	2	55%	18%	13%	12%	1.5 X
1992	3	66%	11%	23%		2.5 X
1994	4	76%	6%	18%		4.0 X

Note 1: Table 20-2 was synthesized from data reported in Dion [2], Haley [4], and Lyndon [8]. *Note 2:* Effort for first-run tests and prevention were collapsed into one category in 1992. *Note 3:* Productivity growth is in factors compared to the 1988 baseline.

As evident in these data, productivity was heavily affected by the amount of rework. The proportion of rework is usually high prior to initiating an improvement program, with reports of 41 percent at Raytheon, 30 percent at TRW [14], 40 percent at NASA [15], and 33 percent at Hewlett Packard [3]. Stabilizing baselines and commitments enabled developers to work in a more disciplined, professional manner, reducing mistakes and rework and thereby improving productivity. The amount of initial testing stayed the roughly the same, while the retesting required after fixing mistakes declined. The extra effort devoted to the improvement program (prevention) was more than offset by reduced rework. Accompanying productivity growth was a 40 percent reduction in development costs per line of code by level 3.

The size of Raytheon's productivity growth in moving from level 3 to level 4 is difficult to explain from quantitative management practices alone. Further investigation revealed a reuse program that reduced the effort required to develop systems. Corroborating results on the productivity impact of reuse at level 4 were reported by Omron [11] and Boeing Computer Services [13]. Standardized processes at level 3 appear to create the necessary foundation of rigorous development practices and trusted quality outcomes needed to convince developers it is quicker to reuse existing components than develop new ones.

Updating Maturity Practices for an Agile-DevOps Environment

In the early 2000s the U.S. Department of Defense and aerospace community expanded the CMM to include system engineering practices. The new architecture of the Capability Maturity Model Integration (CMMI) dramatically increased the number of practices and reflected the ethos of large defense programs. In the opinion of many, including some authors of the original CMM, CMMI was bloated and required excessive practices for many software development environments that occasionally bordered on bureaucracy. At the same time, the rapid iterations of agile methods were replacing lengthy development practices that were insufficient to handle the pace of change affecting most businesses.

In theory, agile methods solve the level 1 commitment problem by freezing the number stories to be developed at the beginning of a sprint. New stories can only be added during the planning of a subsequent sprint. Consequently, it was disconcerting to hear developers at the Agile Alliance conferences in 2011 and 2012 complain about stories being added during the middle of sprints at the request of marketing or business units. These in-sprint additions created the same rework-inducing schedule pressures that had plagued low maturity waterfall projects. Enforcing controls on commitments is a critical attribute of level 2 to protect developers from chaotic circumstances that degrade the productivity and quality of their work.

In a session at the Agile Alliance Conference in 2012, Jeff Sutherland, one of the creators of the Scrum method, commented that perhaps as many as 70 percent of the companies he visited were performing scrumbut. "We are doing Scrum, *buut* we don't do daily builds, *buut* we don't do daily standups, *buut* we don't do...." As Jeff observed, they clearly weren't doing Scrum. When performed rigorously across an organization's development teams, Scrum and other agile or DevOps methods can provide the benefits of standardized processes characteristic of a level 3 capability. However, when these methods lack discipline, development teams are exposed to the typical level 1 problems of uncontrolled baselines and commitments, as well as patchy development practices that sap their productivity.

In 2015 Fannie Mae, a provider of liquidity for mortgages in the U.S. housing market, initiated a disciplined agile-DevOps transformation across their entire IT organization [12]. The transformation involved replacing traditional waterfall processes with short agile sprints and installing a DevOps tool chain with integrated analytics. Although they did not use CMMI, their improvement program mirrored a maturity progression from stabilizing changes on projects (level 2) to synthesizing standard practices, tools, and measures across the organization (level 3). Productivity was measured using Automated Function Points [11] delivered per unit of time and was tracked to monitor progress and evaluate practices.

After the transformation was deployed organization-wide, Fannie Mae found that the density of defects in applications had decreased by typically 30 percent to 48 percent. Productivity gains attributed to the transformation had to be calculated by collating data across several sprints whose combined duration and effort were comparable to previous waterfall release cycles (the baseline). The initial sprints were often less productive while the team adjusted to short-cycle development methods. However, when combined with results from several succeeding sprints, the average productivity was found to have increased by an average of 28 percent across applications compared to the waterfall baseline.

Summary

Improvement programs based on the Process Maturity Framework have improved productivity in software development organizations globally. Practices are implemented in evolutionary stages, each of which creates a foundation for more sophisticated practices at the next maturity level. Although development methods evolve over time, many of the problems that reduce their effectiveness are similar across generations. Thus, the maturity progression of Stabilize–Standardize–Optimize–Innovate provides an approach to improving productivity that is relevant to agile-DevOps transformations.

Key Ideas

The following are the key ideas from the chapter:

- Immature, undisciplined development practices can severely constrain productivity.

- Staged evolutionary improvements in an organizations' development practices can dramatically increase productivity.

- Modern development practices can suffer from weaknesses that hindered the productivity of earlier development methods.

References

[1]   Crosby, P. (1979). *Quality Is Free*. New York: McGraw-Hill.

[2]   Dion, R. (1993). Process improvement and the corporate balance sheet. *IEEE Software*, 10 (4), 28–35.

[3]   Duncker, R. (1992). *Proceedings of the 25th Annual Conference of the Singapore Computer Society*. Singapore: November 1992.

[4]   Haley, T., Ireland, B., Wojtaszek, E., Nash, D., & Dion, R. (1995). *Raytheon Electronic Systems Experience in Software Process Improvement (Tech. Rep. CMU/SEI-95-TR-017)*. Pittsburgh: Software Engineering Institute, Carnegie Mellon University.

[5]   Herbsleb, J., Zubrow, D., Goldenson, D., Hayes, W., & Paulk, M. (1997). Software Quality and the Capability Maturity Model. *Communications of the ACM*, 40 (6), 30–40.

[6]   Humphrey, W. S. (1989). *Managing the Software Process*. Reading, MA: Addison-Wesley.

[7]   Liker, J. K. (2004). *The Toyota Way: 14 Management Principles from the World's Greatest Manufacturer*. New York: McGraw-Hill.

[8]   Lydon, T. (1995). Productivity drivers: Process and capital. *In Proceedings of the 1995 SEPG Conference*. Pittsburgh: Software Engineering Institute, Carnegie Mellon University.

[9]   Object Management Group (2014). *Automated Function Points*. www.omg.org/spec/AFP.

[10] Paulk, M. C., Weber, C. V., Curtis, B., & Chrissis, M. B. (1995). *The Capability Maturity Model: Guidelines for Improving the Software Process*. Reading, MA: Addison-Wesley.

[11] Sakamoto, K., Kishida, K., & Nakakoji, K. (1996). Cultural adaptation of the CMM. In Fuggetta, A. & Wolf, A. (Eds.), *Software Process*. Chichester, UK: Wiley, 137–154.

[12] Snyder, B. & Curtis, B. (2018). Using analytics to drive improvement during an Agile- DevOps transformation. *IEEE Software, 35* (1), 78–83.

[13] Vu. J. D. (1996). Software process improvement: A business case. In *Proceedings of the European SEPG Conference*. Milton Keynes, UK: European Software Process Improvement Foundation.

[14] Barry W. Boehm (1987). Improving Software Productivity. *IEEE Computer*. 20(9): 43-57.

[15] Frank McGarry (1987). Results from the Software Engineering Laboratory. Proceedings of the Twelfth Annual Software Engineering Workshop. Greenbelt, MD: NASA.

CHAPTER 21

Does Pair Programming Pay Off?

Franz Zieris, Freie Universität Berlin, Germany

Lutz Prechelt, Freie Universität Berlin, Germany

Introduction: Highly Productive Programming

Immerse yourself in the following software development scenario: You're implementing a new feature in a large, GUI-heavy information system. You found a close match among the existing features and decided to duplicate and tweak the respective code and to eventually refactor it to get rid of unwanted duplications. You already made the copy and are starting to adapt it. You feel most productive, undistracted by your surroundings, deep in the zone, focused, *in the flow.*

You look at the code and read:

editStrategy.getGeometryType()

You notice something odd.

That's wrong, no need to call a method here.

You understand why it feels odd.

It's always the same!

You see the parts before your inner eye, see how they fit together.

It's: Polygon.

You start typing.

[tap tap]

You read the IDE's auto-completion and have second thoughts.

Or is it MultiPolygon?

You consider it. It would be the more general solution.

Could be. That's an open question.

There could be many reasons in favor or against. You make a decision.

Polygon is fine for now.

You write the code.

[tap tap]

You are satisfied and did all of this in just 15 seconds; life is great.

If you are a software developer, you know focus phases like this one. It's a great feeling when the ideas appear to be flowing directly from your brain through your fingers to become code. Who would spoil such an experience by adding another developer? At every point there would be endless discussions about which way is the best; and where there is no disagreement, there is misunderstanding because your colleagues often just don't get it.

Well, you are in for a surprise. The previous scenario was not a fictional inner monologue of a single developer. It is in fact an *actual dialogue* of two pair programmers, the two taking turns with the quotes. And it did indeed finish within 15 seconds.

Studying Pair Programming

Pair programming (PP) means that two programmers work together closely on the same programming task on a single computer.

Although super-efficient focus phases like the one described previously do happen during good pair programming sessions, most of the time pair programming evolves in a more pedestrian manner. So, does pair programming pay off overall?

To answer this, researchers have—multiple times—proceeded roughly like this:

- Devise a small task, let some developers (preferably students) solve it alone and some others in pairs, clock their time to completion, and compare the outcomes.

- Make sure the task is isolated and requires little background knowledge to ensure a level playing field for everyone.

- For greater control, assign partners randomly and set up identical workspaces for all of them.

Unfortunately, such settings do not reflect how pair programming happens in industry. The students work on machines they did not configure themselves and may not even know their partner. Additionally, consider the difference between short-term and long-term effects. In most student PP experiments, *productivity* is reduced to the number of passing (prewritten) test cases per time spent on the task. But that's not what commonly matters in industrial contexts. Here, top priorities might be a short time-to-market or value of implemented features, or they might be long-term goals such as keeping code maintainable and avoiding information silos.

Practitioners have by and large ignored the results of these experiments. You cannot expect to learn much about how PP affects real-world productivity from a setup that so drastically differs from the real world.

In our research, we take a different approach. We talk to tech companies and observe pair programming as it happens in the wild. The pairs are in their normal environment and choose everyday development tasks and programming partners as they always do. The only difference is that we record the interaction of the pair (through webcam and microphones) and their screen content for the duration of their session—typically between one and three hours. Over the years, we have collected more than 60 such session recordings from a dozen different companies.

We analyze this material in great detail by following a qualitative research process based on grounded theory [1]. The following observations are distilled from years of studying pair programming sessions of professional software developers.

Software Development As Knowledge Work

Let's take a step back first, though. What makes programming highly productive? Psychologist Mihaly Csikszentmihalyi described a type of high-productivity mental state, which is much admired (and sometimes achieved) by software developers: flow. He places a *flow* experience in that area between *boredom* and *anxiety* where difficulty (*challenges*) and one's *skills* are on par [2].

In software development, each task is somewhat unique with its own particular challenges. Consequentially, boredom is hardly an issue for software developers. The challenges while developing software, on the other hand, are not just a matter of skill. Many stem from a lack of understanding or *knowledge*. It might take many hours of sifting through modules to finally find the right spot to add that single new if condition required. Or to understand the unfamiliar concepts used by a new library. Or to follow a stacktrace that leads into uncharted territories from the legacy part of the system. The "fluency" of a developer depends on this type of understanding and familiarity with the software system at hand. The lack thereof is what mostly slows down software developers, more or less independent of their general skill level [3].

To work on a given task, developers (solos and pairs alike) need to understand the *system* (not *all* of it, but at least the parts relevant for the task at hand). And last week's understanding of some of these parts may already be outdated! High system understanding, let's call it *system knowledge*, is necessary to fix bugs and to implement new features.

Of course, general software development skills and expertise (we will call them *general knowledge*) are also relevant. General knowledge is about language idioms, design patterns and principles, libraries, technology stacks and frameworks, testing and debugging procedures, how to best use the editor or IDE, and the like. In contrast to the mostly product-oriented and relatively short-lived system knowledge, general knowledge is also process-oriented and more long-lived. (There is not necessarily a clear-cut separation between system and general knowledge—some pieces of knowledge may belong to both types.)

Developers build up system and general knowledge through experience, but it's not the mere number of years under their belt that matters but whether they possess applicable system and general knowledge for the task at hand.

What Actually Matters in Industrial Pair Programming

There are different PP use cases that developers regularly employ.

- *Getting help from a colleague*: One developer has been working on some task for some time and either finds it hard or needs to hand over the results, so another joins.

- *Tackling an issue together*: Two developers sit down to work on a problem together from the start.

- *Ramping up newbies*: A senior developer pairs with a new team member to bring her up to speed.

We found that it's not so much the particular PP use case that characterizes the dynamics of a session but what the two developers know and don't know—more precisely, their respective level of system knowledge and general knowledge **concerning today's specific task**. That's because most of the work in programming consists of steps to get your system knowledge to what is needed to solve the task (general knowledge may be helpful along the way). Once you have that, actually solving the task is usually a piece of cake—the kind of thing we described in the initial scene at the beginning. Therefore, it is the relevant *knowledge gaps* that count in programming.

Framing PP situations in terms of the involved system and general knowledge gaps helps to understand why some constellations are more beneficial than others and where pair programming actually pays off. There are three particularly interesting pair constellations we will discuss here. All of the examples in this chapter are real cases we saw in our data; we just left out some details and changed the developers' names.

Constellation A: System Knowledge Advantage

In this setting, one developer has a more complete or more up-to-date understanding of the task-relevant system parts. This is normal for the "getting help" use case but can occur in the other two as well.

Consider the scenario of developer Hannah who has been working on some task and is at one point joined by Norman. Hannah already looked at the code relevant for the current issue and performed some changes. Norman might have a better understanding of the system in general, but this does not cover all the details relevant for this task and of course not Hannah's recent code changes. Overall, Hannah has a *system knowledge advantage*.

If developers want to work as a pair, they need to address their relative system knowledge gap. Only if Norman understands what Hannah already found out and which changes she performed can they properly discuss ideas and agree on how to proceed.

But some of the pairs we observed, including this one, did not address the system knowledge advantage. Norman takes great pride in his programming skills and assumes he understands everything Hannah did. Hannah tries to explain an intricate matter she encountered, but Norman doesn't pay attention. It takes almost half an hour until Norman realizes his misconception of the status quo, lets Hannah explain it, and, at last, the pair becomes productive.

A pair situation where one partner has a system knowledge advantage (for whatever reason) is challenging because the relative system knowledge gap might be hardly visible but still needs to be addressed before the pair can move together at any speed. Better pairs therefore address the matter proactively at the beginning of their session. If your co-developer already worked on the issue, appreciate her system knowledge advantage, regardless of your own (perceived) seniority, and let her explain what she already has done and learned. We have heard that some developers with high system knowledge may also be reluctant to share what they know, but we did not observe such behavior in our pairs.

Constellation B: Collective System Knowledge Gap

When two developers start on a new task together (but not only then), they also usually both begin with an incomplete system understanding. The pair has a *collective system knowledge gap.*

Consider Paula and Peter who picked a new story card to work on. Both know their way around the system, so it doesn't take long until they find a place where to put the new feature. There are still some dependencies that need to be understood, so they navigate through the source code to complete their mental model. One time it's Paula who sees an important detail or relationship first, and the next time it's Peter. They are not deliberately taking turns here; one of them just happens to have a particular relevant idea first and will then explain it to the other. Sometimes Paula sees no need to dig deeper into the class inheritance graph, but Peter isn't as familiar with the current subsystem so he prefers to keep reading. Paula cuts him some slack and lets him take his time. In any case, both make sure their partner always stays on the same page so they can reach a high system understanding together.

Compared to the one-sided scenario of Hannah and Norman, Peter and Paula are better off. There are multiple strategies how they can build up the necessary system understanding as they don't depend on the knowledge flowing in one direction. The developers may stay closely together for a period of time, building up system knowledge in what we call an episode of knowledge "co-production" [4]. Alternatively, one developer may dig deeper in a self-paced manner, while the other is temporarily more passive ("pioneering production"). Either way, the development work done in such constellations can be very effective—*if* the pair takes care of maintaining their collaborative understanding as it grows, e.g., by explaining ("push") or getting asked about ("pull") what one of them just found out during his or her pioneering episode.

Constellation C: Complementary Knowledge

Every time a new developer joins the team, her system knowledge will be very low. But, depending on the partner's background and the nature of the current task, being low on system knowledge can occur in every PP use case. How well a pair performs then is limited by the general knowledge level of the low-system-knowledge developer. At least for the ramping-up use case, one would usually expect a twofold deficit, but this is not necessarily the case. Remember, what matters is the applicable knowledge for the current task, so with the right choice of task, even a fresh team member can score high on general knowledge, perhaps higher than a given senior. We've seen developers on their first work day teaching their programming partner design patterns and neat tricks in the IDE. Senior developers pair up in complementary constellations as well, since neither system understanding nor generic software development skill is evenly distributed in development teams.

Andy and Marcus, for instance, have quite different competencies. Andy advocates always writing clean, readable, and maintainable code, whereas Marcus has a pragmatic approach of patching things together that get the job done. A particular module that Marcus wrote a year ago needs an update, but since Marcus has trouble figuring out how it actually works, he asks Andy for help. Their session is a complementary one: Andy has a general knowledge advantage but is low on system knowledge, as he knows next to nothing about Marcus's module; Marcus, as the module's author, has a system knowledge advantage but lacks general knowledge to systematically improve its structure. Their session is mutually satisfactory, as they get the job done *and* Marcus learns a lot about code smells and refactorings.

So, Again: Does Pair Programming Pay Off?

You probably now appreciate that "Does pair programming pay off?" is an entirely inappropriate question, because

- It is hard to tell since too many different benefits have to be quantified and added up with respect to code functionality, code and design quality, and learning within the team.

- It depends, because different knowledge and task constellations provide very different opportunities for being efficient as a pair.

The key aspects are the knowledge gaps the developers have to deal with. To succeed with the task, the pair as a whole can benefit from various pieces of pertinent-for-this-task general software development knowledge and absolutely must possess or build the pertinent-for-this-task system knowledge. As system knowledge is more short-lived, it is usually the scarcer resource.

If the task-relevant knowledge of a pair is highly complementary, a pair programming session will probably pay for its cost multiple times. But even if it is not and the pair's visible work output is less than the two could have produced as two solo programmers, the PP session's midterm benefits in terms of learning provide ample opportunity for time saved in the future and mistakes not made in the future to pay off the higher expense today.

From an industrial perspective, an answer to the question might be this: given the dominant role of system knowledge for productive development, companies may not like to let their top-general-knowledge developer go, but they are *terrified* of losing their single top-system-knowledge developer. And frequent pair programming is an excellent technique to make sure system knowledge spreads continuously across a team.

Key Ideas

The following are the key ideas from this chapter:

- Pair programming will tend to pay off if the pair manages to have high process fluency.

- Pair programming will pay off if the pair members' knowledge is nicely complementary.

References

[1]   Stephan Salinger, Laura Plonka, Lutz Prechelt: "A Coding Scheme Development Methodology Using Grounded Theory for Qualitative Analysis of Pair Programming," Human Technology: An Interdisciplinary Journal on Humans in ICT Environments, Vol. 4 No. 1, 2008, pp.9–25

[2]   Mihaly Csikszentmihalyi: "Flow: The Psychology of Optimal Experience," Harper Perennial Modern Classics, 2008, p.74

[3]   Minghui Zhou, Audris Mockus: "Developer Fluency: Achieving True Mastery in Software Projects," Proceedings of the 18th ACM SIGSOFT International Symposium on Foundations of Software Engineering (FSE '10), 2010, pp.137–146

[4]   Franz Zieris, Lutz Prechelt: "On Knowledge Transfer Skill in Pair Programming," Proceedings of the 8th ACM/IEEE International Symposium on Empirical Software Engineering and Measurement, 2014

CHAPTER 22

Fitbit for Developers: Self-Monitoring at Work

André N. Meyer, University of Zurich, Switzerland

Thomas Fritz, University of Zurich, Switzerland

Thomas Zimmermann, Microsoft Research, USA

Self-Monitoring to Quantify Our Lives

Recently, we have seen an explosion in the number of devices and apps that we can use to track various aspects of our lives, such as the steps we walk, the quality of our sleep, or the calories we consume. People use devices such as the Fitbit activity tracker to increase and maintain their physical activity level by tracking their behavior, setting goals (e.g., 10,000 steps a day), and competing with friends. Generally, the miniaturization of self-tracking devices and their ubiquitousness make it possible to carry them around all the time and track more and more aspects of our lives. At the same time, studies have shown that these approaches can successfully encourage people to change their behavior, often motivated through persuasive technologies, such as goal-setting, social encouragement, and sharing mechanisms [3].

Notably, the interest for self-monitoring tools at the workplace is also increasing, and approaches to get insights into one's behavior and habits during work have emerged. Tools, such as RescueTime, allow users to get insights into the amount of time they spend in different applications on their computer, or Codealike visualizes to developers how they spent their time inside the IDE working in different code projects. Yet, little is known about developers' expectations of, their experience with, and the experience of self-monitoring in the workplace.

© The Author(s) 2019

C. Sadowski and T. Zimmermann (eds.), *Rethinking Productivity in Software Engineering*,
https://doi.org/10.1007/978-1-4842-4221-6_22

Self-Monitoring Software Developers' Work

There are numerous factors that impact a software developers' success and productivity at work: interruptions, coordinating work with the team, requirements that change, the infrastructure and office environment, and many more (see Chapter 8). Developers are often not aware of how these factors impact both their own productivity and the work of others [1]. The success of self-monitoring approaches in other domains suggests that self-monitoring can improve the awareness of developers about their work. Developers can reflect about their actions and factors that increase or decrease their productivity and make informed decisions to improve their productivity. The captured data about developers' work and productivity could further allow developers to compare themselves to other developers with similar job profiles.

This idea is related to Watts Humphrey's work on the Personal Software Process (PSP) that aims to help developers better understand and improve their performance by tracking their estimated and actual development of code [2]. The research conducted to evaluate PSP showed promising results, including more accurate project estimations and higher code quality. Today, with sensors and data trackers being more ubiquitous and accurate, we can give developers the ability to measure their work and behavior changes automatically and provide a much broader set of insights.

To learn the requirements and best practices for self-monitoring systems for software developers, we ran a mixed methods study: a literature review, a survey with more than 400 developers, and an iterative feedback-driven approach with 5 pilot studies and a total of 20 software developers. The study revealed developers' expectations of features, measures of interest, and possible barriers toward the adoption of self-monitoring systems. We then built PersonalAnalytics, a self-monitoring tool targeted to developers and studied its impact and use with 43 professional software developers who used it during three workweeks.

PersonalAnalytics consists of three components: the monitoring component, the self-reporting pop-up, and the retrospection. The monitoring component captures information from various individual aspects of software development work, including application use, documents accessed, development projects worked on, websites visited, and collaborative behaviors from attending meetings, as well as using e-mail, instant messaging, and code review tools. The data collection runs nonintrusively in the background, requiring no additional input from the developer. In addition, PersonalAnalytics prompts developers to reflect on their work periodically and to-self report their perceived productivity using a pop-up. To enable more multifaceted insights, the captured data is visualized in a daily retrospection (see Figure 22-1), which also provides a higher-level overview in a weekly summary and allows users to relate various data with each other.

In this chapter, we share the lessons that we learned from building and evaluating PersonalAnalytics and the insights that users received from using the tool. We describe why these insights are sometimes not enough for a behavior change. Chapter 16 further extends the discussion on dashboards in software engineering, by debating about their need and risks.

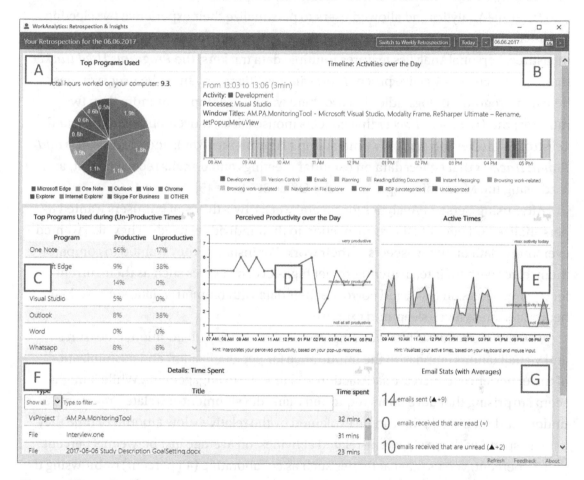

Figure 22-1. *Daily retrospection in PersonalAnalytics. (A) displays the distribution of time spent in the most used programs, (B) shows a timeline of time spent in different activities, (C) depicts the most used programs and the amount of time the user self-reported feeling productive/unproductive while using them, (D) illustrates the user's self- reported productivity over time, (E) visualizes the user input from mouse and keyboard, (F) shows a detailed breakdown of how much time was spent on different information artefacts (including web sites, files, e-mails, meetings, code projects, code reviews), and (G) summarizes e-mail-related data such as the number of e-mails sent/received.*

Supporting Various Individual Needs Through Personalization

In our preliminary studies, developers expressed an interest in a large number of different measures when it comes to the self-monitoring of their work. To support these individually varying interests in work measures, we included a wide variety of measures into PersonalAnalytics and allowed users to personalize their experience by selecting the measures that were tracked and visualized. To capture the relevant data for these measures, PersonalAnalytics features multiple data trackers: the *Programs Used tracker* that logs the currently active process and window titles every time the user switches between programs or logs "idle" in case there was no user input for more than two minutes; the *User Input tracker* that collects mouse clicks, movements, scrolling, and keystrokes (no key logging, only time-stamp of any pressed key); and the *Meetings and E-mail trackers* that collect data on calendar meetings and e-mails received, sent, and read using the Microsoft Graph API of the Office 365 Suite [5].

After using PersonalAnalytics for several weeks, two-thirds of our users wanted to personalize and better fit the retrospection to their individual needs. They also wanted even more data on other aspects of their work. For instance, they wanted to compare themselves with their team members, get high-level measures such as their current focus or progress on tasks, and correlate their data with biometric data, such as their heart rate, stress level, sleep, and exercise.

The diverse requests for extending PersonalAnalytics with additional measures and visualizations emphasize the importance for personalization and customization of the experience to increase satisfaction and long-term engagement. While it might seem surprising that developers requested many development-unrelated measures to understand their work, this can be explained by the relatively low amount of time they usually spend with development-related activities, on average just between 9 percent and 21 percent, versus other activities such as collaborating (45 percent) or browsing the Web (17 percent) [4].

Self-Reporting Increases Developers' Awareness About Efficiency

PersonalAnalytics asks users to answer a pop-up survey once an hour on their computer. The collected data allows us to learn more about productivity and the tasks that developers work on. During the pilot studies, users expressed aversion toward the pop-up, as it included too many questions. After refining the pop-up to include only one question asking users to self-report productivity for the past hour, most started to like the pop-up. Two-thirds of the users mentioned that the brief self-reports increased their awareness about work and helped them assess whether they had spent their past work hour effectively, whether they had spent it working on something of value, and whether they had made progress on their current task:

"The hourly interrupt helps to do a quick triage of whether you are stuck with some task/problem and should consider asking for help or taking a different approach."

PersonalAnalytics does not automatically measure productivity but rather lets users self-report their productivity. This was highly valued by users as many do not think an automated measure can accurately capture an individual's productivity, similar to what is discussed in Chapters 2 and 3.

"One thing I like about [PersonalAnalytics] a lot is that it lets me judge if my time was productive or not. So just because I was in a browser or Visual Studio doesn't necessarily mean I was being productive or not."

These findings emphasize that self-reporting can be of value to users as it increases their awareness about work. It is yet to be seen how long the positive effects of self-reporting last and whether users lose interest at some point.

Retrospection About Work Increases Developers' Self-Awareness

The users of PersonalAnalytics liked the ability to self-reflect on work and productivity with the retrospection that visualizes a personalized list of measures; 82 percent said that the retrospection increased their awareness and provided novel insights. The insights included how developers spend their time collaborating or making progress on tasks, their productivity over the course of a day, or the fragmentation at work. The time spent further rectified some misconceptions users had about their work, such as how much time they actually spent with e-mails and work-unrelated browsing (for example, Facebook):

"[PersonalAnalytics] is awesome! It helped confirm some impression I had about my work and provided some surprising and very valuable insights I wasn't aware of. I am apparently spending most of my time in Outlook."

"I did not realize I am as productive in the afternoons. I always thought my mornings were more productive but looks like I just think that because I spend more time on e-mail."

Actionable Insights Foster Productive Behavior Changes

Naturally, most users of self-monitoring tools don't just want to learn about themselves but also want to improve themselves. We asked the users of PersonalAnalytics about what behaviors they changed. Interestingly, this study resulted in ambivalent responses. Roughly half of the users changed some of their habits based on what they learned from reflecting about their work. This includes trying to better plan their work, e.g., by taking advantage of more productive afternoons, trying to optimize how they spend their time with e-mails, or trying to focus better and avoid distractions, e.g., by closing the office door or listening to music when the background noise is distracting. However, the other half of our users didn't change their behavior, either because they didn't want to change something or because they were not sure what to change. These users reported that some of the new insights were not concrete and actionable enough for knowing what or how to change:

"While having a retrospection on my time is a great first step, I gained interesting insights and realized some bad assumptions. But ultimately, my behavior didn't change much. Neither of them have much in way of a carrot or a stick."

"It would be nice if the tool could provide productivity tips, ideally tailored to my specific habits and based on insights about when I'm not productive."

To improve the actionability of the insights, users asked for specific recommendations that encourage more focused work, e.g., to start a focused work block using the Pomodoro technique, to recommend a break from work for when they were stuck on the same task for too long, all the way to intervening and blocking certain applications or websites for a certain time:

"Warnings if time on unproductive websites exceeds some amount, and perhaps provide a way for the user to block those sites (though not forced)."

Besides providing developers with personalized recommendations for improvements based on their work behavior, allowing them to benchmark and compare themselves with their team or other developers could lead to insights that are actionable enough to change a behavior. For example, PersonalAnalytics could collect anonymized measures about developers' work habits, such as fragmentation, time spent on activities, and achievements; correlate the measures with other developers with similar job profiles; and present the comparisons to the developer. Insights could reach from letting a developer know that others spend more time reading development blogs to further educate themselves, all the way to informing them that they spend way more time in meetings than most other developers.

Increasing Team Awareness and Solving Privacy Concerns

One drawback of giving developers insights only into their own productivity is that their behavior changes might have negative impact on the overall team productivity. As an example, a developer who blocks out interruptions at inopportune times to focus better could be blocking a co-worker who needs to ask a question or clarify things. Also receiving insights into how the team coordinates and communicates at work could help developers make more balanced adjustments with respect to the impact their behavior change might have on the team. For example, being aware of co-workers' most and least productive times in a workday could help to schedule meetings during times where everybody is the least productive and where interrupting one's work for a meeting has the least effect. Being more aware of the tasks each member of the team is currently working on and how much progress they are making could also be useful for managers or team leads to identify problems early, e.g., a developer who is blocked on a task or uses communication tools inefficiently, and take appropriate action.

However, these additions to a workplace self-monitoring tool would require aggregating and analyzing the data from multiple developers, which could result in privacy concerns given the possibly sensitive nature of the data. When creating tools that include data from multiple users, tool builders need to ensure privacy, e.g., by giving users full control over what data is being captured and shared, by properly obfuscating the data, and by being transparent about how the data is being used. If not done properly, this could severely increase pressure and stress for developers.

A recurring theme during the pilots and initial survey was the users' need to keep sensitive workplace data private. Some users were afraid that sharing data with their managers or team members could have severe consequences on their employment or increase pressure at work. To account for privacy needs at work, PersonalAnalytics, among other precautions, stores all logged data only locally on the user's machine, rather than having a centralized collection on a server. This enables users to retain full control of the captured data. While a few users were initially skeptical and had privacy concerns, no privacy complaints were received during the study, and the majority even shared their obfuscated data with us for analyzing it. While some users mentioned that they voluntarily exchanged their visualizations and insights with teammates to compare themselves, others mentioned that they would start to game the tool or go as far as leave the company, in case their manager would force them to run a tracking tool that would ignore their privacy concerns.

We think that the chances of misuse of the data and developers' sensitivity will decline if managements establish an environment where the data is used for process improvements only and not for HR-related evaluations. Also, making comparisons across teams with absolute data might lead to wrong conclusions since conditions can differ so much between different teams, projects, and systems. Hence, the delta improvements such as behavior changes and trends are important to consider. Nonetheless, further research is required to determine how workplace data can be leveraged to improve team productivity, while respecting and protecting employee privacy, including data protection regulations such as the GDPR [7]. This topic is explored in more depth in Chapter 15.

Fostering Sustainable Behaviors at Work

One way to foster software developers' productivity is to increase their self-awareness about work and productivity through self-monitoring. We found that regular self-reflection using the retrospection and minimal-intrusive self-reports allows developers to increase their awareness about time spent at work, their collaboration with others, their productive and unproductive work habits, and their productivity in general. You also learned that developers are interested in a large and diverse set of measurements and correlations within the data and that the insights gained from looking at the visualized data is not always concrete and actionable enough to motivate behavior changes. Detailed descriptions of the studies and more findings can be found in the corresponding paper [6]. In the future, we could imagine that self-monitoring tools for developers at their workplace will be extended to include an even richer set of measures that can be correlated with each other. For example, by allowing integrations with development tools (e.g., GitHub, Visual Studio, or Gerrit) and biometric sensors (e.g., Fitbit), developers could be warned to carefully review their changes again before checking in a breaking code change after having slept badly in the night before. Another possibility to foster productive behavior changes is goal-setting. Workplace self-monitoring tools could be extended to not only enable developers to gain rich insights but also motivate them to identify meaningful goals for self-improvements and allow them to monitor their progress toward reaching them. Finally, anonymized or aggregated parts of the data could be shared with the team, to increase the awareness within the team and reduce interruptions, to improve the scheduling of meetings, and to enhance the coordination of task assignments.

We open-sourced PersonalAnalytics on Github (`https://github.com/sealuzh/ PersonalAnalytics`), opening it up to contributions and making it available for use.

Key Ideas

Here are the key ideas from this chapter:

- Self-monitoring personal behavior at work can improve developers' performance for a substantial proportion of developers.

- Self-reporting productivity allows developers to briefly reflect about their efficiency and progress at work and take timely actions that improve productivity.

- Developers have a diverse interest in measures about their work, ranging from development related data to data about their collaboration in the team, all the way to biometric data.

References

[1]   Dewayne E. Perry, Nancy A. Staudenmayer, and Lawrence G. Votta. 1994. People, Organizations, and Process Improvement. IEEE Software 11, 4 (1994), 36–45.

[2]   Watts S. Humphrey. 1995. A discipline for software engineering. Addison-Wesley Longman Publishing Co., Inc.

[3] Thomas Fritz, Elaine M Huang, Gail C Murphy, and Thomas Zimmermann. 2014. Persuasive Technology in the Real World: A Study of Long-Term Use of Activity Sensing Devices for Fitness. In Proceedings of the International Conference on Human Factors in Computing Systems.

[4] André N. Meyer, Laura E Barton, Gail C Murphy, Thomas Zimmermann, and Thomas Fritz. 2017. The Work Life of Developers: Activities, Switches and Perceived Productivity. Transactions of Software Engineering (2017), 1–15.

[5] Microsoft Graph API. https://graph.microsoft.io.

[6] André N. Meyer, Gail C Murphy, Thomas Zimmermann, and Thomas Fritz. 2018. Design Recommendations for Self-Monitoring in the Workplace: Studies in Software Development. To appear at CSCW'18, 1–24.

[7] European General Data Protection Regulation (GDPR). 2018. https://www.eugdpr.org.

CHAPTER 23

Reducing Interruptions at Work with FlowLight

Manuela Züger, University of Zurich, Switzerland

André N. Meyer, University of Zurich, Switzerland

Thomas Fritz, University of Zurich, Switzerland

David Shepherd, ABB Corporate Research, USA

The Cost of Interruptions at Work

In today's collaborative workplaces, communication is a major activity and is important to achieve a company's goals. Especially given the sociotechnical nature of software development, communication between stakeholders is important to successfully complete projects. Communication thereby takes many forms, such as e-mail and instant messaging, phone calls, or talking to colleagues in person. Despite the overall importance of communication, it can also impede productivity of knowledge workers (see Chapter 7 for a definition of knowledge work). In fact, around 13 times a day, a knowledge worker gets interrupted and suspends his or her current activity to respond to a co-worker asking a question, to read an e-mail, or to pick up a call. Each of these interruptions takes an average of 15 to 20 minutes and leads to an increased work fragmentation. Not surprisingly, interruptions are considered one of the biggest impediments to productivity, costing substantial time and money ($588 billion per year in the United States) [1]. Additionally, interruptions have been shown to cause stress and frustration for the interrupted person and lead to an increase in the errors created after resuming the interrupted task [2, 3]. These negative effects and costs of

© The Author(s) 2019

C. Sadowski and T. Zimmermann (eds.), *Rethinking Productivity in Software Engineering*,
https://doi.org/10.1007/978-1-4842-4221-6_23

interruptions are particularly high when the interruptions happen at inopportune moments and cannot be postponed. This is why in-person interruptions are one of the most disruptive types of interruptions. Compared to other types of interruptions such as an e-mail notification or an instant message, it is difficult to ignore a person waiting next to the desk and first finish the current task at hand. Yet, the interruption cost can be reduced significantly by mediating interruptions to more opportune moments, e.g., moments when the mental load is lower, when the worker might have taken a short break anyways, after just finishing a task or during work on less demanding tasks. Refer to Chapter 9 for more details on interruptions.

FlowLight: A Light to Indicate When to Interrupt

The FlowLight is an approach we developed to optimize the timing of interruptions and reduce the cost of external interruptions. The FlowLight is a physical desk "traffic light" and an application that computes and indicates the current availability to co-workers (see Figure 23-1) [4]. Similar to the colors of a traffic light and the status colors of instant messaging services, the FlowLight has four states: away (yellow), available (green), busy (red), and do not disturb (red pulsating). The physical LED lamp is usually mounted on a person's desk, cubicle separator, or office entrance to be easily visible by co-workers. Depending on personal preference, the light can be places so that it is visible for the workers themselves, for use as a personal flow monitor, or on a less visible place, to prevent distraction. After installing the FlowLight application on a user's computer, it calculates the users' "flow status"—the availability for interruptions—based on the user's current and historical computer interaction data. A change in flow status results in an update of FlowLight's LED color, as well as an update to the user's Skype status, resulting in muted notifications at times of low availability for interruptions.

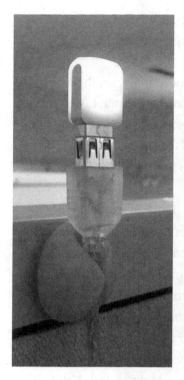

Figure 23-1.   FlowLight in use at the office

Evaluation and Benefits of FlowLight

We evaluated the effects of FlowLight in a large-scale field study with 449 participants from 12 countries and 15 sites of a multinational corporation. The participants worked in various areas such as software development, other engineering, or project management and evaluated FlowLight while working normally for several weeks. Our goal was to investigate how knowledge workers were using it and how interactions and perceptions of productivity changed after introducing the FlowLights. Overall, the FlowLight reduced the amount of interruptions significantly, by 46 percent, without eliminating important interruptions, and participants continued using the FlowLight even long after the study period ended. Participants also stated that the FlowLight increased awareness of the potential harm of interruptions, that they generally paid attention to their colleagues' FlowLight, were more respectful of each other's work and focus, and either waited for a more convenient time or switched to a different media to communicate with their colleague when the interruption was not urgent.

"The pilot increased the sensitivity to interruption[s]. Team members think more about whether an interrupt is necessary and try to find a suitable time."

"People ask each other if they are available, even when the light is green, even to people with no light. When I see the colleague I want to ask a question (...) has a red light, then I wait a while, or write an e-mail."

These positive effects also led to an increased feeling of productivity, on the one hand because of the increased amount of undisrupted time to work on one's own tasks, and on the other hand because some participants actually liked to observe their status and felt motivated when they realized that the algorithm detected that they were "in flow."

"I definitely think it resulted in less interruptions both in person and via Skype. This resulted in more focus and ability to finish work."

"When I notice that my light is turning yellow, and I'll feel like, 'Oh yeah, I've been idle' and then I do something...I think the other way, yeah, there's some effect there too. Like, if I see that it's red, or even flashing red, then I'm like, 'Yeah, I've been very active, or productive, I should keep that going.' At the same time, I think it's also a little bit distracting too. Sometimes just because the light is there, I turn around to check it."

Finally, most participants stated that their FlowLight's automatic state changes were accurate. Nonetheless, there is potential for improvement. For instance, in situations when a knowledge worker experiences a high cognitive load but is not interacting with the mouse or keyboard intensely (e.g., when reading complicated text or code), the FlowLight will signal the user to be available for interruptions. One way to improve the algorithm is to integrate more fine-grained data, such as application usage or biometric data. Application usage data could, for instance, allow the algorithm to tailor to specific development activities, such as indicating no availability during debugging or availability after code commits. Data from biometric sensors, such as heart rate variability, could be used to more directly measure cognitive load or stress, which in turn influences a person's availability for interruptions.

Key Success Factors of FlowLight

The iterative process of developing and evaluating FlowLight revealed many insights on the factors that contributed to the FlowLight's success.

Pay Attention to Users

For the development of the FlowLight, we followed an iterative, user-driven design process. In particular, we made sure to roll out early versions of the FlowLight to receive user feedback and to improve the approach iteratively. This iterative design helps to identify issues that might be small with respect to the underlying concept of the approach but might have a big impact on user acceptance. For instance, in the beginning we set the FlowLight to busy (red) and do not disturb (red pulsating) for approximately 19 percent of the day based on previous research. However, early users perceived the FlowLight to be red too often and noted that the state switched too frequently so that it was almost annoying. Therefore, we decreased the percentage and introduced and refined a smoothing function.

Furthermore, the early pilot studies revealed that the FlowLight needs to account for specific job roles, such as managers. While software developers value time spent on coding tasks without any interruptions and Skype messages muted (the "do not disturb" mode) and sometimes wanted to increase this undisrupted time, managers want to be available at all times. Therefore, we added a feature to manually set the do not disturb mode for longer periods as well as a feature to completely disable the do not disturb mode for managers.

Finally, the user feedback also illustrated how the company culture and office layout can impact the value of the approach. While the FlowLight was valuable to almost all teams, there were two smaller teams of people sitting very close together in the same office who were generally interested in reducing interruptions but did not want to spend the extra effort of looking up and checking for the FlowLight status before asking a question to a colleague. In these two teams, the FlowLight did not have any value despite the teams' wish to reduce interruptions, so we uninstalled it shortly after.

Focus on Simplicity

A lot of time and effort during the development of the FlowLight went into creating an easy and simple setup and installation process. For instance, the application can be installed by running an installer in the course of a few seconds. To set up the FlowLights in an office, we further had a member of the research-team visit the team, introduce the functionality to the whole office site, and assist users in placing the lamps in highly visible spots for the co-workers.

We further focused on creating an application that is intuitive and runs smoothly without user interaction. Knowledge workers have used manual strategies for indicating availability before, e.g., using manual busy lights or headphones, but often abandoned them because of the additional effort. The automatic nature of the FlowLight for changing the availability status appealed to the participants and led to the continued usage of the light long after the end of the study. Furthermore, the intuitive design of the FlowLight that combined the idea of a traffic light with availability states common in instant messaging applications made it easy for users and co-workers to pick up the meaning and reason of the FlowLight and contributed to its success.

Pay Attention to Privacy Concerns

Productivity is a sensitive topic in the work environment and monitoring sensitive work-related data for productivity reasons can quickly result in privacy concerns. Since FlowLight harnesses sensitive and work-related data to calculate a person's availability state, we provide transparency of the data tracking and store the collected data only locally on the users' computers. We asked users to share their data with us only at the end of the study and at the same time gave them the opportunity to delete or obfuscate any data they did not want to share.

We further focused on tracking as little data as possible. While we considered leveraging application usage data from the beginning, we ended up only tracking mouse and keyboard interaction to reduce invasiveness and privacy concerns that users raised in the beginning. Once users appreciated the FlowLight and its value, they themselves asked for refining the algorithm by taking into account further data using additional tracking methods. For instance, users asked us to integrate application usage data to avoid getting into the do not disturb or busy state when reading social media during lunchtime or to make sure they are in busy when they focus on debugging in the IDE. By letting users drive the data collection, users see a clear value from using a rich data set and privacy concerns can be reduced. With productivity in the workplace, peer pressure and competition among team members is another concern. Participants were concerned about being the one who is never "busy" and therefore considered as not very focused by their peers. We designed the FlowLight in a way that reduces the possibility for competition or peer pressure. In particular, we set the FlowLight to be approximately the same amount of time in the busy and do not disturb states for each participant and day by setting the thresholds for changing the states based on historical data of each individual. We further allowed users to change their light manually and broadly communicated that the available state is not representative of "not working" but that it only indicates the availability for interruptions.

Focus on Value First, Not on Accuracy

While each study participant mentioned ways in which the FlowLight's accuracy could be improved, the accuracy of our approach was good enough to lead to a large and quick adoption. We found that as long as the FlowLight provided some value to its users, was easy to understand by everyone, and did not require much effort, the accuracy was only a secondary concern. Therefore, our focus on simplicity and value first paid off, and now that we have a large user base and can test different options, we have time to improve the accuracy of the flow algorithm.

Let Users Surprise You

The main intention of the FlowLight was to foster awareness of a person's availability for interruptions to co-workers. However, many users found their own way of using it. For instance, they used it as a personal monitor to reflect on their own productivity or also to check whether someone is in the office before going over to a colleague's desk either via checking the light bulb from a distance or looking up the person's Skype status. Getting feedback from users early on allowed us to identify and potentially extend such new use cases that were not anticipated by the creators.

Summary

FlowLight is a traffic-light-like LED that indicates when knowledge workers are available for a chat or to answer a question. A study with 449 participants has shown that the FlowLight decreases interruptions, improves productivity, and promotes awareness on the topic of interruptions. Overall, the FlowLight project was very successful, picked up by various media (`http://sealuzh.github.io/FlowTracker/`), and study participants continue to use it. We believe that the key factors for successful adoption are to ensure that the approach addresses a problem of its users in a way that is easy to install and operate, respects privacy concerns, and is adapted to the users' needs and use cases.

Get Your Own FlowLight

Do you want to get your own FlowLight? We are happy to collaborate with Embrava (`https://embrava.com/flow`) to bring FlowLight to a wider audience. The office productivity company licensed the FlowLight software and plans to offer a subscription for an integration of the automatic algorithm into their own products, such as the BlyncLight status light or the Lumena headset with status light.

Key Ideas

The following are the key ideas from the chapter:

- Interruptions, and especially in-person interruptions, are one of the biggest impediments to productivity.

- FlowLight indicates the availability for interruptions to co-workers in the office with a traffic light like LED.

- FlowLight reduced interruptions by 46 percent and increased the awareness on interruptions, and users felt more productive.

- Success factors of FlowLight are its simplicity and continued development using a user-driven design process.

References

[1] Spira, Jonathan B., and Joshua B. Feintuch. "The cost of not paying attention: How interruptions impact knowledge worker productivity." Report from Basex (2005).

[2] Bailey, Brian P., and Joseph A. Konstan. "On the need for attention-aware systems: Measuring effects of interruption on task performance, error rate, and affective state." Computers in human behavior 22.4 (2006): 685–708.

[3] Mark, Gloria, Daniela Gudith, and Ulrich Klocke. "The cost of interrupted work: more speed and stress." Proceedings of the SIGCHI conference on Human Factors in Computing Systems. ACM, 2008.

[4] Züger, Manuela, Manuela Züger, Christopher Corley, André N Meyer, Boyang Li, Thomas Fritz, David Shepherd, Vinay Augustine, Patrick Francis, Nicholas Kraft, and Will Snipes. "Reducing Interruptions at Work: A Large-Scale Field Study of FlowLight." Proceedings of the 2017 CHI Conference on Human Factors in Computing Systems. ACM, 2017.

CHAPTER 24

Enabling Productive Software Development by Improving Information Flow

Gail C. Murphy, University of British Columbia, Canada

Mik Kersten, Tasktop Technologies, Canada

Robert Elves, Tasktop Technologies, Canada

Nicole Bryan, Austin, Texas, USA

At its core, software development is an information-intensive knowledge generation and consumption activity. Information about markets and trends are analyzed to create requirements that describe what a desired software system needs to do. Those requirements become information for software developers to use to produce models and code that, when executed, provide the behavior desired for the system. The execution of a system creates more information that can be analyzed as to how the software performs, and so on.

We are interested in how software tools can enable the productive development of software. Our hypothesis has been that software development productivity can be increased by improving the access and flow of information between the humans and tools involved in creating software systems. In this chapter, we review an evolution of technologies that we have introduced based on this hypothesis. These technologies are in use by large software development organizations and have been shown to improve

© The Author(s) 2019

C. Sadowski and T. Zimmermann (eds.), *Rethinking Productivity in Software Engineering*,
https://doi.org/10.1007/978-1-4842-4221-6_24

software developer productivity. The description of these technologies highlights how productivity can be considered at the individual (the Mylyn tool), team (the Tasktop Sync tool), and organizational levels (the Tasktop Integration Hub).

Mylyn: Improving Information Flow for the Individual Software Developer

A software system cannot exist without code that executes to provide the behavior of the software system. To produce code for a system, a software developer must deal with an amazing amount of information, such as written requirements, documentation about libraries and modules, and test suites. The result for a developer can be information overload. Figure 24-1 shows a snapshot of an integrated development environment as a software developer works on a bug fix. The developer is consulting a description of the bug (A), the other hidden tabs in the main portion of the screen hold source code already accessed as the developer is investigating the bug, the result of a search on a portion of a method name described in the stack trace is shown in the bottom part of the screen (B), and the left side provides access to the many bits of code making up the system (C). Within this environment, to produce code for a new feature or a fix for a bug, the developer must perform many navigation steps to access the contextual information needed. The friction just to get started on a task can be significant. The more complex the system, the more information a developer may need to find and cognitively maintain to start work on the task. If the developer worked on only one task a day, the friction might be manageable. However, studies have shown that developers, on average, work on approximately five to ten tasks per day, spending only a few minutes at any one time on a particular task before switching to another task [3]. As a result, developers constantly spend time finding, and re-finding, the bits of information they need to work on a task, impeding their productivity.

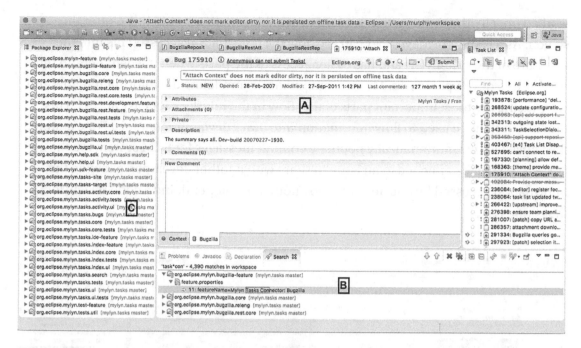

Figure 24-1. *Information overload in integrated development environment*

To address these points of information flow friction for an individual software developer, we created the Mylyn task-focused interface for integrated development environments [2]. Mylyn changes the paradigm with which a developer interacts with the artifacts making up a software system by framing a developer's work explicitly around the tasks performed. With Mylyn, a developer begins work on a task by activating a task description. A task description may be a description of a bug or a new feature to develop in an issue tracker. Once a task is activated, Mylyn begins tracking the information a developer accesses as part of the task, modeling the developer's degree of interest in information using an algorithm based on the frequency and recency with which information is accessed. For instance, if a developer accesses a particular method definition only once as part of a task, as work on the task progresses, the interest level of that method in the degree-of- interest model will reduce. If another method is edited heavily by the developer as part that task, the interest level will remain high. These degree-of-interest values can be used in several ways. For example, the model can be used to focus the development environment on just the information that matters for a task. Figure 24-2 shows the development environment interface when focused on the same bug-fixing task introduced earlier. In this view, the development environment provides easy access to just the information that the developer needs for the task being worked on: all other information is easily accessible but does not visibly clutter the screen. As a result, the developer can see how the information accessed fits into the structure of the system (A) and has easier access to the parts when needed. Behind the scenes, as a developer works, Mylyn is automatically modeling the information flow and is surfacing the most important parts of that flow in the interface for easy access. This model can then be used to flow information into other development tools. For example, the active task can automatically populate commit messages for SCM systems such as Git. Or it can be attached to an issue to share with another developer, allowing the information accessed by one developer to another developer doing a code review for that same issue.

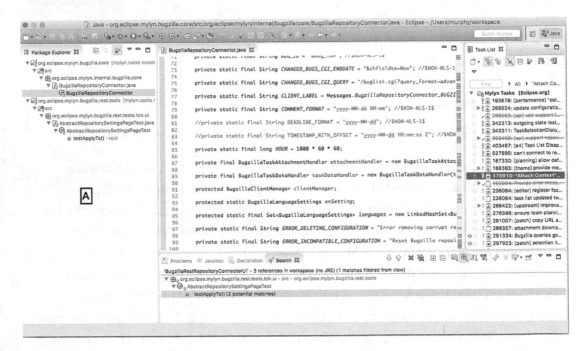

Figure 24-2. *Mylyn's task-focused interface active in integrated development environment*

To determine whether Mylyn helps improve productivity by giving developers access to information when it is needed, we conducted a longitudinal field study. In this study, we recruited 99 participants who were practicing software developers using the Eclipse integrated software development environment. For the first two weeks of the study, participants worked with the integrated development environment as normal. The development environment was instrumented to collect logs of how the developer worked. Once the developer had reached a threshold of coding activity, the developer was invited to install the Mylyn tool within their integrated development environment. Further logs of coding activity were then collected as the developer worked using Mylyn. To ensure we could reasonably compare the activities before and after the installation of Mylyn, we defined thresholds of coding activity for acceptance into the study. Sixteen participants met our thresholds for study acceptance. For these participants, we compared their edit ratios—–the relative amount of edit and navigation events in their logs—both before and after Mylyn use. We found that the use of Mylyn improved the edit ratio of developers, adding support that Mylyn reduces friction of accessing information and improves productivity when looked at through the lens of actions performed. In other words, developers coded more, and navigated around looking for information less, when the tool focused their coding and supported their context switching. Mylyn is an open source plugin for the Eclipse integrated development environment (`www.eclipse.org/mylyn`) and has been use by developers around the world for more than 13 years.

Tasktop Sync: Improving Information Flow for the Development Team

In working with organizations using the open source Mylyn tool, and a commercial version of Mylyn our company (Tasktop Technologies Inc.) produced called Tasktop Dev, we learned about additional friction for accessing information that was occurring at the team level. Increasingly, companies have been moving away from the use of one vendor's tools to support all development activities to the use of best-of-breed tools for each development activity, chosen individually by the different teams in the organization. As a result, business analysts who focus on requirements gathering may be using a tool from one vendor, the developers writing code using another vendor's tool, the testers a tool from a third vendor, and so on. While each best-of-breed tool may enable productive work, the information flow between teams is impeded as information must be manually re-entered into a tool used by another team or moved in some other form, such as via a spreadsheet or an e-mail. Information can also fail to flow, causing difficulties in the development, such as errors when a given team may not have access to needed information. With the increasing agility and need for speed of delivery in software development, a lack of automation of information flow between teams is a major impediment. A Forester survey in 2015 identified that gaps in the process of integrating tools had become the number-one source of failure and cost overruns of efforts to modernize the software lifecycle in organizations. The impact on the productivity of teams due to friction in the flow of information between teams leads to a decrease in team productivity.

Through our work on Mylyn and Tasktop Dev, we have gained expertise on the variety of ways in which tasks—a unit of work—are described in the best-of-breed tools used by different teams in large software development organizations. We realized it was possible to abstract the notion of a task across these tools and to enable automatic movement of task information between tools. In 2009, we introduced a tool called Tasktop Sync. Figure 24-3 provides an abstraction of what Tasktop Sync supports. By serving as a platform, Tasktop Sync enables the flow of task information between tools from many different kinds of teams, from the project management office through to handling service requests.

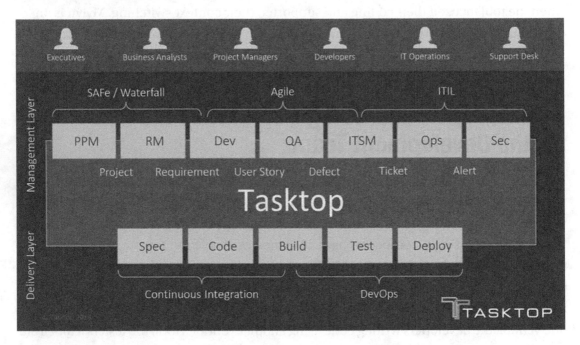

Figure 24-3. *Tasktop Sync Platform view*

Tasktop Sync works in the background, synchronizing information across tools in near real time. Tasktop Sync accesses information in the tools via each tool's API. As each tool represents task information using a different schema and within a different workflow, Tasktop Sync relies on configuration information to map and transform data between the tools. For example, a task in a tool used by a business analyst may be a requirement with a short-form identifier and a longer name. When synchronized to a developer's tool, the title of the associated task in a developer's tool may become a concatenation of the identifier and the longer name from the requirements tool. The synchronization rules extend beyond simple data transformations, such as concatenation. When a data value indicates workflow status, such as whether a defect is new or has just been reopened, the status of the information must be appropriately mapped to workflow in other tools. Sometimes the matching of workflow information may require multiple changes of state of the data in another tool, such as requiring a task to move from a created state automatically into an open state.

Synchronizing information between tools also requires the interpretation and management of context of tasks between tools. In a business analyst's tool, a task (a requirement) may exist within a hierarchy. This hierarchical context must be mapped appropriately to other tools. For instance, an issue tracker used by a developer may need this information represented in an epic and user story structure. As tools can sometimes represent contextual information in multiple ways, including as links to information in other tools, maintaining context during a synchronization requires careful handling.

As software development is not a linear activity, to support teams appropriately, Tasktop Sync enables bidirectional synchronization. For instance, if tasks created by a business analyst in their tool have been synchronized to a developer's tool and the developer subsequently starts working on the task and adds a comment requiring clarification on the nature of the task, the comment can be automatically synchronized back to the business analyst's tool. Combined, these capabilities of Tasktop Sync means that a team member can work in a best-of-breed tool optimized for the work they perform, yet they can interact directly with other team members in near real time in their own best-of-breed tool choices.

Tasktop Sync has been used both within and between organizations to improve the flow of information between teams involved in a software development project. A credit card processing company used Tasktop Sync to integrate the results of tests from a testing automation tool into a tool used by the organization to chart project progress. A major automotive manufacturer used Tasktop Sync to synchronize change request and defect data between their suppliers' tools and the tools used in their organization. An important factor in the automotive manufacturer's case was the ability to configure workflow differences between multiple repositories in use in particular instances of a given tool by a supplier. The manufacturer reported times of less than three seconds to synchronize information between a supplier and themselves, providing much needed transparency between software that would be integrated into the manufacturer's product.

Tasktop Integration Hub: Improving Information Flow for a Software Development Organization

As we have been working to improve the flow of information in software development, there have been substantial changes in the approaches taken by organizations to develop software, largely catalyzed by the DevOps movement. Over the last ten years, the DevOps movement has helped organizations consider how to increase automation in all parts of the software life cycle and to increase the focus on simultaneously achieving quality in software with faster delivery times [1]. Thinking about the overall software delivery process has led to the emergence of a consideration of the value stream of software delivery in which the delivery process is considered as an end-to-end feedback loop of flowing value to customers in a way that optimizes for business value. As a simple example, consider an organization with two software development delivery teams: one that delivers a mobile app and another that delivers a web-based app to the company's insurance business. The first team is able to deliver more customer-facing features per month than the second team. By analyzing the value stream of software delivery for each delivery team, it is determined that the mobile app team uses an automated testing process that speeds the creation of new features with high quality compared to the web-based app team. The organization may use this information to improve the software development processes across more of its teams.

At Tasktop, our products have continued to evolve. Our focus remains on improving information flow across the organization, and our latest product offering, Tasktop Integration Hub, has replaced the Sync and Dev products. Tasktop Integration Hub enables visibility across an organization's value stream of software delivery. Building on our knowledge of synchronizing data across the tools used by different teams, Tasktop Integration Hub provides insight into what information flows are occurring between different tools for different projects. Figure 24-4 shows a sample Tasktop Integration Landscape drawn automatically from the integrations various teams have set up between their tools. A landscape enables an organization to consider, and optimize, the steps that are occurring in their software development process. As it executes, Tasktop Integration Hub captures data about how information is flowing across tools used by the development teams. This data enables cross-toolchain reporting so that such aspects of development as the time to value from requirement being specified to being deployed can be tracked. The need for Tasktop Integration Hub came from the sheer number of teams and tools that an enterprise IT organization needs to connect in order to support the flow and access of information across their software delivery value streams.

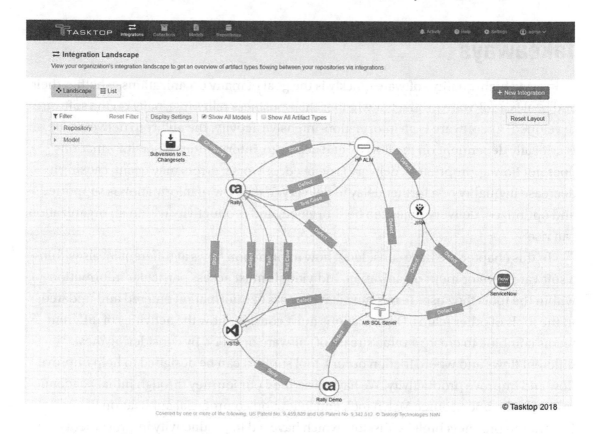

Figure 24-4. *Tasktop integration landscape*

By supporting visibility into the software life cycle and by supporting an ability to track metrics as changes to the life cycle are introduced, Tasktop Integration Hub enables a determination of where friction is occurring in the life cycle, a precursor to being able to implement changes to reduce the friction and improve productivity at an organizational level.

Returning to the example of the mobile app and web-based app delivery teams within an organization, Tasktop Integration Hub provides an explicit view of how information flows across the tools used by each delivery team and can report metrics on how many customer-facing features are progressing through each of the tools used by different parts of the delivery teams. Differences between various teams in this flow of information through the value stream can be used to question different approaches

289

being taken and to identify where there are opportunities for improving productivity through process changes, such as introducing automated testing.

Takeaways

Delivering high-quality software quickly is the goal of many organizations, whether their end goal is a software product or whether their business relies internally on the software developed. As software is an information-intensive activity, the ability to deliver value is critically dependent on the flow of, and access to, information. When information does not flow appropriately, delivery is delayed, or worse, errors may occur, causing a decrease in quality or a further delay in delivery. If the flow of information is supported and optimized, delivery times can be shortened, and productivity within an organization can rise.

In this chapter, we have considered how information flows at different levels within a software development organization. Individuals must access particular information within the tools they use. Teams must have access to information entered and updated in the tools of other teams. Organizations must consider how the activities of different teams combine to create a value stream of software delivery. By considering these different flows and where friction occurs, tool support can be designed to help improve flow and improve productivity. We have described our journey through initial academic research, the open source Mylyn tool, and follow-on commercial application life-cycle integration products built by Tasktop, which have led to productivity improvements at the individual, team, and organization levels. Given how much software has penetrated into every kind of business, improving the productivity of creating software means improving the productivity of a vast number of businesses. Further analysis of information flow may lead to additional productivity improvements in the future that can have far reaching impacts into healthcare, commerce, and manufacturing domains to name just a few.

Key Ideas

The following are the key ideas of this chapter:

- The flow of information among software developers is directly related to productivity.

- When the flow of information is adequately supported, delivery times on software can be shortened, and productivity within an organization can rise.

- Individuals, teams, and organizations need different kinds of support for information flow.

- Individuals, teams, and organizations can benefit from information flow that respects the best-of-breed and individual tools in which they can work most effectively.

References

[1]   Humble, J. Continuous delivery sounds great, but will it work here. CACM, 61 (4), pp. 34–39.

[2]   Kersten, M. and Murphy, G.C., Using task context to improve programmer productivity. In Proc. of FSE, 2006, pp. 1–11.

[3]   Meyer, A.N., Fritz, T., Murphy, G.C., Zimmermann, T. Software Developers' Perceptions of Productivity. In Proc. of FSE, 2014, pp. 19–29.

CHAPTER 25

Mindfulness as a Potential Tool for Productivity

Marieke van Vugt, University of Groningen, The Netherlands

A Definition of Mindfulness

No day passes without seeing mindfulness mentioned in popular blogs as *the* solution for productivity. Many large companies offer mindfulness classes. Why would mindfulness be useful for productivity? Before discussing that question, it is important to first define mindfulness. Traditionally it has been defined by the originator of the mindfulness movement Jon Kabat-Zinn as "paying attention in a particular way, in the present moment, nonjudgmentally" [5]. A common way you could go about this is by bringing your attention to your breath and then gently monitoring whether it is still there. Before you know it, you will realize that your attention has wandered to a different location. Once you notice your attention has wandered (which can occur after two minutes but also after half an hour!), you are to simply drop the thought and return to the breath. This is the way in which you pay attention, and it is in the present moment because you do not linger on the past nor anticipate the future. This way of paying attention also has a quality of nonjudgmentalness because when you realize you have been distracted, you are not to get frustrated with yourself and blame yourself for being a terrible mindfulness practitioner, but instead you can realize that this is the natural thing the mind does and then start again by paying attention to the breath. You can say that you try to become friends with your mind, monitoring what it does with a sense of chuckle and amusement (one traditional Buddhist way of phrasing that is "be like an old man, watching a child play"). Mindfulness tends to be practiced in sessions ranging from three minutes to one hour.

© The Author(s) 2019
C. Sadowski and T. Zimmermann (eds.), *Rethinking Productivity in Software Engineering*,
https://doi.org/10.1007/978-1-4842-4221-6_25

Mindfulness is a secular contemplative practice that was developed by Jon Kabat-Zinn on the basis of (mostly) Buddhist meditation techniques. It is only one of many meditative techniques that vary among others in the object of the meditation (which is not limited to the breath but could be anything, including code on a computer screen), the width of the attentional focus, and the desired outcome [7]. While mindfulness is typically used by people to make themselves feel better and less stressed, the traditional goal of mindfulness is to make the mind more pliable such that it is less overpowered by the negative emotions of greed, hatred, and delusion (the three main negative emotions in the Buddhist context). A mindful state is thus traditionally not a goal in itself but rather a means to live one's life more ethically and to become a more kind and compassionate human being.

Mindfulness for Productivity?

Mindfulness is widely used in hospitals to reduce stress and support healing. It has also been touted as a solution for employees to allow them to maintain well-being in a very stressful environment. The idea is that you learn to relax by bringing your attention to your breath and not taking your thoughts so seriously. Some preliminary evidence for mindfulness' effect on stress reduction was given by a seminal study [3], which showed that employees of a biotech firm, when given a mindfulness intervention, felt less stressed and showed an improved immune response.

In addition, it is generally thought that mindfulness helps to counteract distraction and mindlessness and thereby allow one to concentrate for longer periods of time without interruption. For this claim there is much less evidence, as will be discussed in the next section. While the practice of mindfulness can be considered to be a training of attention, this is not the main point of mindfulness. Moreover, it is not clear that the small amounts of attention training in mindfulness are in fact sufficient to actually substantially improve concentration. This chapter will therefore critically evaluate the cognitive benefits of mindfulness, discuss the benefits of mindfulness for emotional resilience, and then suggest how mindfulness may be specifically applied in the context of software engineering.

Cognitive Benefits of Mindfulness

There has been an increasing amount of laboratory research investigating the cognitive benefits of mindfulness. Overall the benefits are modest, as indicated by a meta-analysis [11]. One important reason for this is that most likely a large amount of practice is needed before cognitive functions are improved. Nevertheless, to understand whether and how mindfulness could potentially be beneficial for software productivity, it is useful to review exactly where cognitive benefits have been observed with respect to attention, distraction, and memory.

First and foremost, mindfulness has been studied in the context of attention training. This is logical, because attention features prominently in the definition of mindfulness as paying attention in a particular way, nonjudgmentally. Scientifically speaking, attention can be subdivided into different faculties, each measured with its own task. Perhaps the most convincing attentional effects have been observed in the domain of sustained attention: the ability to maintain attention on a stimulus for a relatively long duration. A seminal study of practitioners on a three-month retreat showed that while normally people's attention declines over the course of a task, this effect had virtually gone away after 1.5 months of intense practice and stayed like that even after the retreat had ended [8]. Of course, a three-month training is not something that is feasible for the average software engineer.

Other aspects of attention that have been reported to change with mindfulness practice are the ability to orient it to the desired location, the ability to engage it at the right time, and the ability to deal with conflicting inputs. All three aspects have been measured in a single cognitive task: the attention network task. In different meditator populations, improvements in all three components have been observed, although the conflict monitoring effect is the most frequently and consistently reported [13]. A final attentional capacity is the ability to allocate it flexibly to rapidly changing stimuli. It has been observed that attention becomes more flexible after an intensive three-month meditation retreat [12]. For this effect, it does matter what kind of meditation you practice, since we found that this occurred only when practitioners engaged in meditation practices that involve a general monitoring of the environment, without a single specific focus such as the breath [15].

Another aspect of attention that can be measured is the tendency to get distracted, which is quantified by asking people at random moments during a boring task whether they are in fact doing the task or instead are distracted (see Chapter 14 for more details about these tasks). Mrazek and colleagues [10] observed that participants in such a task reported fewer attentional lapses after a short mindfulness induction compared to a relaxation induction. Moreover, improvements in test scores on measures such as working memory capacity seemed to depend on an individual's tendency to get distracted. Given that mindfulness involves a constant monitoring of one's distraction, this makes a lot of sense.

A third cognitive skill is memory. Several studies have demonstrated that working memory—the ability to keep recent information active in mind and manipulate it—is improved by mindfulness [14]. Working memory in software engineering is crucial for tasks such as visualizing the impact of a particular control structure on the software architecture or keeping in mind the complete design for a complex program. It is likely that the mindfulness-related improvements in working memory arise from the reduction in distraction that has been reported to be an effect of mindfulness. Compared to working memory, much less is known about the effects of mindfulness on long-term memory—the ability to store and retrieve information more permanently. This memory skill is crucial in software engineering for being able to remember the relevant commands in a programming language, for example, and to remember how a software architecture changes over time. In this domain of long-term memory there have been few studies. One of those studies demonstrates an improvement in recognition memory, which is the ability to remember you have seen something before, after a very brief mindfulness induction [1].

Mindfulness and Emotional Intelligence

It has also been suggested that mindfulness can enhance emotional intelligence, which may be helpful for managers or teams working together. Emotional intelligence is a fairly fuzzy concept. The term was coined by Peter Salavoy and John Mayer and subsequently popularized by Daniel Goleman. It refers to the ability to recognize, understand, and manage your own and others' emotions. It is easy to see that spending some time watching your thoughts and emotions when you are practicing mindfulness could help you to enhance this ability. What is crucial about mindfulness is that the intention is to cultivate a very friendly and nonjudging attitude toward your thoughts and emotions, which is an effective way to manage these emotions. Our normal way of managing our emotions is to try to either suppress or enhance them, and most of the time this results in the emotion spinning out of control. The mindfulness practitioner learns that by simply observing the thoughts and emotions, these emotions will simply disappear by themselves when not fed by attention.

In the context of software productivity, a crucial emotional intelligence skill is *resilience*, the ability to deal with setbacks. Resilience relies crucially on recognizing that while your emotions may seem intense, they too are fleeting. When you are criticized, this may feel like a disaster, but with the perspective of impermanence gleaned from mindfulness, you realize that the emotional impact is just temporary. Not being too caught up in catastrophizing emotions is a crucial component of cognitive resilience, and is likely to benefit productivity.

Furthermore, much of programming work these days involves significant team collaboration. With team collaboration, especially in a competitive environment, comes significant potential for interpersonal friction. Although little research has been done in this area, a recent study showed that a brief mindfulness intervention in agile teams improved the ability to listen to each other [4], which is crucial for preventing and reducing interpersonal friction. Traditionally, mindfulness is used as a natural method to increase compassion, thought to arise naturally when you develop a sense of kindness and nonjudgmentalness toward your own thoughts. In fact, one experimental study provided empirical evidence for such compassion: when faced with a confederate of the experimenters who was on crutches, people gave up their chair more often after a mindfulness intervention than a wait-list control [2].

Pitfalls of Mindfulness

The preceding sections demonstrated the positive effects that have been reported of mindfulness and meditation practices on cognitive and emotional skills that are crucial for productivity. However, it is important to note that also adverse effects of mindfulness are starting to be reported [6]. These effects have not yet been systematically inventorized, but a large number of interviews with meditation teachers and serious practitioners indicate that adverse effects of mindfulness can range from sleep disturbances to emotional problems to resurfacing of past trauma and many more. One may think that those adverse effects will arise only after long hours of mindfulness practice, but in fact they have also been reported in first-time meditators taking part in mindfulness interventions. It is therefore important to engage in mindfulness under the supervision of a well-trained teacher who can recognize signs of adverse effects and halt the intervention if necessary. Moreover, mindfulness interventions should never be rolled out as a blanket intervention for a whole company because they may not be suitable for every individual. Future research will ideally develop an overview of personality traits for whom mindfulness is a less desirable intervention.

Mindfulness Breaks

Now if we want to implement a mindfulness intervention in the workflow of a software engineer, how could we go about this? These more practical recommendations follow primarily from my own experience as a mindfulness practitioner and as a meditation teacher. First it should be emphasized that, given its potential adverse side effects, it is not advisable to force it upon software engineers. It is also important to set the expectations right; as mentioned, the cognitive benefits are limited, and the first gains are likely to arise in emotional resilience.

Having established these boundary conditions, if software engineers would like to engage in a mindfulness practice at work, in my experience, the best approach is a combination of substantial practice before the day starts and small mindfulness breaks during the day itself. The longer mindfulness session (ideally at least 20 minutes) serves to cultivate and develop cognitive skills, while the shorter sessions serve as reminders and refreshers during the workday. In fact, it has been suggested that these short—less than three-minute—sessions may be the most effective breaks (i.e., more effective than, for example, browsing social media for the same amount of time). One could take such a short mindfulness break after completing a subtask such as writing a routine. Alternatively, it is possible to set a timer to interrupt a debugging session, which may help to give a fresh view of your program.

For most people, using the breath as a meditation object works well because it reconnects you to your body. For some, however, the breath can be a little claustrophobic. In that case, focusing attention on a sound can be helpful (especially because there are probably many sounds to choose from). Focusing on sounds has the added benefit that you may learn to develop a more friendly attitude toward sounds that you would otherwise consider to be annoying or disturbing.

Perhaps surprisingly, for most people, taking short mindfulness breaks during a workday is not easy in practice. Even for a seasoned meditator, the thought frequently creeps in: "Should I not be doing something more useful?" There is always more to accomplish, and often having more tasks makes us feel more worthwhile. Even social media can sometimes be justified as being more useful than a mindfulness break because at least you are doing something. Nevertheless, my own experience and that of others [9] indicates that when you muster the courage to actually take a break, you are able to zoom out and get a better sense of priority in your work, and you are able to build a deeper connection with your inner kindness and therefore with your co-workers. To have a productive mindfulness break, it is important to not completely close yourself off from what is going on but instead to perceive it mindfully. A mindful attitude involves not only having some sense of kind attention toward it but also a sense of curiosity. You can investigate your gut reactions to the current situation, or you can investigate your intention. Also realize that a brief mindfulness break won't always lead to feelings of calm and bliss. The trick is to be present and OK with whatever shows up in these moments. The goal is not to be a perfect meditator!

A final consideration to incorporating mindfulness in work is paying attention to your intention. Intention is much less discussed in the popular literature on mindfulness than focus. Nevertheless, cultivating a good intention is a crucial component of mindfulness [5]. Mindfulness practice is typically engaged with an intention to not just feel better oneself but to also benefit other sentient beings. In my own personal experience, this attitude, when reinforced at the beginning and end of a working day, creates a tremendous sense of space and peace of mind. Suddenly work is not primarily to get ahead oneself, but also has a larger purpose. When work is not just done for yourself then also setbacks are less frustrating because you realize you are not working alone.

Conclusion

In conclusion, it is fair to say that mindfulness has the potential to be beneficial for software engineers. Mindfulness has been associated with limited cognitive benefits such as a reduction in distraction and more substantial emotional benefits, such as improved ability to manage emotions and resilience in the face of setbacks. Nevertheless, it is important to realize that it is not a panacea. Mindfulness is not something that begets immediate results with no effort. Moreover, mindfulness may not be beneficial for every individual. Incorporating mindfulness in the software engineer's workflow has to be done with skill, and then it can make a large difference.

Key Ideas

Here are the key ideas from this chapter:

- Mindfulness has limited benefits for cognition but may improve emotional intelligence.

- Short mindfulness breaks could lead to better productivity.

- For some people mindfulness can also have adverse effects.

References

[1] Brown, Kirk Warren, Robert J Goodman, Richard M Ryan, and Bhikkhu Analayo. 2016. "Mindfulness Enhances Episodic Memory Performance: Evidence from a Multimethod Investigation." *PLoS ONE* 11 (4). Public Library of Science:e0153309.

[2] Condon, P., G. Desbordes, W. B. Miller, and D. DeSteno. 2013. "Meditation Increases Compassionate Responses to Suffering." *Psychological Science* 24 (10):2125-7. `https://doi.org/10.1177/0956797613485603`.

[3] Davidson, R. J., J. Kabat-Zinn, J. Schumacher, M. S. Rosenkranz, D. Muller, S. F. Santorelli, F. Urbanowski, A. Harrington, K. Bonus, and J.F. Sheridan. 2003. "Alteration in Brain and Immune Function Produced by Mindfulness Meditation." *Psychosomatic Medicine* 65:564–70.

[4] Heijer, Peter den, Wibo Koole, and Christoph J Stettina. 2017. "Don't Forget to Breathe: A Controlled Trial of Mindfulness Practices in Agile Project Teams." In *International Conference on Agile Software Development*, 103–18. Springer.

[5] Kabat-Zinn, J. 1990. *Full Catastrophe Living: The Program of the Stress Reduction Clinic at the University of Massachusetts Medical Center*. Dell Publishing.

[6]   Lindahl, Jared R, Nathan E Fisher, David J Cooper, Rochelle K Rosen, and Willoughby B Britton. 2017. "The Varieties of Contemplative Experience: A Mixed-Methods Study of Meditation-Related Challenges in Western Buddhists." *PLoS ONE* 12 (5). Public Library of Science:e0176239.

[7]   Lutz, Antoine, Amishi P Jha, John D Dunne, and Clifford D Saron. 2015. "Investigating the Phenomenological Matrix of Mindfulness-Related Practices from a Neurocognitive Perspective." *American Psychologist* 70 (7). American Psychological Association:632.

[8]   MacLean, K. A., E. Ferrer, S. R. Aichele, D. A. Bridwell, A. P. Zanesco, T. L. Jacobs, B. G. King, et al. 2010. "Intensive Meditation Training Improves Perceptual Discrimination and Sustained Attention." *Psychological Science* 21 (6):829–39.

[9]   Meissner, T. n.d. "https://www.mindful.org/Get-Good-Pause/." Accessed 2017.

[10]   Mrazek, M. D., J. Smallwood, and J. W. Schooler. 2012. "Mindfulness and Mind-Wandering: Finding Convergence Through Opposing Constructs." *Emotion* 12 (3):442–48. https://doi.org/10.1037/a0026678.

[11]   Sedlmeier, P., J. Eberth, M. Schwarz, D. Zimmermann, F. Haarig, S. Jaeger, and S. Kunze. 2012. "The Psychological Effects of Meditation: A Meta-Analysis." *Psychological Bulletin* 138 (6). American Psychological Association:1139.

[12]   Slagter, H. A., A. Lutz, L. L. Greischar, A. D. Francis, S. Nieuwenhuis, J. M. Davis, and R. J. Davidson. 2007. "Mental Training Affects Distribution of Limited Brain Resources." *PLoS Biology* 5 (6):e138.

[13]   Tang, Yi-Yuan, Britta K Hölzel, and Michael I Posner. 2015. "The Neuroscience of Mindfulness Meditation." *Nature Reviews Neuroscience* 16 (4). Nature Publishing Group:213–25.

[14]   van Vugt, M. K., and A. P. Jha. 2011. "Investigating the Impact of Mindfulness Meditation Training on Working Memory: A Mathematical Modeling Approach." *Cognitive, Affective, & Behavioral Neuroscience* 11 (3):344–53.

[15]   van Vugt, M. K., and H. A. Slagter. 2013. "Control over Experience? Magnitude of the Attentional Blink Depends on Meditative State." *Consciousness and Cognition* 23C:32.

Index

A

A/B testing, 150
Achievement method, 60
Aggregate information, 182
Agile
    Alliance conferences, 246
    development
        cost of productivity, 129, 131
        global out-sourcing, 126–127
        planning, 127–128
        stressful environment, 128–129
    methodology, 125–126, 128, 130
    principles, 125–127, 129–131
Agile-DevOps environment
    automated function points, 247
    CMMI, 246
    waterfall projects, 247
Albrecht's FPA method *vs.* cosmic
        method, 193
Albrecht's function point analysis, 192
Atlassian tool, 183
Automated awareness mechanisms
    collaborative software development, 176
    developers goal, 176
    quantitative/qualitative information, 176
Automated methods, 175
Awareness
    aggregating information
        development life cycle, 173
        development tasks, 174

        expected events, 174
        number of issues/commits, 173
        numbers, 173
        status updates, 174
        text, 174
        unexpected events, 175
    categories, 171
        collaboration awareness, 171
        context awareness, 171
        location awareness, 171
        situation awareness, 172
        social awareness, 171
        workspace awareness, 172
    collaborative software
        development, 172
    collaborative working, 169
    design, tools, 170
    high-level status information, 170

B

Balanced developers, 143
Base population, 6
Benchmarking
    COSMIC method, 207
    definition, 205
    false incentives, 214
    framework, 209
    inward focus, 208
    ISO-standard, 210

© The Author(s) 2019
C. Sadowski and T. Zimmermann (eds.), *Rethinking Productivity in Software Engineering*,
https://doi.org/10.1007/978-1-4842-4221-6

S